Contesting
the Philippines

The **ISEAS – Yusof Ishak Institute** (formerly Institute of Southeast Asian Studies) is an autonomous organization established in 1968. It is a regional centre dedicated to the study of socio-political, security, and economic trends and developments in Southeast Asia and its wider geostrategic and economic environment. The Institute's research programmes are grouped under Regional Economic Studies (RES), Regional Strategic and Political Studies (RSPS), and Regional Social and Cultural Studies (RSCS). The Institute is also home to the ASEAN Studies Centre (ASC), the Singapore APEC Study Centre, and the Temasek History Research Centre (THRC).

ISEAS Publishing, an established academic press, has issued more than 2,000 books and journals. It is the largest scholarly publisher of research about Southeast Asia from within the region. ISEAS Publishing works with many other academic and trade publishers and distributors to disseminate important research and analyses from and about Southeast Asia to the rest of the world.

Philippines Update Series

Contesting the Philippines

EDITED BY

STEVEN ROOD
VERONICA L. TAYLOR

YUSOF ISHAK INSTITUTE

First published in Singapore in 2024 by
ISEAS Publishing
30 Heng Mui Keng Terrace
Singapore 119614
E-mail: publish@iseas.edu.sg
Website: http://bookshop.iseas.edu.sg

All rights reserved. No part of this publication may be reproduced, stored in a retrieval system, or transmitted in any form or by any means, electronic, mechanical, photocopying, recording or otherwise, without the prior permission of the ISEAS – Yusof Ishak Institute.

© 2024 ISEAS – Yusof Ishak Institute, Singapore

The responsibility for facts and opinions in this publication rests exclusively with the authors and their interpretations do not necessarily reflect the views or the policy of the publisher or its supporters.

ISEAS Library Cataloguing-in-Publication Data

Name(s): Rood, Steven, editor. | Taylor, Veronica L., editor.
Title: Contesting the Philippines / edited by Steven Rood and Veronica L. Taylor.
Description: Singapore : ISEAS-Yusof Ishak Institute, 2024. | Includes bibliographical references and index.
Identifiers: ISBN 978-981-5104-91-2 (soft cover) | 978-981-5104-92-9 (PDF) | 978-981-5104-93-6 (epub)
Subjects: LCSH: Philippines—Economic conditions. | Philippines—Social conditions. | Philippines—Politics and government.
Classification: LCC DS686.614 C77

Cover design by Lee Meng Hui
Index compiled by Raffaie Bin Nahar
Typesetting by International Typesetters Pte Ltd
Printed in Singapore by Markono Print Media Pte Ltd

Contents

About the Contributors ... vii

1. Introduction: Contesting the Philippines ... 1
   Steven Rood and Veronica L. Taylor

PART I: ECONOMIC RESURGENCE

2. Structural Fiscal Reforms to Support Strong, Sustainable Growth with Equity ... 11
   Benjamin E. Diokno

3. Political and Economic Update: DU30 at 2 ... 22
   Ronald U. Mendoza

4. The Philippine Economy: Sustained Economic Growth amidst Short-Term Disturbances? ... 35
   Myrna S. Austria

5. The Philippine Service Export Economy and Prospects of Manufacturing ... 60
   Antoinette R. Raquiza

6. The Philippine Climate Change Commitments and the Energy Transition to a Low-Carbon Future ... 78
   Manuel P.S. Solis

7. Hey Big Spender: Filipino Migrants, Consumption and Social Change, 1980–2018 ... 107
   Mina Roces

PART II: WAGING LAWFARE IN THE PHILIPPINES

8. Impeachment under Duterte: Liberal Tool or Illiberal Weapon? — 129
   Cristina Regina Bonoan and Björn Dressel

9. Tipping the Balance? Politics, Personalities and Institutions in the Philippine Supreme Court — 149
   Imelda Deinla and Maria Lulu Reyes

10. Contesting Duterte's Drug War: Truth, Politics, Ethics — 171
    Nicole Curato and Bianca Ysabelle Franco

11. Prioritizing Prison Reform: The Real Challenges behind Managing Violent Extremist Prisoners in the Philippines — 190
    Clarke Jones and Raymund Narag

PART III: RESHAPING THE STATE UNDER DUTERTE

12. Local Civil-Military Relations during Emergency: Lessons and Norming from Marawi — 209
    Rosalie Arcala Hall

13. Emergency Mental Health and Psychosocial Support Provision for Marawi's Internally Displaced Persons — 236
    Gail Tan Ilagan

14. A Tale of Two Towns: Patterns of Violent Conflict in Maguindanao since the Framework Agreement on the Bangsamoro — 253
    Georgi Engelbrecht

15. The ARMM Is Gone: Long Live the BARMM — 276
    Steven Rood, Veronica L. Taylor and Imelda Deinla

Index — 292

About the Contributors

Myrna S. Austria is a University Fellow and Full Professor at the School of Economics, De La Salle University (DLSU). She has published journal articles, monographs, book chapters and policy briefs on trade, investment and industrial policy, development economics, competition policy, and regional economic integration. She earned her master's degree and PhD in economics from the Australian National University. She has served DLSU in various capacities: Vice-Chancellor for Academics (May 2010–July 2015); Dean of the College of Business & Economics (May 2006–May 2010); and Director of the Center for Business and Economics Research and Development (January 2003–May 2006). She has served several top universities in ASEAN as Chief and Lead Quality Assurance Assessor under the ASEAN University Network (AUN).

Cristina Regina Bonoan is a lawyer and Senior Lecturer at the University of the Philippines (UP) College of Law. Her research interests revolve around rights, access to justice and the rule of law. She received her master's degree in international affairs, specializing in human rights and development, from the Columbia University School of International and Public Affairs. In addition, she holds a Bachelor of Laws from the UP College of Law and a Bachelor of Science in Legal Management from the Ateneo de Manila University. She has worked as a consultant for the Commission on Human Rights, the Asian Development Bank, and other international and non-governmental organizations, specializing in governance, the rule of law reform and human rights.

Nicole Curato is Professor of Political Sociology at the Centre for Deliberative Democracy and Global Governance at the University of Canberra. She is the author of *Democracy in a Time of Misery: From Spectacular Tragedy to Deliberative Action* (2019) and *A Duterte Reader: Critical Essays on Rodrigo Duterte's Early Presidency* (2017).

Imelda Deinla is currently Senior Lecturer at the School of Law, University of New England and Visiting Senior Fellow at the School of Government, Ateneo de Manila University. She was previously Associate Professor at the School of Government at Ateneo de Manila University and Convenor of BOSES Pilipinas, the first university-based public opinion survey outfit in the Philippines. Her research interests include rule of law, justice and democracy in ASEAN, Southeast Asia and the Philippines. Her current research is on electoral violence, misinformation, and crime and punitiveness. She is the author of *The Development of the Rule of Law in ASEAN: The State and Regional Integration* (2017), co-editor of *From Aquino to Duterte: Change, Continuity and Rupture* (2017), and co-editor of *Philippine Conglomerates and Inclusive Development: Tracking a Unique Trajectory in Asia* (forthcoming, March 2024).

Benjamin E. Diokno is an economist and has served as the Secretary of Finance under the administration of President Ferdinand 'Bong Bong' Marcos Jr. since June 2022. He previously served as Secretary of Budget and Management under the administration of President Rodrigo Duterte (2016–19) and under President Joseph Estrada (1998–2001). He has also served as the Governor of the Central Bank of the Philippines (Bangko Sentral ng Philipinas) and ex officio chairman of the Anti-Money Laundering Council (2019–22) under President Duterte. He holds a bachelor's degree in public administration from the University of the Philippines (UP) Diliman, master's degrees in public administration and in economics from UP Diliman, a MA in political economy from the Johns Hopkins University, USA and a PhD in economics from Syracuse University, USA.

Björn Dressel is an Associate Professor and inaugural Director of the Philippines Institute at the Australian National University (ANU). His research is concerned with comparative constitutionalism, judicial politics and governance, and public sector reform in Asia. He has published in a range of international journals, including *Governance, Administration &*

Society, *International Political Science Review* and *Pacific Review*. He is the editor of *The Judicialization of Politics in Asia* (2012) and co-editor of *Politics and Constitutions in Southeast Asia* (2016) and *From Aquino II to Duterte: Continuity, Change–and Rupture* (2019).

Georgi Engelbrecht is a Senior Analyst with the International Crisis Group. He is based in Manila. Before joining the International Crisis Group in late 2019, Georgi worked in Mindanao as part of a multinational peacekeeping mission monitoring the ceasefire between the Philippine government and the Moro Islamic Liberation Front.

Bianca Ysabelle Franco graduated with a master's degree in sociology from the University of the Philippines Diliman. She was formerly a research associate at the Development Studies Program of the Ateneo de Manila University where she worked on projects about human rights, deliberative democracy and conflict studies. Her written work has been published on the academic blogs *New Mandala* (Australian National University) and *Broad Agenda* (University of Canberra) and on the news websites *Globe Post* (United States) and *Rappler* (Philippines).

Rosalie Arcala Hall is Professor of Political Science and Scientist III at the University of the Philippines Visayas (UPV) in Miagao, Iloilo. She earned her Masters and PhD from Northeastern University, Boston, USA. She has completed research projects and published extensively on civil-military relations, security in the Bangsamoro area and rebel integration with grants from Toyota Foundation, the Nippon Foundation, The Asia Foundation and the Australian National University. She is a member of the Philippine Commission on Higher Education Technical Panel for Political Science and past president of the Philippine Political Science Association (2019–21).

Gail Tan Ilagan retired in 2023 from the chair of the Department of Psychology at Ateneo de Davao University. She was the Director of the Davao-based Center of Psychological Extension and Research Services (COPERS) from 2011 to 2018. She headed the Psychological Association of the Philippines' Task Force for Emergency MHPSS Response to the Marawi Crisis from June 2017 to March 2018.

Clarke Jones is a criminologist and senior research fellow based at the School of Medicine and Psychology at the Australian National University (ANU). His expertise includes interventions/rehabilitation, radicalization/prison radicalization, correctional reform and prison gangs. Dr Jones has applied his research to prison and jail reform in the Philippines correctional system over the past 15 years and continues to advise Philippines correctional agencies—the Bureau of Corrections (BuCor), the Bureau and Jail Management and Penology (BJMP)—on areas such as the management of high-risk offenders and prison gangs. He has also worked as a senior consultant for the United Nations Development Program (UNDP) and the United Nations Office of Drugs and Crime (UNODC). Before moving into academia in 2010, he worked for over 16 years in several areas of Australian national security, including police, military and intelligence. In 2002, he was awarded the Chief of the Australian Defence Force Fellow and, based on this fellowship, completed a PhD at the University of New South Wales in 2010.

Ronald U. Mendoza is Regional Director for Southeast Asia at IDinsight, a policy research organization focused on international development policy and programmes, with a menu of data-driven technical assistance and capacity-building services. Dr Mendoza is a governance and institutional reforms specialist with over 25 years of experience in development policy and public administration reforms. Prior to joining IDinsight, he served as Dean and Professor at the Ateneo de Manila University School of Government. Between August 2020 and July 2022, he also served as Chief of Party of PARTICIPATE, a three-year USAID project that focused on supporting citizens' participation in governance and strengthening democratic and governance institutions. From 2011 to 2015, he was an Associate Professor of Economics at the Asian Institute of Management (AIM) and the Executive Director of the AIM Rizalino S. Navarro Policy Center for Competitiveness. His research background includes work with UNICEF, UNDP, the Federal Reserve Bank of Boston, the Economist Intelligence Unit (EIU), and several Manila-based non-governmental organizations. In early 2021, the United Nations Economic and Social Council (UN ECOSOC) approved Dr Mendoza's appointment to serve with the 24-person UN Committee of the Experts on Public Administration (CEPA 2021–2025). And in early 2023, he was listed among the Philippines' top 100 scientists in the AD Scientific Index 2023 based on the total number of citations in the last five years.

Raymund E. Narag is an Associate Professor at the School of Justice and Public Safety in Southern Illinois University Carbondale. His research interests include court and correctional management, comparative criminal justice systems and qualitative research. He implemented the Community Bail Bond programme in the Philippines where Persons Deprived of Liberty (PDLs) and Persons with Drug Use Disorders (PWDUDs) are released under the supervision of community volunteers. He also serves as a consultant with the United Nations Office of Drugs and Crime (UNODC) on correctional concerns in the Philippines.

Antoinette R. Raquiza is Professor at the Asian Center, University of the Philippines Diliman, where she teaches Southeast Asian Studies and Philippine Development Studies. She received her PhD in political science from the City University of New York Graduate Center and has written on comparative political economy and political institutions, including *State Structure, Policy Formation, and Economic Development in Southeast Asia: The Political Economy of Thailand and the Philippines*, as well as on Philippine politics, governance and development. She is the convenor of the Political Economy Program of the UP Center for Integrative and Development Studies, vice president of the Manila-based think tank, Asia-Pacific Pathways for Progress Foundation, Inc. (APPFI), and chair of the Consortium for Southeast Asian Studies in Asia (SEASIA), a network of 15 leading area studies institutions in the region.

Maria Lulu Reyes is Professor of Law at the Saint Louis University in Baguio City, Philippines, where she also heads its Master of Laws programme. She is active in non-government and civil society work in the Cordillera region of the Philippines, and her research interests include justice and indigenous people, law and violence against women.

Mina Roces is a Professor of History at the School of Humanities and Languages, University of New South Wales, Sydney, Australia. A PhD graduate from the University of Michigan, she is the author of five monographs: *Women, Power and Kinship Politics: Female Power in Post-war*

Philippines (1998), *Kinship Politics in Post-war Philippines: The Lopez Family, 1946–2000* (2001), *Women's Movements and the Filipina, 1986–2008* (2012), *The Filipino Migration Experience: Global Agents of Change* (2021, which won the 2022 NSW Premier's General History Prize), and *Gender in Southeast Asia* (2022). She is the recipient of the 2019 Grant Goodman Prize for Excellence in Philippine Historical Studies given by the Philippine Studies Group, Association for Asian Studies, USA. In 2016 she was elected to the Australian Academy of the Humanities.

Steven Rood is Fellow-in-Residence at the Social Weather Stations and Visiting Fellow at the Australian National University. He was Professor of Political Science at the University of the Philippines Baguio from 1981 to 1999 and Philippine Country Representative for the Asia Foundation from 1999 to 2017. From 2009 to 2013, he was a member of the International Contact Group for the negotiations between the Philippine government and the Moro Islamic Liberation Front, and from 2013 to 2017 he was on the International Monitoring Team examining the progress of the agreements reached in those talks. He is the author of *The Philippines: What Everyone Needs to Know* (2019).

Manuel Solis is currently a Senior Lecturer of Law at Deakin University and Law Course Coordinator at the National Indigenous Knowledges Education Research Innovation (NIKERI) Institute in Australia. He has been a Senior Research Fellow at the Manila Observatory since 2019. Dr Solis is also an Adjunct Professor on Climate Change Law and Energy Transition at the San Beda University Graduate School of Law and the University of Santo Tomas Graduate School of Law in the Philippines. He was a Japan Foundation Visiting Scholar at Waseda University, Tokyo, Japan in 2022.

Veronica L. Taylor is a socio-legal scholar and Professor of Law and Regulation in the School of Regulation and Global Governance (RegNet) at the Australian National University. She is a former Dean of the ANU College of Asia and the Pacific, an ANU Public Policy Fellow and the designer of the University's education programs in Regulation and Governance. Her work focuses on the professional practice of regulation, regulatory justice, rule of law, institutional reform and corporate governance. She specializes in the design and evaluation of legal reform projects in authoritarian and volatile settings and for transition economies, including Afghanistan, China, Indonesia, Mindanao, Myanmar and Vietnam. In Australia, Professor Taylor is the Senior Academic Advisor to the National Regulator Community of Practice and an Expert Advisor to the Regulatory Reform Division of the Department of Finance. She is a non-Executive Director of ANU Enterprise and of the Social Research Centre. She received the Japanese Foreign Minister's Citation in 2017.

1

Introduction: Contesting the Philippines

Steven Rood and Veronica L. Taylor

The Duterte administration in the Philippines (2016–22) marked the return of authoritarian rule in the Philippines. It was also accompanied by an economic recovery that was better than many expected, at least until the onset of the COVID-19 pandemic. Both during and following the Duterte period, the country was buffeted by a series of internal and external shocks that called into question the state's legal and social policy contract with its citizens.

We think of this as "contesting the Philippines"—an intense normative and practical struggle to shape (or reshape) some of the Philippines' most critical institutions: the Constitution, the presidency, the Supreme Court, the free press, regional autonomy and independent regulatory institutions. That contestation intensified under the Duterte administration and continues to the present.

One of President Rodrigo Roa Duterte's signatures was a Manila-centric show of strength through martial law in Mindanao, the roll-out of a punitive anti-drugs policy and asserting executive control over other branches of government and independent agencies. Not surprisingly, the national commitment to the rule of law and human rights was called into question. President Duterte aimed to remove the executive from the constraints of both domestic and international rule of law while using law as a repressive policy tool. The most dramatic expression of this was Duterte's "war on drugs", which targeted drug dealers but also swept up men in the streets, with the police acting with apparent impunity. At the same time, the administration launched legal attacks on media outlets, journalists and politicians critical of their policies. This period also saw the administration apparently abandoning international law, announcing a withdrawal from the International Criminal Court and declining to exploit the Philippines' arbitral tribunal victory over China regarding territorial claims in the South China Sea. The result was a precipitous decline in the Philippines' ranking in the World Justice Project's Rule of Law Index.

At the same time, the Philippines is also particularly vulnerable to regional and transnational influences. The Duterte government initially embraced China as its bilateral partner of choice, notwithstanding China's incursion into Filipino maritime territory. But, by the end of Duterte's term, relations with the United States had improved. The 2017 Marawi siege and its aftermath underscored the vulnerability of the southern Philippines to external terrorist groups, becoming a major setback to achieving sustainable peace in Mindanao and affecting the political settlement in Muslim Mindanao (the Bangsamoro).

All of these developments energized many other domestic policy actors: technocrats, the business sector, civil society organizations, the police and the military, armed groups and religious leaders across the spectrum of Filipino politics.

The following chapters, drawn from a conference in 2018, consider some of the key sites of contestation since 2016 between and among domestic policy actors, including the executive. The authors analyse the key institutions under stress and the actors competing to reshape them in the aftermath of the Duterte presidency.

ECONOMIC RESURGENCE

The Philippines' economy has unequivocally shed its image as "the sick man of Asia". The opening chapter of this volume is based on the conference's keynote address. In chapter 2, Finance Secretary Benjamin

E. Diokno outlined the (then) Duterte administration's medium-term goals to drastically reduce the incidence of poverty to 14 per cent by 2022 through fiscal initiatives, an expansionary policy for an economy that would outgrow its debt burden, comprehensive tax reform (begun with the 2017 Tax Reform for Acceleration and Inclusion [TRAIN] law) and a rapid expansion of spending on infrastructure to 7.3 per cent of GDP by the end of its term in 2022. These policies were to be paired with an increase in social sector spending to 9.2 per cent. A host of reforms in public finance management were pursued, including a cash-based budget beginning in 2019. In this way, the administration aimed for public spending that could drive growth in the Philippines while addressing poverty and inequality. The continuing role of Diokno illustrates continuity in economic policymaking: during the Duterte administration, Diokno became the Governor of the *Bangko Sentral ng Pilipinas* (Central Bank of the Philippines) and, since 2022, in the new administration of Ferdinand Marcos Jr., he has been Secretary of Finance.

In chapter 3, Ronald U. Mendoza assesses two full years of the Duterte administration as of the middle of 2018. Writing before the politicking towards the May 2019 mid-term elections had heated up, the political update discussion focuses on the efforts (ultimately unavailing) towards a federal constitution, a long-term advocacy priority of President Duterte. The economic update focuses on how the economy continues to be robust—as it has been for some years—and the tax reform and infrastructure emphasis outlined by Secretary Diokno in his chapter. The 2018 rise in inflation is noted, particularly the impact on the poor. The replacement of quantitative restrictions on the import of rice with more liberal trade with a tariff imposed ("tariffication") was aimed at easing this problem. In the end, the question is: can more than 6 per cent growth be sustained over a couple of decades, and can economic growth become more inclusive?

Myrna Austria in chapter 4 presents the other side of this improved economic performance, with some concerns about short-term disturbances such as a weakening peso, inflation and the trade deficit. The Philippines' sustained growth has been driven by more investment than in the past, along with growth in manufacturing. The peso's weakening has been largely the result of global conditions and can contribute to inflation as imports become more expensive in peso terms. Inflation surged and then receded in 2018 as the effects of the TRAIN law took effect, and a rice shortage briefly hit the country in mid-year. The trade deficit is driven by an expanding economy and the importation of equipment and materials for the government's focus on infrastructure under its "Build, Build, Build" initiative. In the face of these economic challenges and uncertainties, she outlines reforms the government can take, including its Manufacturing Resurgence Program.

In chapter 5, Antoinette R. Raquiza picks up the story of the Manufacturing Resurgence Plan, launched in 2014 and continued by the current Marcos administration. She analyses the rise in the export of services from the Philippines, which may be under threat from current global economic trends and growing protectionism. She describes how government initiatives helped business process outsourcing and how the emphasis on manufacturing has led to faster growth and the belated beginning of a structural shift in the economy, with slower growth in services.

Manuel P.S. Solis in chapter 6 highlights the challenges of achieving policy coherence in the energy sector, given the trilemma among energy security, energy equity and environmental sustainability, while pursuing growth policies. Solis looks at the prospect of a transition to a low-carbon energy regime in light of the 2001 Electric Power Industry Reform Act (EPIRA) and the 2008 Renewable Energy Act. The growing issue of climate change was partly addressed in the Philippines through the 2009 Climate Change Act. However, there are evident contradictions between, for instance, government projections of increased use of coal for power generation and the aspirations of the Renewable Energy Act.

In chapter 7, Mina Roces focuses on some unanticipated consequences of affluence in the Philippines. She explores a cultural practice evolving out of Filipino labour migration and remittances over the past decades—the recently invented tradition of *balikbayan* boxes (large boxes full of gifts and food) sent by overseas Filipino workers to their families at home. The practice has shifted the traditional norm of reciprocity since this is a one-way flow of gifts. Sending the boxes has become both a symbol of love and proof that the worker overseas is successful. The pressures of this consumption behaviour also undermine individual capacity for investment or better financial management. This requires another norm change—"How to say 'No'" to both the cultural practice and the expectations of relatives.

WAGING LAWFARE IN THE PHILIPPINES

Part of the international perception of a steep decline in the quality of the rule of law in the Philippines was shaped by the events surrounding the removal of the chief justice of the Philippine Supreme Court in mid-2018. Cristina Regina Bonoan and Björn Dressel in chapter 8 address the problems caused when impeachment, a tool intended as an accountability mechanism, is wielded in an authoritarian manner by a presidential administration as a weapon against critics who would otherwise be in a position to hold the executive accountable. They review the history of impeachment attempts in the Philippines under the 1987 Constitution, both successful and unsuccessful. Under the Duterte administration, impeachment attempts were launched against Vice President Leni Robredo (the running mate of one of Duterte's opponents during the 2016 elections) and three Constitutional officers: Commission on Elections Chair Andres Bautista, Ombudsman Conchita Carpio-Morales and (then) Supreme Court Chief Justice Lourdes Sereno. This last attempt was overtaken by the novel *quo warranto* proceedings, where the Supreme Court ruled that Sereno's appointment as chief justice was invalid. Bonoan and Dressel are critical of the reliance on impeachment as a tool of legal governance when it is politicized in the way it has been in the Philippines. They argue that the ability of the president at the time to wield a supermajority in the legislature and influence the Supreme Court to achieve this result point to a "weakness in Philippine democratic practice".

In chapter 9, Imelda Deinla and Maria Lulu Reyes go deeper into the removal from office of the chief justice of the Supreme Court of the Philippines, something that they argue has become intertwined with the presidential transitions since the turn of the millennium. Their chapter looks at how impeachment and other legal tools have evolved from mechanisms of legal accountability to ones of political weaponry, directed particularly against chief justices. They examine the confluence of politics, leadership and personalities within the court, the legislature and the presidential palace that have allowed the law to be used in this way, both within and outside the Supreme Court.

In chapter 10, Nicole Curato and Bianca Ysabelle Franco begin with the central fact about the war on drugs launched nationwide by Duterte immediately upon being elected in 2016: that thousands have been killed extrajudicially. Yet, surveys showed that the effort was popular among citizens. Then they go beyond this simple narrative to look into contestation about truth, politics and ethics. Rooted in, but different from, Duterte's previous efforts as mayor of Davao City, the national drug war's first site of contestation was numbers, both of addicts and deaths involved. Political contestation occurred as officials declined to cooperate with the bloody campaign and through social protests that expressed solidarity with victims or pointed to connections to authoritarianism of the past and possible future. Ethical stances discovered in their fieldwork in urban poor communities range from unqualified support for the "war on drugs" through ambivalence to outright dissent based on violations of due process and the inequities of a campaign in which victims were largely the poor. The authors end by raising questions for democratic practice embodied in the contestations and the capacity of elites to learn from the war on drugs experience.

In chapter 11, Clarke Jones and Raymund Narag are concerned with some of the ways in which the Duterte administration's tough-on-crime stance also corrodes the correctional system in the Philippines. Jones and Narag use the issue of violent extremist offenders in the Philippines' correctional system as a lens to examine vulnerabilities in corrections that are compounded by the higher prison and jail populations. Overcrowding impacts prisoner mental and physical health but also erodes correctional management efforts by government agencies. Inmates must rely on their own resources and informal coping mechanisms such as gang co-management of facilities. International actors looking to help the Philippines with its "war on terror" must first address overcrowding as part of any effort to deal with high-risk offenders. The authors suggest that beyond addressing the issue of overcrowding, the informal mechanisms that have grown up in Filipino prisons might be formalized in a shared governance model that reduces discretion and possible abuses.

RESHAPING THE STATE UNDER DUTERTE

Part of the legacy of President Duterte's predecessor, President Benigno Aquino, was the unresolved issue of securing an end to the civil conflict in Mindanao and a sustainable peace that would allow for full regional autonomy and a power-sharing arrangement with Manila. Duterte delivered that deal, and Imelda Deinla, Steven Rood and Veronica Taylor analyse progress to date in chapter 15 of this volume. What no one could have anticipated, however, was the interpolation of an Islamic State-influenced terror attack in 2017 on the Islamic City of Marawi, followed by a five-month military siege of the city.

The after-effects of that military action have been far-reaching, and in chapter 12 Rosalie Arcala Hall evaluates some of the lessons of the siege by analysing civil-military relations during that emergency. She tells a story of frayed coordination, with separate military and civilian coordination platforms evolving (including those of the Philippine government and UN cluster system). The military undertook its own relief operations, both because of the fraught security situation and to improve its image with local civilians. Non-government organizations and local governments distributed aid via their channels, encountering some restrictions from the military. Coordination forums that had been set up were ignored. By the end of 2018, progress on the reconstruction of the main battle area was minimal.

In chapter 13, Gail Tan Ilagan assesses the capacity to provide emergency mental health during emergencies, reflecting on the experience of Marawi's internally displaced persons (IDPs). During the five-month siege of Marawi City in 2017, the needs of the more than 300,000 IDPs strained the systems attempting to respond. Ilagan focuses on mental health and psychosocial support (MHPSS). The Department of Health is the lead agency for this service in the Philippines' disaster management structure but generally lacks resources. Ilagan traces some of the weaknesses in the system—reaching home-based IDPs (the vast majority in this instance), difficulties of government systems coordinating with non-government organizations and lack of skills among organizations that have a presence on the ground in the affected areas. She indicates that more activity addressing IDPs' trauma was accomplished than was reflected in reporting by official government or international organizations and concludes that the

Department of Health must enhance its working relationships with community-based organizations. She also argues that local governments must emphasize MHPSS services to a greater degree in anticipation of future emergencies.

All conflicts, however, are not created equal. Georgi Englebrecht in chapter 14 reminds us that there remains considerable variation in the history and trajectory of violence within and across communities within Muslim-majority Mindanao. Englebrecht leverages his on-the-ground experience with other data sources to compare and contrast the situation since 2012 in two municipalities in Maguindanao province. While the framing (and most international attention) concerns violence between armed rebels and the state, there are also incidents of "horizontal" conflict among clans or over resources, as well as political violence related to elections and political offices. These are crowded spaces: a heavy government military presence and many different actors (including the Moro Islamic Liberation Front, private armed groups and the Bangsamoro Islamic Freedom Fighters) make it hard to control conflict in a volatile environment. Particular incidents over recent years highlight how violence can flare up and change direction. Some progress on peace at the local level is being made, particularly in Datu Piang municipality, where local governance is more robust. Englebrecht discusses the contributing factors to this.

This volume closes with an analysis of one of the high points of the Duterte administration to date—a relatively successful plebiscite on regional autonomy in early 2019 and the implementation phases of the Bangsamoro peace deal for the warring actors in Muslim Mindanao. In chapter 15, Imelda Deinla, Steven Rood and Veronica Taylor analyse the new agreement and its anticipated contribution to remaking Muslim autonomy in Mindanao. They consider what legal and political institutional reforms this will require and think whether and how the current administration is likely to deliver these.

These contributions by leading Filipino and international scholars of the Philippines were developed and presented as part of the Australian National University (ANU)'s Philippines Update series, a project supported by the Australian Department of Foreign Affairs and Trade through the ANU Philippines Project. The views of the contributing authors and the editors of this volume are their own.

PART I

Economic Resurgence

2

Structural Fiscal Reforms to Support Strong, Sustainable Growth with Equity

Keynote Address
Philippine Update Conference 2018

Benjamin E. Diokno[1]

ABSTRACT

The Rodrigo Roa Duterte administration seeks a safer, fairer, richer, greener and more beautiful Philippines. Specifically, it aims first, that the economy grows strongly and sustainably at 7 to 8 per cent in the medium term and second, that poverty incidence be cut from 25 per cent in 2015 to 14 per cent in 2022, its steepest decline in Philippine history. In order to achieve these lofty goals, the new administration has adopted an expansionary fiscal policy, reformed its weak and unresponsive tax system and redesigned its dysfunctional budget system. Most of these fiscal reforms need to be institutionalized, enacted into law, so the next president(s) will be constrained from undoing them. With the imminent Congressional approval of the Budget Reform Bill, which embodies most of the structural fiscal reforms planned by the Duterte administration, the Philippine budget system has the promise of becoming one of the best budget institutions in the world in terms of openness, allocative efficiency and accountability.

THE PHILIPPINE GROWTH NARRATIVE

For many decades, the Philippines had seen wild swings of booms and busts brought forth by various crises, whether political or economic in nature. Since 2010, however, the Philippine economy has grown at a rapid and sustained pace above 6 per cent. This growth momentum was sustained last year as full-year growth reached 6.7 per cent, despite it being a post-election year.

Remarkable dips were recorded in previous post-election years. Growth decelerated from 6.7 per cent in 2004 to 4.7 per cent in 2005. Likewise, growth skyrocketed to 7.6 per cent in 2010, another election year, before falling back to 3.7 per cent in 2011.

For the Duterte administration, this is not quite applicable. GDP (Gross Domestic Product) growth was a robust 6.9 per cent in 2016, an election year, but was sustained the year after with 6.7 per cent GDP growth—the difference being a mere 0.2 percentage points.

More importantly, we can say that Philippine growth is now more diversified and sustainable. Economic expansion is increasingly being driven by investments on the demand side and industry on the supply side.

Multilateral organizations like the International Monetary Fund, the World Bank and the Asian Development Bank all project the Philippines to grow steadily in the near term. All three organizations peg our growth to reach almost 7 per cent (about 6.7 per cent to 6.9 per cent) from 2017 to 2019. In their forecasts, this is the highest among the ASEAN-5 countries.

We are more ambitious than these forecasts. As enshrined in our Medium-Term Development Plan, this administration aims to ramp up the Philippine economy to a 7 per cent to 8 per cent growth rate from 2018 to 2022, pushing the country into upper-middle income status by 2022 while reducing poverty incidence to 14 per cent from 21.6 per cent in 2015.

In order to ensure the achievement of our medium-term goals, we are pursuing an expansionary fiscal policy and an aggressive fiscal reform agenda.

EXPANSIONARY FISCAL POLICY

For much of the past three decades, our fiscal position has been volatile, affected by high levels of public debt and weak macroeconomic fundamentals, making the economy susceptible to external risks (e.g., the Asian Financial Crisis in 1997 and Sovereign Debt Woes in 2008). Hence, we have been unable to finance our development priorities. Of course, it did not help that we had a string of fiscal conservatives running our fiscal policy.

From 1987 to 2016, disbursements only averaged 17.1 per cent of GDP; revenues remained flat at 15.1 per cent of GDP; which means our deficit as per cent of GDP averaged at 2 per cent.

Revenues reached PHP 2.48 trillion in FY (fiscal year) 2017, equivalent to 15.7 per cent of GDP. We intend to raise this to PHP 4.49 trillion or 17.5 per cent of GDP by 2022 with the implementation of the Tax Reform Program and more effective tax administration. On the other hand, disbursements reached PHP 2.82 trillion in FY 2017, roughly 17.9 per cent of GDP. This will rise to as much as PHP 5.26 trillion or 20.5 per cent of GDP.

On balance, this means that we are aiming for a deficit level of 3 per cent of GDP.

To make sure we can finance our development priorities, we will maintain this deficit target until 2022. This implies a deficit target of PHP 523 billion in 2018 to PHP 774 billion in 2022. This increases the fiscal space available to government programs from PHP 175 billion in 2018 to PHP 258 billion in 2022.

The deficit will be financed through borrowings following a 75–25 mix in favour of domestic sources. This strategy ensures minimal exposure to foreign exchange fluctuations and to other potential external shocks.

Although the total debt stock of the government will increase, the government is exercising aggregate fiscal discipline. There is little to worry about when we have a low and falling debt profile, one that earns the envy of many developing nations with higher debt-to-GDP ratios. In fact, our debt-to-GDP ratio is expected to decline progressively over the medium term from 42.1 per cent in 2017 to 38.9 per cent in 2022. Simply put, our economy will continue to outgrow its debt.

The government's financing strategy will be complemented with the projected increase in revenue collection from improvements in tax policy and tax administration efforts through a Comprehensive Tax Reform Program (CTRP). The five packages of the CTRP seek to raise additional revenues and to correct a number of deficiencies in the tax system. The reforms seek to make the tax system simpler, fairer and more efficient.

The first package of the CTRP has already been enacted into law. Its main features include lowering personal income tax rates, expanding the Value-Added Tax base, increasing excise taxes on petroleum products and automobiles and introducing a tax on sugar-sweetened beverages.

The Tax Reform for Acceleration and Inclusion (TRAIN) law will contribute additional revenues ranging from PHP 125 billion in 2018 up to PHP 215 billion in 2022, totalling close to PHP 1.0 trillion (PHP 960 billion) over the medium term. The combined effect of the higher deficit ceiling and the TRAIN law will generate fiscal space of about PHP 300 billion in 2018 up to PHP 473 billion in 2022.

Sustainable debt management and tax reforms have enabled the government to increase the national budget by 12.4 per cent, from PHP 3.35 trillion in 2017 to PHP 3.767 trillion in 2018. This is our largest budget to date, almost three times the budget ten years ago. The expansionary fiscal policy enables the leveraging of the national budget to fund its two spending priorities—infrastructure development and human capital development.

SPENDING PRIORITY: INFRASTRUCTURE

According to the World Economic Forum (WEF) Competitiveness Rankings, the Philippines has had the worst overall infrastructure among the ASEAN-5 countries since 2010. Over time, our overall infrastructure global ranking has deteriorated: from 96 in 2009 to 112 in 2017. By contrast, Indonesia, our closest competitor, has significantly improved its overall infrastructure ranking from 96 in 2009 to 80 in 2017.

This is the result of historical underinvestment in infrastructure. From 1983 until 2006, infrastructure and other capital spending amounted to less than 3 per cent of GDP. It doubled to 3 per cent from 2007 to 2016, although such a level is still well below the suggested 5 per cent of GDP threshold for developing countries. From 2011 to 2016, government spending on infrastructure as a percentage of GDP averaged a measly 3 per cent. The Philippines has consistently fallen short of the suggested threshold for developing countries of 5 per cent of GDP for infrastructure spending.

To catch up with its regional neighbours and to open up economic opportunities to the lagging parts of the country, the Duterte administration has embarked on a massive infrastructure development programme—the "Build, Build, Build". We plan to spend PHP 8 to 9 trillion (USD 160 to 180 billion) in public infrastructure for the next six years to make up for past neglect and to realize what we call the "Golden Age of Infrastructure".

For FY 2018 alone, we have allocated PHP 1.06 trillion or 6.1 per cent of GDP for infrastructure development. The annual infrastructure spending will be ramped up, reaching as much as 7.3 per cent of GDP in 2022.

There are 75 big-ticket projects under the flagship "Build, Build, Build" programme—31 roads and bridges, 12 rail and urban transport projects, six air transport projects, four water transport projects, four flood management projects, 11 water supply and irrigation projects, four power projects, and three other public infrastructure projects.

This year three major transport infrastructure projects provide a glimpse of how the "Build, Build, Build" programme will accelerate growth and development—the Metro Manila Subway Project (MMSP), the Clark International Airport Expansion Project and the Mindanao Railway Project.

In the 4th quarter of 2018, the Department of Transportation (DOTr) shall commence the implementation of Phase 1 of the MMSP. This is a 25.3-kilometre subway, the first of its kind in the Philippines. It will have 13 stations connecting the north and the south of Manila (from Mindanao Avenue, Quezon City, to Food Terminal Inc.), including the Ninoy Aquino International Airport (NAIA). This subway is expected to accommodate around 370,000 passengers in its first year of operations, significantly decongesting Metro Manila. This project will cost approximately PHP 357.0 billion, financed through Japanese Official Development Assistance (ODA). The project is expected to be completed in 2027, but partial operations is expected to commence by the 4th quarter of 2025.

On the other hand, the PHP 9.4-billion Clark International Airport Expansion Project involves the construction of a new passenger terminal building to accommodate eight million passengers annually. This also includes the construction and installation of all required associated facilities—both landside and airside—to support the operations of the Clark International Airport. This airport is expected to complement the existing NAIA complex.

Meanwhile, the first phase of the Mindanao Railway Project or the Tagum–Davao–Digos (MRP-TDD) segment is expected to commence by the 3rd quarter of 2018. It is expected to reduce travel time from Tagum City, Davao del Norte to Digos City, Davao del Sur, from 3.5 hours to 1.3 hours once it starts operating in 2022. The MRP-TDD is expected to make travel not only faster but also safer, more convenient and comfortable for passengers in the said corridor. The project will cost PHP 35.91 billion.

The DOTr expects the daily ridership of the Tagum-Davao-Digos segment to increase to 134,060 by 2022 upon project completion. Further, the department projects the daily ridership to increase to 237,023 by 2032 and 375,134 by 2042.

Of course, infrastructure development alone cannot fulfil the president's promise of having a safer, prosperous and just society. In order to genuinely transform the lives of the Filipino people, the government will continue its sizeable investments in human capital development.

SPENDING PRIORITY: HUMAN CAPITAL DEVELOPMENT

In the 2018 budget, the social services sector (e.g., education, health care and social protection) remains to have the lion's share of the budget with PHP 1.42 trillion or 37.8 per cent of the total budget.

This sum supports the increase in the allocations of the government's flagship social service programmes such as the Conditional Cash Transfer (CCT) Program, the National Health Insurance Program, universal access to quality tertiary education, the full implementation of the K–12 Program for basic education, and employment safety nets, among others.

The government will sustain this level of support. In fact, the share of social sector expenditures to GDP is planned to rise from 8.5 per cent of GDP this year to 9.2 per cent of GDP by 2022. In a developing country with a median age of 23 years old, increased spending on human capital development is key to producing an agile, competitive and productive workforce that will sustain the growth of the economy. This is consistent with the government's aim of developing the country's most important resource—its people.

To ensure that our expanding national budget leads to actual delivery of public goods and services, we are continually improving our budget process.

IMPROVING CAPACITY TO DELIVER THROUGH KEY PFM REFORMS

The Philippine government needs to solve its perennial problem of underspending, defined as the difference between actual spending versus planned spending. In 2014 and 2015, government recorded underspending rates of 13.3 per cent and 12.8 per cent, respectively, or around PHP 300 billion annually.

In order to improve spending and to promote greater fiscal transparency and accountability, several key Public Financial Management (PFM) reforms have been introduced.

First, the release and management of funds have been streamlined. Through the General Appropriations Act (GAA) As-Allotment-Order (GAAAO) starting in 2017, the GAA serves as the official fund release document, eliminating discretion and streamlining budget release processes. This enables departments and agencies to utilize their authorized appropriations as early as the first working day of the fiscal year. As a result, on January 3, the first working day of 2017, the Department of Budget and Management (DBM) comprehensively released PHP 1.64 trillion, or 83.5 per cent of the total PHP 1.969 trillion agency-specific budget. At the end of 2017, this resulted in releases totalling PHP 3.246 trillion or 96.9 per cent of the PHP 3.35 trillion national budget.

Second, DBM and the Bureau of the Treasury (BTr) have adopted several cash management reforms to promote efficient spending and active cash management. DBM has comprehensively released the Notices of Cash Allocation (NCAs), covering four quarters, at the beginning of 2018—shifting from the quarterly and semestral releasing. This streamlined release of cash authority, corresponding to the operating cash requirements of departments and agencies, allows for prompt payment of delivered goods and services.

To further curb underspending, the quarterly cash allocation of agencies is credited by the government-servicing banks on the first day of every quarter, and the validity of checks issued by these banks has been reduced from six to three months. In addition, the DBM and the BTr are continuously pushing for the use of the Advice to Debit Account (ADA) facility to eliminate the need for paying through checks.

Third, the Implementing Rules and Regulations (IRR) of the Procurement Reform Act (Republic Act No. 9184) were revised to simplify and standardize the rules to ensure contracts are awarded on time and public goods are delivered efficiently. Restrictive provisions were identified and amended to be more flexible and adaptable to the procurement environment without sacrificing the integrity of the process. This ensures that a broader portion of the private sector is able to participate and bid for government contracts.

Some of the salient changes introduced in the revised IRR include strengthening the provisions on procurement planning and budget linkage and Early Procurement, short of award, to fast-track procurement. Submission to the Government Procurement Policy Board (GPPB) of the annual procurement plan (APP) and changes thereto are now required to improve procurement planning and enhance procurement assessment and monitoring. Conduct of pre-bid conferences in person or face-to-face via videoconferencing, webcasting or similar technology, or a combination thereof is now allowed to increase competition and enhance the transparency of the procurement process.

Several measures have also been included to facilitate eligibility checks and to avoid disqualification of bidders or failures of bidding. One such measure is mandatory registration under Platinum Membership with the Philippine Government Electronic Procurement System (PhilGEPS). To further streamline the process for the use of alternative methods of procurement, the Consolidated Guidelines for the Alternative Methods of Procurement have been included in the IRR. The revised IRR ensures a more efficient and effective public procurement system that will result in better public spending and quality public service.

Fourth, the 2018 national budget includes a refinement of the Performance-Informed Budget (PIB) through the adoption of a Program Expenditure Classification (PREXC), a global best practice. In place of an output-based budget structure, recurring activities and projects that contribute to a particular common objective or outcome are grouped into a programme. In addition, output and outcome targets are included for every programme of an agency. This allows for (a) a budget structure that is easier to understand and is more transparent; (b) a stronger link of the annual budget to the Philippine Development Plan; and (c) clearer monitoring of the use of public funds and their corresponding results.

Fifth, technology is being used to enhance the existing PFM system. The Budget and Treasury Management System (BTMS), a financial management information system that links the budget operations of DBM with the Treasury Single Account (TSA) and cash management operations of the Bureau of the Treasury (BTr), is currently being developed. The DBM and the BTr are now pilot testing the Budget Execution Module of the BTMS while the BTr is also using the Treasury Management Module. The Commission on Audit (COA) is also being engaged to support the development of the Accounting Module to fully integrate the complete PFM cycle into the BTMS. This builds on the use of the government's Unified Accounts Code Structure so that all government financial transactions are tracked from budgeting to payment and auditing.

This year the largest agencies, such as the Department of Education (DepEd), the Department of Public Works and Highways (DPWH) and the Department of Health (DOH), are being engaged to help in the pilot testing of the BTMS. This ensures that the system can capture the government's largest financial transactions more efficiently. The plan is to have a fully installed Integrated Financial Management Information System by 2022.

Sixth, the national government will be shifting from an obligation-based budget to an annual cash-based budget in 2019. An annual cash-based budget will limit the time horizon of delivery and payment for goods and services appropriated in the budget to just one fiscal year. This is the logical progression of the one-year validity of appropriations instituted in 2017 and 2018. This shift is envisioned to increase the pace of government spending and to enforce the intent of the national budget—that programmes and projects are completely delivered within the year of the appropriation. As part of the change management of this shift, DBM is embarking on a nationwide campaign to push for better planning and procurement capacity in departments and agencies to improve discipline in managing resources.

Lastly, the government is pushing for the passage of the Budget Reform Bill (BRB), a measure that seeks to modernize budgetary practices in the Philippines. It is an encompassing reform initiative covering the entire budget process—from budget planning to budget execution and accountability. The bill institutionalizes many of the reforms introduced and currently being implemented by the Executive to improve the quality of government spending, such as (a) the one-year validity of appropriations, (b) the shift to annual cash-based budgeting, (c) the Treasury Single Account (TSA), (d) stronger enforcement of internal controls by the DBM and the COA, (e) the strengthening of Congress' power of the purse through greater oversight of agencies' financial and physical performance and (f) clearer rules regarding the landmark Supreme Court decision on the use of savings.

Through these substantial PFM reforms, the spending pattern of government has been improving. In 2016, underspending narrowed down to 3.6 per cent. And the forecast for 2017 is a lower underspending level than the previous year. Instituting the above-mentioned reforms is now more critical than ever to sustain these gains.

To meet the ambitious goals of the administration, the marching order of the president is clear—to transform how business is done in the government. Simply, this means a government that listens to and serves the people, a government free from corruption and a government that gets things done promptly and properly. These PFM reforms embody this transformation in the government.

A SAFER, FAIRER, RICHER, GREENER AND MORE BEAUTIFUL PHILIPPINES

Public spending is now one of the biggest drivers of growth in the Philippines. But growth for growth's sake is empty. Rather, economic development should benefit everyone and address the pervasive poverty and inequality in the country. Thus, the expansionary but responsible fiscal policy of the government, coupled with its continued strengthening of the PFM system, ensures that sizeable investments in infrastructure development and human capital development are felt by all.

The Duterte administration understands that for the public to truly feel the dividends of their hard-earned taxes, major public sector reforms in the government's budgeting system are necessary. This overhaul ensures that public institutions have the capacity to fully implement the increasing national budget. At the heart of this is the institutionalization of PFM reform through the BRB that will ensure that the budgeting system of government is truly transparent, accountable and participatory. This landmark bill shows that the fulfilment of the president's vision relies not only on political will but also on the strength of democratic institutions.

Soon, we will get a glimpse of what a modern Philippines would look like—first-world infrastructure; better trained and flexible labour force; more decent jobs and higher wages; open, effective and accountable governance—a safer fairer, richer, greener and more beautiful Philippines for all Filipinos.

Note

1. As delivered on 25 May 2018 while Benjamin E. Diokno was Secretary of Budget and Management.

3

Political and Economic Update: DU30 at 2

Ronald U. Mendoza[1]

This chapter draws on a presentation made at a policy conference held in Canberra, Australia in mid-2018, when the focus was on the status of the Philippines as of the second full year of the Duterte administration. Since then, further political and economic developments may have changed the landscape but are not extensively discussed here.[2]

GENERAL ECONOMIC OUTLOOK

Since Rodrigo Duterte won the presidential race in 2016, the Philippine government has been implementing key reforms. The emphasis on continuing and ramping up some of the previous administration's economic reforms has also strengthened inter-administration policy coherence and continuity. The Duterte administration immediately adopted *Ambisyon* 2040—the country's long-term development vision and an initiative of Arsenio Balisacan, a socioeconomic planning secretary and chief economist under the Aquino administration, and carried on by Ernesto Pernia, President Duterte's socioeconomic planning secretary and chief economist. Hence, this sent a strong signal to development partners and observers of policy continuity. The Duterte administration's 0+10 policy framework, as fleshed out in the 2017–2022 Philippine Development Plan, added President Duterte's concern with the war on drugs to economic and social policies with roots in past initiatives.

Under the Duterte administration, some of the key legislative reforms include the Tax Reform for Acceleration and Inclusion (TRAIN) Act (Republic Act [RA] 10963); the Ease of Doing Business Act (RA No. 11032), which shortens the number of days in processing permits and licenses for all business-related transactions; and the Universal Access to Quality Tertiary Education Act of 2017, which provides free tuition and other school fees in state universities and colleges (Avendaño 2018).

The passage of TRAIN was crucial because it bolstered the country's fiscal position by adding PHP 80 billion in tax revenues annually to the country's coffers based on one estimate. When it was released, it immediately contributed to a more positive sovereign credit outlook for the Philippines. Revenues can be deployed to further fuel the country's ambitious infrastructure build-up; however, as noted later, this does not come without costs.

TABLE 3.1
GDP Breakdown (in millions PHP)

	2015	Percentage	2016	Percentage	2017	Percentage
Agriculture	719,742.4	9.47	710,926.4	8.75	739,029	8.53
Industry	254,5411	33.49	2,750,034	33.86	2,947,103	34.01
Service	4,335,022	57.04	4,661,781	57.39	4,979,575	57.46

Source: Philippine Statistics Authority.

The Philippine economy remains generally strong, with growth driven by the country's services sector (Metro Manila accounts for 53.43 per cent of the services sector). While some analysts (Austria and Raquisa, this volume) point to nascent increases in industry,[3] the Asian Development Bank maintained its growth projection for the Philippine economy at 6.8 per cent and 6.9 per cent for 2018 and 2019, respectively. If realized, this would fall below the government's 7 to 8 per cent goal set for 2018 until the end of President Duterte's six-year term (Cigaral 2018). However, there are signs of overheating, and there is a debate on whether and to what extent the tax reforms have contributed to the increasing prices of basic commodities. Regardless, analysts are now emphasizing that the government can turn to some practical solutions to help address rising food prices, including rice tariffication (signed into law in early 2019) and more effective investments in the agricultural sector. This would all depend not simply on policy direction, but also in actual reform implementation.

Along with these policy reforms come risks that should be accounted for by the Philippine government. Reforms have had distributional implications that do not necessarily favour poor and low-income households. TRAIN increased the price of certain commodities and was programmed to be accompanied by a small unconditional cash transfer to poor households, but the implementation of this provison of the law was delayed. Hence, this is one area where Duterte's supposed populism—or at least his economic populism—is debunked.

The initial approach to emphasize rice self-sufficiency and the mismanagement of the National Food Authority contributed to rising food (particularly rice) prices in 2018. Such inflation hits the poor most severely as they spend a larger proportion of their income on food. The economic team responded by lobbying for the passage of the rice tariffication law that would shift the country from a quota-based to a tariff-based system for importing rice. This reform, finally accomplished after decades of advocacy by economists and development planners, is predicted to lower the price of rice to help mitigate the impact of rising food prices on the poor. Nevertheless, the full benefits of this reform will also depend critically on its implementation. Importation of rice could be loosened; but the concurrent supply side support for farmers requires strong governance and reform emphasis, and this latter aspect has always been a challenge in previous administrations and perhaps even President Duterte's.

Inflation

FIGURE 3.1
Inflation Rate (Base Year = 2012)

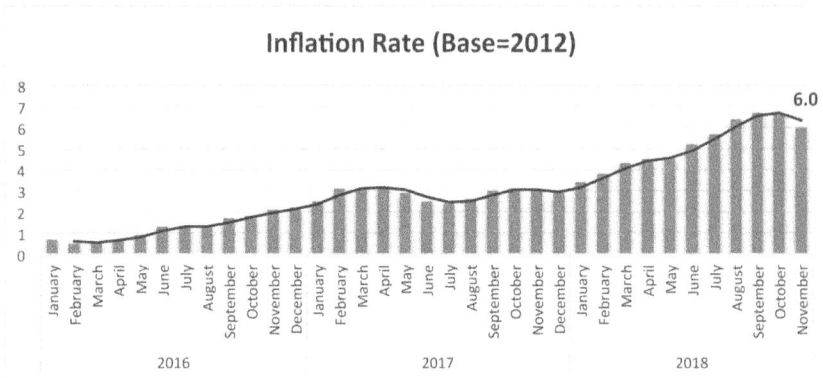

Source: Bangko Sentral ng Pilipinas (BSP).

There is an increasing risk of the economy overheating. The Philippines' annual inflation is expected to hit a six-year high by the end of 2018, at 4.3 per cent (de Vera 2018a). The spikes in food and transport prices are particularly anti-poor given the importance of these two parts of the poor households' budget. Rice, in particular, was a major driver of the country's inflation rate, which stood at a five-year high of 5.2 per cent in June 2018 (Philippine Daily Inquirer 2018). Administration economists and the Bangko Sentral ng Pilipinas (Central Bank) maintain that this is a transitory problem and point to lower rates at the end of 2018 as evidence.

Infrastructure

While the emphasis on infrastructure investments in the "Build-Build-Build" flagship programme of the Duterte administration is a much-welcomed signal—particularly given the importance of infrastructure as one of the key challenges constraining development in the country (Salaverria 2017)—there appear to be major delays in the roll-out of the key flagship projects under the Duterte administration.

Other analysts point to possible governance issues in infrastructure, particularly with rising emphasis on Chinese-funded projects and the seeming deprioritization of public-private partnerships (Mendoza and Cruz 2017).

A growing number of analysts also point to the lack of transparency in the government's infrastructure projects. The Philippine Center for Investigative Journalism (PCIJ) criticized the lack of transparency in public procurement in the Duterte administration, highlighting major gaps in the disclosure of critical documents related to public works contracting (Mangahas and Ilagan 2018).

For example, regarding the much ballyhooed Metro Manila Subway project, hardly any official documents assessing the proposed alignment were publicly available. The Department of Transportation itself has stated that the project's final feasibility study was still being conducted as of June 2018 (DOTR-DM DOTR 2018). It is highly unusual that the project was already greenlighted by the National Economic and Development Authority (NEDA), given that NEDA operations manuals emphasize that full feasibility studies are a mandatory documentary requirement for the evaluation of major infrastructure projects (Mendoza and Cruz 2018). Some analysts wondered whether the Japanese-funded projects were going to progress in any real way until after the Tokyo Olympics in 2020 (after which their contractors could fully engage in projects outside of Japan) (Chanco 2018).

Some of these analysts have since called on the government to engage the public with more transparency (quoted in Cruz et al. 2018):

> Only through a "golden age of transparency" can the public be completely assured that Duterte's "golden age of infrastructure" will not end like the one during the Marcos period—a parade of unviable debt-driven ventures, dragging down our country's fortunes, and resulting in two lost decades of growth and development.

Foreign Direct Investment and Employment

Finally, there is a mixed picture of investments and job creation. As of January 2018, 2.3 million unemployed and 7.5 million underemployed

FIGURE 3.2
Foreign Direct Investments, 2010–17 (in millions USD)

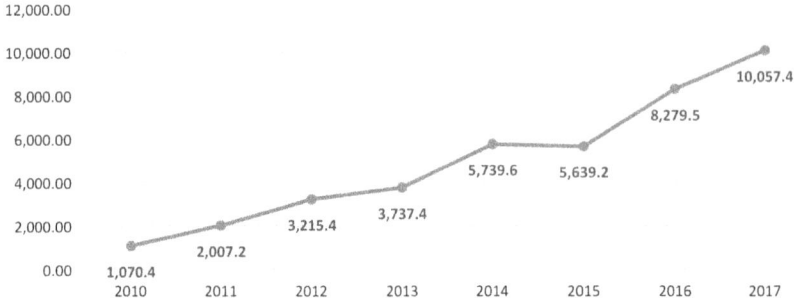

Source: Bangko Sentral ng Pilipinas (BSP).

added to around 10 million unemployed or underemployed workers in the country (out of 44 million workers in the labour force). Annual new jobs created in the first two years of the Duterte administration reached roughly 800,000. But this does not yet account for job destruction, which appears to be a risk thanks to the automation of manufacturing and services sector jobs. Economic think tank IBON Foundation (2019) calculated the overall employment increase as only 81,000 per year in 2017 and 2018—a claim the Duterte administration disputed. The "net job creation" rate needs to be monitored by the government, particularly in the context of the fourth industrial revolution (Business Mirror 2018).

On the other hand, foreign direct investments hit a near-term high of about US$10 billion in 2017 (Bangko Sentral ng Pilipinas 2018). However, this remains small relative to the Philippines' regional neighbours. This may also reflect the growth momentum built up over past years—and not simply the accomplishments under the Duterte administration—but the continuity is reassuring. More worrying, perhaps, are the emerging wait-and-see attitudes due to the government's proposed tax reforms under the second tranche of TRAIN, particularly focused on fiscal incentives for investors (Cuaresma 2018), as well as the downside risks attached by credit rating agencies and analysts to the possible switch to federalism, which is discussed below (Cordero 2018).

Given all these risks, the fundamentals are still strong. Debt management is still sound (as long as Chinese and other loans do not get out of hand), and growth forecasts are still upbeat. The clear challenges here include the following:

- Elevated ambition (Can the Philippine economy grow faster, and can this be sustained over, say, twenty years?) and
- Increased inclusiveness (Can more Filipinos benefit from the growth, and can more regions in the Philippines become linked to emerging economic growth engines?)

A respectable growth (of about 5 per cent per annum) is likely already achievable merely on remittances, business process outsourcing (BPO) and consumption spending—but the real test is whether the Philippine economy can do more to meet the aspirations of its citizens.

Nevertheless, there are risks on the horizon. As noted earlier, there are clear governance challenges, whether in the speed of implementation of infrastructure projects, deficiencies in the business environment (which the Ease of Doing Business Act is intended to address), or policy coherence.

A little-noticed decision of the Philippine Supreme Court overturned how the national government has been calculating its fiscal transfers to local government for the last quarter century under the 1991 Local Government Code. The Mandanas-Garcia ruling required the central government to include customs revenue in "national wealth" in determining the Internal Revenue Allotment to localities (Buan 2018). This mandate to remit larger intergovernmental transfers in favour of the provinces, cities, municipalities, and *barangay*s (villages) may raise fiscal risks. Even though the decision is prospective, the fiscal flexibility of the national government will be constrained. However, local officials will likely be delighted with a substantial revenue increase, and that too will raise governance and accountability challenges, along with opportunities to ramp up investments in public services. Eventually the rebalancing of central-local financing and mandates for public services provision will need to be navigated. Nevertheless, a much larger wave of potential central-local rebalancing could be triggered by the administration's federalism push (discussed next).

FEDERALISM INITIATIVE

Duterte began his pre-campaign presidential exploration with a nationwide campaign in 2014 and 2015 to discuss the possibility of a transition to federalism. While not spelling out the details of his proposed new governance framework, he repeatedly reverted to the topic throughout his presidency (Rood 2019).

The consultative committee tasked to review the 1987 Constitution was formed by President Duterte in 2017. Still, the first nineteen members of this committee were appointed only in January 2018, over a year after creating this group (Ranada 2018). Chaired by former Supreme Court Chief Justice Reynato Puno, the committee had less than six months to produce the draft *"Bayanihan* Constitution" (the name given to the proposed constitution). It was submitted to President Duterte on 3 July 2018 shortly before his third State of the Nation Address (SONA) (Philstar.com 2018).

Perhaps there are at least two levels of discussion and debate regarding the effort to push for charter change. First, one can focus on the substance surrounding this initiative—the draft has triggered an intense discussion of whether and to what extent the *Bayanihan* Constitution improves on the 1987 Constitution. There are several things worth noting here. First, the *Bayanihan* Constitution contains important self-executory reforms that the 1987 Constitution had in aspirational form but left to Congress to enact. These include a clause to regulate political dynasties, provisions for promoting political party reforms and rules to punish turncoatism. These are not linked to federalism but address the longstanding reforms Congress should have passed. Congress failed to enact these reforms, to the detriment of the full implementation of democratic aspects of the 1987 Constitution.

Second, the *Bayanihan* Constitution attempts to open the door for lifting the economic restrictions embedded in the 1987 Constitution. It roughly maintains the ownership restrictions in key sectors like education, media and mining. Still, it also contains the following phrase: "Congress may, by law, change the voting capital requirement under this section considering public welfare and national security, and for this purpose, such entities shall be managed by citizens of the Philippines." By allowing Congress to change the voting capital requirements, this provision follows a similar track to the 2013 proposal by former House Speaker Feliciano Belmonte to ease restrictions in the 1987 Constitution (Salaverria 2013). Economic analysts were dismayed that these proposed provisions were not self-executing (fearing the same fate as occurred with the democratic aspirations of the 1987 Constitution).

Third, the *Bayanihan* Constitution contains bold provisions to form a layer of regional governments to create region-based agglomerations that could have positive and negative side effects. Presumably, the intention is to provide a layer of governance that facilitates more coherent regional growth that province-level strategies alone could not accomplish. It could also lessen the tendency for fractionalized projects and development planning. Ostensibly, this could also form part of a broader decentralization effort that further weakens the dominance of the central government over taxing and spending decisions—channelling some of this power to the regions (and more specifically to a new layer of regional government) that could, in turn, foster greater synergy in their development policy and strategy.

However, the formation of regional governments (as well as other government agencies and deep structural reforms such as more courts) under the proposed *Bayanihan* Charter triggered a strong response from economists, including within the Duterte administration. Economic and Development Secretary Ernesto Pernia noted how federalism might wreak havoc on the Philippine economy by pushing up spending and the fiscal deficit (Rivas 2018). Finance Secretary Carlos Dominguez III later added more fuel to this critique by noting how the country's current investment-grade credit rating status and stable interest rate environment "will go to hell" under the draft federal Constitution (Leyco 2018). Analyses by credit rating agencies like Moody's have also raised concerns about federalism—considering this initiative's possible credit downgrade risk (de Vera 2018b).

Beyond substantive discussions on the draft's content, there were concerns over the process and the governance environment under which federalism was being pushed. Media reports on the president's 2018 SONA focused more on the change of House speakership broadcast live on television from one Duterte ally to another rather than on the president's address that included an endorsement of federalism.

President Duterte was constrained to wait in a holding room until members of the House of Representatives could sort out the power dynamics enough to allow the speech to go forward. The resurgence of the former president, now House Speaker, Gloria Macapagal Arroyo, as a political player has also raised questions about possible ambitions to use the constitutional reform to introduce a parliamentary system that would allow her to run for head of state.

In fact, at the time of finalizing this chapter in late 2018, the Philippine House of Representatives passed on third and final reading of the "House version" of charter change—one that did not include an anti-dynasty regulation and removed term limits for politicians. These are anathema to the democratic reforms while endorsing some economic liberalization, so that this draft exposes rifts in the ruling administration's broad alliance.

Similar concerns over "conflict of interest" have been raised by leaders from academia and other sectors, pointing to the lack of credibility in the process if leaders push for a Constituent Assembly (Professors for Peace 2018) where members of the House and Senate vote to propose a constitution to be ratified by plebiscite. The business community also joined the fray by raising deep concerns over the speed of this reform, calling for more debate and analyses to ensure that economic concerns are amply addressed. In particular, they raised the issue of the possible sizeable extra cost of expanding government. Citing preliminary estimates of the Philippine Institute for Development Studies, the groups said the would-be multi-level government under a federal system is estimated to incur a cost of PHP 72 billion to PHP 130 billion (Desiderio 2018).

International attention to the Duterte administration focused mainly on his brutal war on drugs and his pivot in foreign affairs towards China. But the fate of his administration is likely to be determined more by economic affairs and political currents. As the nation was preparing for the May 2019 mid-term elections of local officials, members of Congress and half of the Senate, the current administration was presiding over a robust economy, had accomplished some but not all of its desired economic reforms, and yet had not changed any of the fundamental political structures put in place by the 1987 Constitution.[4]

Notes

1. The author would like to thank Miann Banaag and Kendrick Uy for their inputs on the draft of this chapter.
2. This version is as of December 2018.
3. Philippine Statistics Authority, Regional GDP (GRDP) Series, 2009–2017.
4. Editors' note: After the 2019 mid-term elections, President Duterte largely abandoned the push for federalism. See Teehankee (2019).

References

Avendaño, Christine O. 2018. "Palace Releases Report on Duterte Administration's Achievements for Past Year". *Philippine Daily Inquirer*, 21 July 2018. https://newsinfo.inquirer.net/1012627/sona-2018-rodrigo-duterte-accomplishment-report-year-2#ixzz5Lw3edhzC (accessed 1 March 2023).

Bangko Sentral ng Pilipinas. 2018. "Full-Year 2017 FDI Hit All-Time High of US$10 Billion". *Facebook*, 12 March 2018. https://www.facebook.com/BangkoSentralngPilipinas/photos/full-year-2017-fdi-hit-all-time-high-of-us10-billiondetails-on-httpwwwbspgovphpu/1679988962064926/ (accessed 1 March 2023).

Buan, Lian. 2018. "Supreme Court: LGU Shares Shall Be Sourced from All National Taxes". *Rappler*, 4 July 2018. https://www.rappler.com/nation/206467-supreme-court-decision-lgu-shares-all-national-taxes/ (accessed 1 March 2023).

Business Mirror. 2018. "Fourth Industrial Revolution: Are We There Yet?" 4 October 2019. https://businessmirror.com.ph/2018/10/04/fourth-industrial-revolution-are-we-there-yet/ (accessed 1 March 2023).

Chanco, Boo. 2018. "Big Projects". *The Philippine Star*, 24 January 2018. https://www.philstar.com/business/2018/01/24/1780664/big-projects (accessed 1 March 2023).

Cigaral, Ian Nicolas. 2018. "ADB Keeps Growth Outlook, Raises Inflation Forecast for Philippines". *Philstar.com*, 19 July 2018. https://www.philstar.com/business/2018/07/19/1834917/adb-keeps-growth-outlook-raises-inflation-forecast-philippines (accessed 1 March 2023).

Cordero, John Ted. 2018. "Moody's Flags Shift to Federalism as 'Downside Risk' to PHL's Fiscal Health". *GMA News Online*, 20 July 2018. https://www.gmanetwork.com/news/money/economy/661241/moody-s-flags-shift-to-federalism-as-downside-risk-to-phl-s-fiscal-health/story/ (accessed 1 March 2023).

Cruz, Jerome Patrick, Carmen Phanuelle Delgra, Jose Miguelito Enriquez, and Ronald U. Mendoza. 2018. "Governing the 'Golden Age of Infrastructure':

Build, Build, Build through an Accountability Perspective". *Ateneo School of Government Working Paper 18-11*, 13 December 2018. https://dx.doi.org/10.2139/ssrn.3300597 (accessed 1 March 2023).

Cuaresma, Bianca. 2018. "Upbeat on Long Term: FDI Rise 43.5% in Q1". *Business Mirror*, 11 June 2018. https://businessmirror.com.ph/upbeat-on-long-term-fdi-rise-43-5-in-q1/ (accessed 1 March 2023).

Desiderio, Louella. 2018. "Business Groups: Weigh Costs, Risks of Federalism". *The Philippine Star*, 13 August 2018. https://www.philstar.com/headlines/2018/08/13/1842117/business-groups-weigh-costs-risks-federalism (accessed 1 March 2023).

De Vera, Ben O. 2018a. "ADB: PH Annual Inflation to Hit 6-Year High of 4.3% in 2018". *Philippine Daily Inquirer*, 19 July 2018. https://business.inquirer.net/254216/adb-ph-annual-inflation-hit-6-year-high-4-3-2018 (accessed 1 March 2023).

———. 2018b. "Moody's: Shift to Federalism a Downside Risk for PH Economy". *Philippine Daily Inquirer*, 20 July 2018. https://business.inquirer.net/254280/moodys-shift-federalism-downside-risk-ph-economy (accessed 1 March 2023).

DOTR (Department of Transportation)-DM DOTR. 2018. "Response to the Request Dated 30 May, 2018 Re Copy of the Feasibility Study for the Metro Manila Subway Project". *e-FOI – Electronic Freedom of Information*, 5 June 2018. https://www.foi.gov.ph/requests/aglzfmVmb2ktcGhyHgsSB0NvbnRlbnQiEURPVHItMjA0NTk1NDgxNDQxDA (accessed 1 March 2023).

IBON Foundation. 2019. "IBON Replies to Presidential Spokesperson on Employment Situation". *IBON.org*, 27 January 2019. https://www.ibon.org/tag/81000-average-annual-job-generation/ (accessed 1 March 2023).

Leyco, Chino. 2018. "Interest Rates 'Will Go to Hell' under Federalism – Dominguez". *Manila Bulletin*, 9 August 2018. https://mb.com.ph/2018/08/09/interest-rates-will-go-to-hell-under-federalism-dominguez/ (accessed 1 March 2023).

Mangahas, Malou, and Karol Ilagan. 2018. "DPWH under Duterte: Corruption, Politics, Slippage Mar Many Projects". *Philippine Center for Investigative Journalism*, 3 September 2018. https://pcij.org/article/1401/dpwh-under-duterte-corruption-politics-slippage-mar-many-projects (accessed 25 February 2023).

Mendoza, Ronald U., and Jerik Cruz. 2017. "Duterte Infra: Bigger, More Imperial and China-linked". *Rappler*, 30 July 2017. https://www.rappler.com/thought-leaders/177140-duterte-infrastructure-bigger-more-imperial-china-linked (accessed 1 March 2023).

———. 2018. "OPINION: Teka-teka vs. Bara-bara: Assessing the Governance of Build-Build-Build". *ABS-CBN News*, 3 July 2018. https://news.abs-cbn.com/

business/07/03/18/opinion-teka-teka-vs-bara-bara-assessing-the-governance-of-build-build-build (accessed 1 March 2023).

Philippine Daily Inquirer. 2018. "EDITORIAL: Surging Rice Prices". *Philippine Daily Inquirer*, 16 July 2018. https://opinion.inquirer.net/114640/surging-rice-prices (accessed 1 March 2023).

Philstar.com. 2018. "Full Text: Consultative Committee's Draft Federal Constitution". 9 July 2018. https://www.philstar.com/headlines/2018/07/09/1832024/full-text-consultative-committees-draft-federal-constitution (accessed 1 March 2023).

Professors for Peace. 2018. "NO TO CON-ASS | Statement on Prospect for Constitutional Reforms". 13 July 2018. https://peaceprofessors.wordpress.com/2018/07/13/no-to-con-ass-statement-on-prospect-for-constitutional-reforms/ (accessed 1 March 2023).

Ranada, Pia. 2018. "Duterte Appoints 19 Members of Charter Change Consultative Committee". *Rappler*, 25 January 2018, https://www.rappler.com/nation/194518-duterte-appoints-members-consultative-committee/ (accessed 1 March 2023).

Rivas, Ralf. 2018. "Federalism Will 'Wreak Havoc' on Philippine Economy – Pernia". *Rappler*, 17 July 2018. https://www.rappler.com/business/207521-federalism-bad-for-economy-ernesto-pernia/ (accessed 1 March 2023).

Rood, Steven. 2019. "Finding Federalism in the Philippines: Federalism—'The Centerpiece of My Campaign'". In *From Aquino II to Duterte (2010–2018): Change, Continuity – and Rupture*, edited by Imelda Deinla and Björn Dressel, pp. 62–98. Singapore: ISEAS – Yusof Ishak Institute.

Salaverria, Leila B. 2013. "Belmonte Files Resolution to Ease Restrictions on Foreign Firms in PH". *Philippine Daily Inquirer*, 9 July 2013. https://newsinfo.inquirer.net/441735/belmonte-files-resolution-to-ease-restrictions-on-foreign-firms-in-ph (accessed 1 March 2023).

———. 2017. "Inflation, Poor Infrastructure are Pinoys' Most Urgent Issues". *Philippine Daily Inquirer*, 21 October 2017. http://newsinfo.inquirer.net/939575/philippine-news-updates-pulse-asia-crime-jobs (accessed 1 March 2023).

Teehankee, Julio C. 2019. "Duterte's Federalist Project Indefinitely on Hold". *East Asia Forum*, 24 July 2019. https://www.eastasiaforum.org/2019/07/24/dutertes-federalist-project-indefinitely-on-hold/ (accessed 27 February 2023).

4

The Philippine Economy: Sustained Economic Growth amidst Short-Term Disturbances?

Myrna S. Austria[1]

INTRODUCTION

Under the Aquino administration (2010–16), the Philippine economy registered high economic growth rates. It was supported by strong macroeconomic fundamentals characterized by a moderate and decreasing inflation rate, a stable and strong peso, low interest rates, declining unemployment rates and a low budget deficit. During the period, the economy also underwent structural transformation, with investment leading growth on the demand side and industry, particularly the manufacturing sector, on the supply side.

The country also experienced a high level of confidence from the international community. The Philippines consistently improved its global competitiveness ranking by moving thirty positions during the period (see Figure 4.1). It earned its first-ever investment grade rating in 2013; its sovereign credit rating has made significant strides since then.[2] The upgrade is due to strong economic growth, robust external balances, an improving fiscal position and the continued inflow of foreign direct investment (FDI).

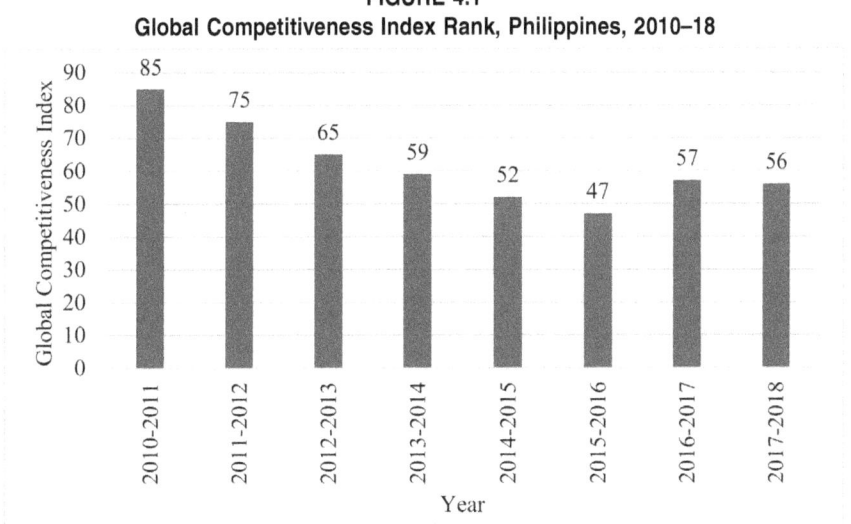

FIGURE 4.1
Global Competitiveness Index Rank, Philippines, 2010–18

Source: World Economic Forum, *Global Competitiveness Reports* (various years).

The favourable economic performance continued under the Duterte administration. However, the economy is facing short-term disturbances coming from internal and external sources that, if not addressed quickly, could endanger the projected growth trajectory of the country. These include the weakening peso, increasing trade deficits and rising inflation rate.

The primary objectives of this chapter are (1) to discuss the country's recent economic performance, (2) to explain the concerns it is facing and the policies and programmes to meet them head-on, and (3) to identify the challenges and uncertainties that lie ahead.

This chapter is structured as follows: Section 2 explains why the country is no longer referred to as the "Sick Man of Asia", the short-term disturbances it is facing and the countermeasures implemented by the government to cushion the adverse effects of such disturbances. Section 3 discusses the major policies and programmes to address the long-standing constraints to growth and steer the economy towards inclusive economic growth in the medium and long term. Section 4 presents the challenges and uncertainties that lie ahead. Section 5 provides a summary and conclusion.[3]

THE PHILIPPINES: NO LONGER THE SICK MAN OF ASIA

Before 2010, the Philippines was often labelled the "Sick Man of Asia". The country missed decades of favourable growth episodes enjoyed elsewhere in the region. The economy's performance contrasted with the vibrant economic growth of its developing country neighbours as they rapidly caught up with the region's developed countries like South Korea, Hong Kong, Taiwan, Singapore and Japan. The Philippines' long-term growth experience is often characterized in the literature as a "boom-bust" cycle of economic growth, where a favourable growth episode is followed by a period of instability and volatility, either political, financial or economic, that erodes the gains achieved, only to be followed by another period of positive growth and then another crisis (Llanto 2012).

Starting in 2013, however, the country shed its negative label as it successfully transitioned to become a rising economic tiger in Asia. No longer a laggard, it remained one of the fastest-growing economies, outpacing Thailand, Malaysia, Indonesia and Vietnam (see Figure 4.2). By 2017, the country was one of East Asia's three leading growth performers, behind only China and Vietnam. The growth rate was down slightly in the second quarter of 2018 to 6 per cent, but economic managers considered the lower-than-expected growth rate as short-term, as explained below.

The acceleration in economic growth is also reflected in the country's unemployment rate, which reached record lows in recent years, signalling less spare labour capacity. From an annual average of 7.4 per cent in 2010, it continued down to an average of 5.7 per cent in 2017 (see Figure 4.3).

FIGURE 4.2
Annual Real GDP Growth, ASEAN, 2010–17 (%)

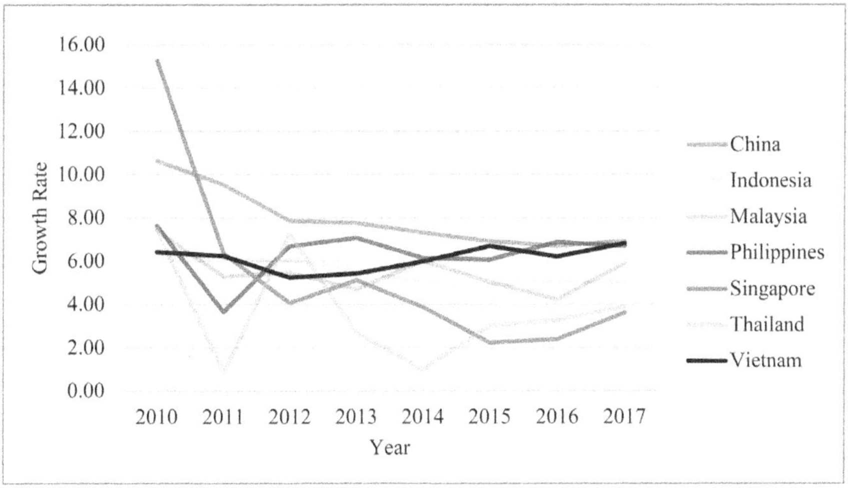

Sources: World Bank Data Indicators (2018); author's calculations.

FIGURE 4.3
Unemployment per Quarter, Philippines, Q1 2010–Q1 2018 (%)

Source: Philippine Statistics Authority.

In general, the favourable economic performance since 2010 has been driven by the cumulative effects of structural reforms and improved macroeconomic and fiscal fundamentals under the various past administrations (World Bank 2018b, p. 10).

Economic growth and structural transformation

Not only is the Philippines' economic growth high, but the sources of growth are now broader and more diversified as the economy undergoes structural transformation, both on the demand and supply sides. On the demand side, growth is now increasingly driven by capital formation or investment (see Figure 4.4). This is in significant contrast to performances over the past two to three decades when growth was led by household final consumption expenditures fuelled by remittances from overseas Filipino workers (OFWs) (World Bank 2018a). While household consumption spending still accounts for the bulk of demand, its contribution to overall demand increased at a lower rate compared to investment. Its share increased by two percentage points from 2010 to 2017 in contrast to the share of investment, which increased by almost five percentage points during the same period. Investment grew the fastest among the components of demand, increasing at double digits for most quarters from 2010 until the second quarter of 2018 (see Figure 4.4). It grew at an average of 15.3 per cent per quarter during the period. On the other hand, Figure 4.4 shows that household consumption grew at a relatively constant rate of 5.8 per cent. Imports as a sector are also growing faster, at an average of 12.1 per cent, another indicator of a growing economy. Also, government expenditures grew relatively more quickly starting in 2017 as the current administration embarked on its massive infrastructure programme under the Build, Build, Build Program (B³P), as will be explained in the next section.

On the supply side, the country is experiencing a resurgence of the industry sector, particularly manufacturing. While the services sector still accounts for the largest share of output (see Figure 4.5), the manufacturing sector has been leading the growth in recent years (see Figure 4.6). The government, under different administrations, has long been promoting the sector. Still, it was not until 2013 that

FIGURE 4.4
Quarterly Real GDP Growth by Expenditure, Philippines, Q1 2010–Q2 2018 (%)

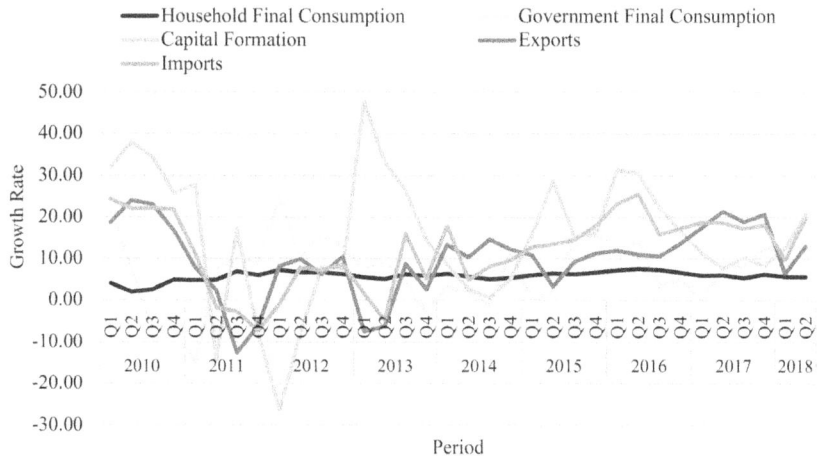

Note: Growth is based at constant 2000 prices.
Source: Bangko Sentral ng Pilipinas.

FIGURE 4.5
Share in GDP by Sector, Philippines, 2010–18 (%)

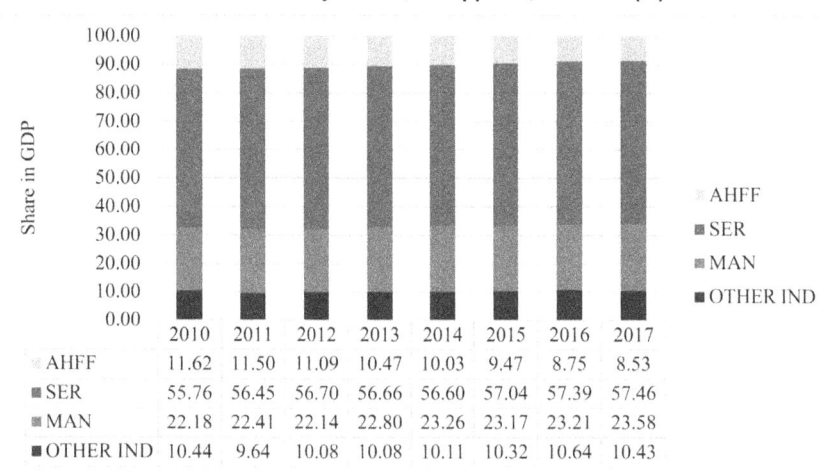

	2010	2011	2012	2013	2014	2015	2016	2017
AHFF	11.62	11.50	11.09	10.47	10.03	9.47	8.75	8.53
SER	55.76	56.45	56.70	56.66	56.60	57.04	57.39	57.46
MAN	22.18	22.41	22.14	22.80	23.26	23.17	23.21	23.58
OTHER IND	10.44	9.64	10.08	10.08	10.11	10.32	10.64	10.43

Notes: AHFF—Agriculture, Hunting, Forestry and Fishing; SER—Service Sector; MAN—Manufacturing; OTHER IND—Mining and Quarrying, Construction and Electricity, Gas and Water Supply
Source: Philippine Statistics Authority.

FIGURE 4.6
Quarterly Real GDP Growth by Sector, Philippines, Q1 2010–Q2 2018 (%)

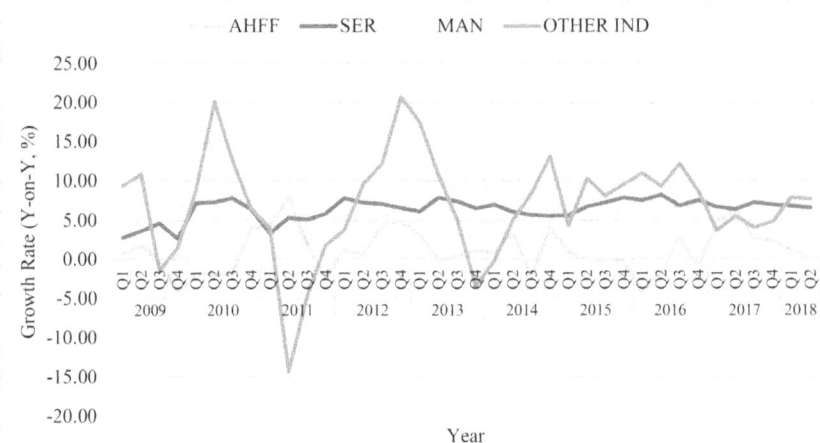

Notes: (i) Notations are the same as for Figure 4.5; (ii) growth is based on constant 2000 prices.
Source: Philippine Statistics Authority.

the sector showed a remarkable growth trend, outpacing the services sector until the second quarter of 2018. On average, manufacturing grew at 7.8 per cent per quarter during the period, while services grew at 6.8 per cent per quarter. As will be discussed in more detail below, the significant shift from a service-driven to a manufacturing-driven economy is the outcome of the government's Manufacturing Resurgence Program (MRP), which commenced under the Aquino administration but continued to have an impact under the Duterte government (Raquiza, this volume).

The ongoing structural transformation is a welcome development for the country. The rise in investment spending increases the country's capital stock which, in turn, enhances the country's productive capacity and creates greater employment opportunities both in the short term and in the medium to long term. On the other hand, the manufacturing sector's resurgence intensifies the economy's forward and backward linkages. These shifts in the drivers of growth on the demand and supply sides create a more inclusive pattern of economic growth for the country, which can eradicate the country's long-time problem of poverty and income inequality when sustained in the long term.

Total factor productivity and sustained economic growth

Recent studies have shown that the structural transformation taking place in the country is accompanied by growth in total factor productivity (TFP). This includes the work done by Llanto (2012), Anand et al. (2014), Glindro and Amodia (2016) and the World Bank (2018b). This recharacterization of the economy's recent performance is another benefit for the Philippines because TFP growth is crucial to sustaining growth in the long run. Because of diminishing returns to scale, an economy cannot rely on capital accumulation alone to sustain growth. The key is TFP growth: how efficiently the inputs are used in production (Blanchard and Johnson 2014).

The study by Glindro and Amodia (2016) shows the increasing contribution of TFP growth to the country's economic growth (see Figure 4.7). From less than 4 per cent in 1989–92 and 15.3 per cent in 1993–2001, its contribution improved substantially to 42.4 per cent in 2010–16. This is consistent with the World Bank's recent study showing that TFP growth has accelerated since 2000. Furthermore, the same study shows that, except for China, the contribution of TFP

FIGURE 4.7
Sources of GDP Growth, Philippines, 1989–Q1 2016 (%)

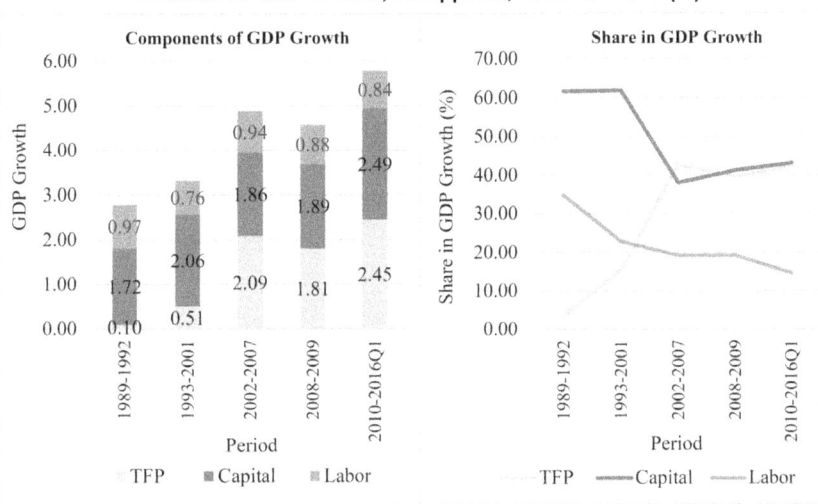

Source: Glindro and Amodia (2016).

growth in the Philippines in 1995–2010 is higher than its neighbours in the region (World Bank 2018b, p. 11). Manufacturing experienced the highest growth in labour productivity among the sectors, again outpacing some of its regional peers (World Bank 2018b, p. 13). This finding supports the structural transformation happening on the supply side, as discussed above.

These findings make clear the significant departure from the country's decades-long past performance of low, if not declining, TFP growth at a time when TFP gained prominence in the economic growth of its neighbours in East Asia (Llanto 2012). In an interview, Socioeconomic Planning Secretary Ernesto Pernia underscored the role of the increase in TFP growth in creating quality growth and employment in the country in the future (de Vera 2018b).

Short-term growth disturbances

However, simultaneously, the Philippine economy is currently experiencing short-term growth disturbances caused by external and internal factors. These include the depreciation of the peso, the rising trade deficit and the increasing inflation rate. These disruptions, considered by the country's economic managers as short term, will test the strength of the domestic economy, depending on the government's response in addressing them.

Depreciation of the Philippine peso. The peso started to depreciate in 2014 (see Figure 4.8) with the increasing demand for imports to meet the requirements of the growing economy. The peso's weakening became more prominent with the volatilities in the global financial markets brought about by Brexit (the decision of the United Kingdom to leave the European Union [EU] in June 2016) and the ongoing interest rate hikes in the United States since 2017. The more favourable return on financial investments in the United States causes capital to move out of the Philippines and depreciate the peso.

The weakening peso puts pressure on the prices of basic commodities and the cost of imported goods, as explained below. Likewise, it increases the cost of payments on the country's foreign-denominated debt. Companies heavily dependent on imported inputs also become highly vulnerable, especially if they do not have dollar-denominated revenues. One sector that benefits from the peso depreciation is the families of OFWs because it increases the purchasing power of the remittances.

FIGURE 4.8
Monthly Peso–Dollar Exchange Rate, Philippines, January 2010–August 2018

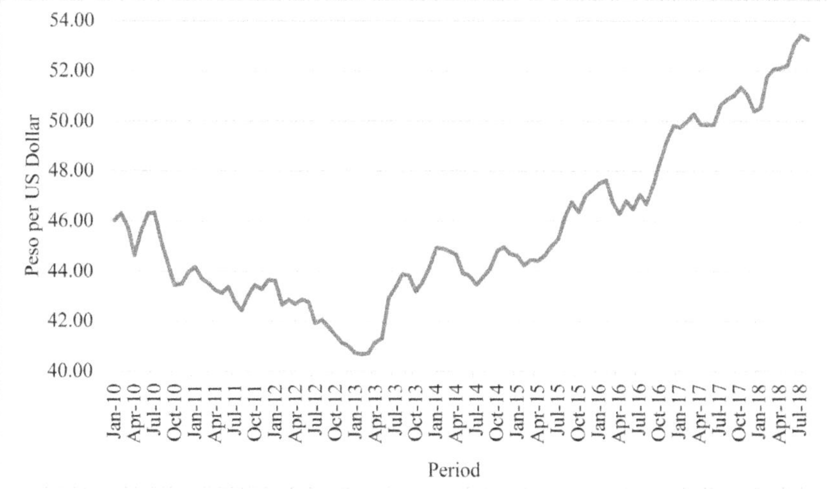

Source: Bangko Sentral ng Pilipinas.

Increasing trade and current account deficits. With imports exceeding exports, the country has been running trade deficits. On an annual basis, the trade deficits narrowed from 9.1 per cent of the gross domestic product (GDP) in 2011 to 6.1 per cent in 2014 (see Figure 4.9). However, the gap widened in 2016 and 2017. From nearly 8 per cent of GDP in 2015, it went up to 11.7 per cent in 2016 and further deteriorated to almost 13 per cent in 2017.

The higher growth in imports compared to exports reflects the expansion of the domestic economy, given the country's high dependence on imports for some of its production requirements. But the deterioration in 2016 and 2017 was due to two primary sources, namely, (1) an increase in the import bill, or more dollars spent on imports, because of the weak peso, and (2) the heavy importation of capital equipment and other materials for the massive infrastructure drive of the government under the B^{3}P.

FIGURE 4.9
Trade Deficit, Philippines, 2010–17 (US$, %)

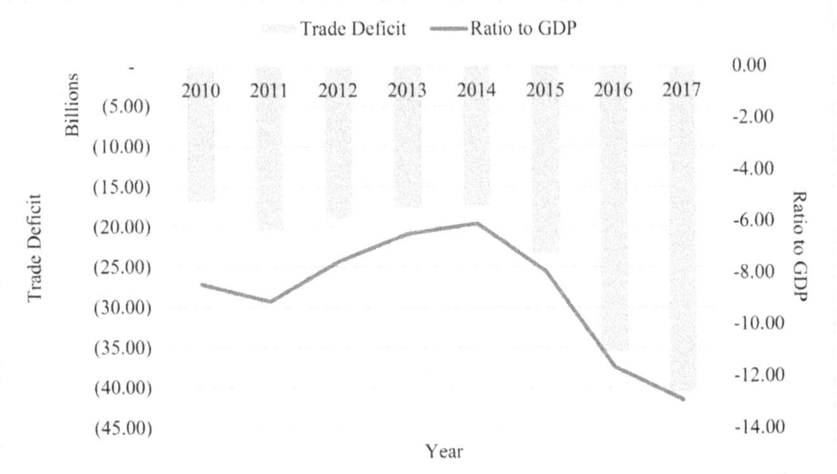

Sources: Bangko Sentral ng Pilipinas; author's calculations.

The worsening trade deficit is currently putting more pressure on the peso. But this can be considered temporary if one looks at the positive long-term effect that the B³P programme may generate on the economy if the implementation succeeds.

Rising inflation rate. The behaviour of the inflation rate somehow mirrors that of the local currency. The inflation rate was mild and stable until 2015 (see Figure 4.10). It went down from a monthly average of 2.6 per cent in 2010 to less than 1 per cent in 2015. But it went up to nearly 3 per cent in 2017 and deteriorated further to a record-high of 6.4 per cent by August 2018.

Both external and domestic shocks cause the higher-than-expected rise in the inflation rate. On the external front, the increase in global fuel prices and the drop in the peso continue to put pressure on domestic prices. The country heavily depends on imports for its oil requirements and raw materials and other inputs for production. Higher prices translate to higher production costs, which are then passed on to domestic consumers. This is exacerbated by the depreciation of the peso mentioned above (see Figure 4.8). According to Bangko Sentral ng Pilipinas (BSP) Deputy Governor Diwa Guinigundo, "As a rule of thumb, every one per cent decline in the value of the peso against the dollar results in an increase in the national inflation rate by 0.06 per cent" (Lucas 2018).

FIGURE 4.10
Monthly Inflation Rate, Philippines, January 2013–August 2018 (%)

Source: Bangko Sentral ng Pilipinas.

On the domestic front, the 2017 Tax Reform for Acceleration and Inclusion Law (TRAIN), a perceived rice shortage and natural calamities contribute to the price increase in basic commodities. As discussed in detail in the next section, the TRAIN law, among other things, reduced personal income taxes and increased the excise tax on sugar-sweetened beverages and petroleum products such as diesel, kerosene and liquified petroleum gas. The increase in take-home pay increased households' demand for goods and services, plus the rise in excise tax, put pressure on the price of basic commodities. Hence, the increase in the inflation rate.

However, the negative effects of TRAIN are considered transitory as the economy adjusts to the new tax scheme (ADB 2018b). On the other hand, natural calamities like typhoons and heavy rains that often visit the country make food and agricultural products highly vulnerable to price fluctuations. As in the past, the adverse effects on food prices are temporary.

Government's response to short-term disturbances

To curb inflation and inflation expectations and defend the peso from speculative attacks, the government has been aggressively tightening monetary policies through the BSP. After maintaining a constant rate for over a year, the BSP raised its reverse repurchase rate (RRP) four times after May 2018 (see Figure 4.11). From 3.0 per cent, the RRP rose to 4.5 per cent or a total increase of 150 basis points over five months. The RRP is the key policy rate on which financial institutions base their lending rates to borrowers. The increase in interest rate will protect the country from investment outflows. At the same time, household consumption expenditures funded by loans were expected to decrease, thus lessening cash circulation and inflationary pressure. The tightening of monetary policy was expected to slow down the inflation rate during the fourth quarter of 2018, barring natural calamities that could affect supply.

Since part of the inflationary pressure is driven from the supply side, the government is also working on non-monetary measures

FIGURE 4.11
BSP's Reverse Repurchase Rate (RRP), February 2017–September 2018 (%)

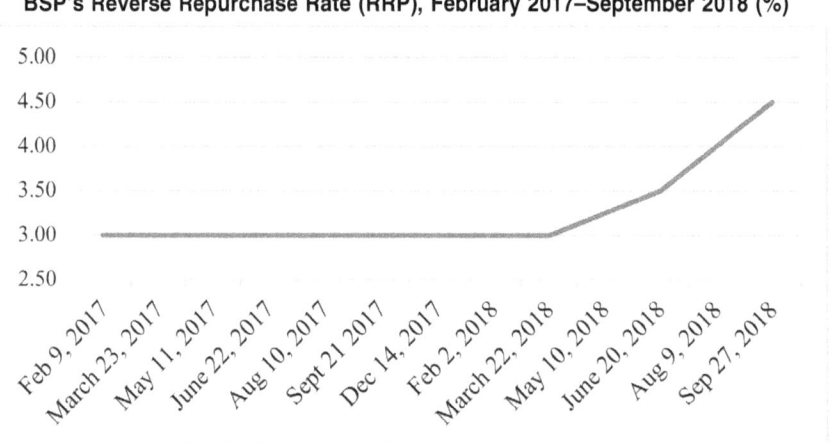

Source: Bangko Sentral ng Pilipinas.

to tame inflation. This includes increasing rice supply by enacting the rice tariffication bill and simplifying the licensing process for rice importation. It is also constantly monitoring the price of basic commodities to prevent unscrupulous businessmen from taking advantage of the shortfall in supply, particularly of rice and other food items.

POLICY REFORMS AND PROGRAMMES FOR SUSTAINED LONG-TERM GROWTH

This section of the chapter will briefly discuss the major programmes and policy reforms the current administration is implementing to address some of the long-standing constraints to the country's long-term inclusive economic growth. As mentioned in the preceding section, while these programmes may generate short-term disruption, their long-term effects will contribute to the sustained economic growth of the country.

Build, Build, Build Program (B3P)

Poor and inadequate infrastructure supply has been holding back growth in the country. The insufficiency affects productivity and increases the cost of doing business in the country. Among the pillars of the World Economic Forum's Global Competitiveness Index (GCI),[4] infrastructure is the second weakest (see Figure 4.12). It also ranked second among the sixteen most problematic factors of doing business in the country, as assessed by the World Economic Forum (see Figure 4.13). According to the latest Japan International Cooperation Agency study, the worsening traffic congestion in Metro Manila, the centre of economic activity in the country, costs PHP 3.5 billion per day in lost opportunities—and it will increase to PHP 5.4 billion a day in 2035 if nothing is done (de Vera 2018a).

Styled the "golden age of infrastructure", the Duterte administration embarked on the Build, Build, Build Program (B³P) to address the long-standing bottlenecks in infrastructure and logistics in the country. Projected to cost the government PHP 9 trillion over a ten-year period, the programme consists of seventy-five flagship projects, including airports, railways, bridges, seaports, bus rapid transits, energy facilities and flood control facilities. Potential benefits from B³P include lower

FIGURE 4.12
Global Competitiveness Index, by Pillars, Philippines, 2017–18

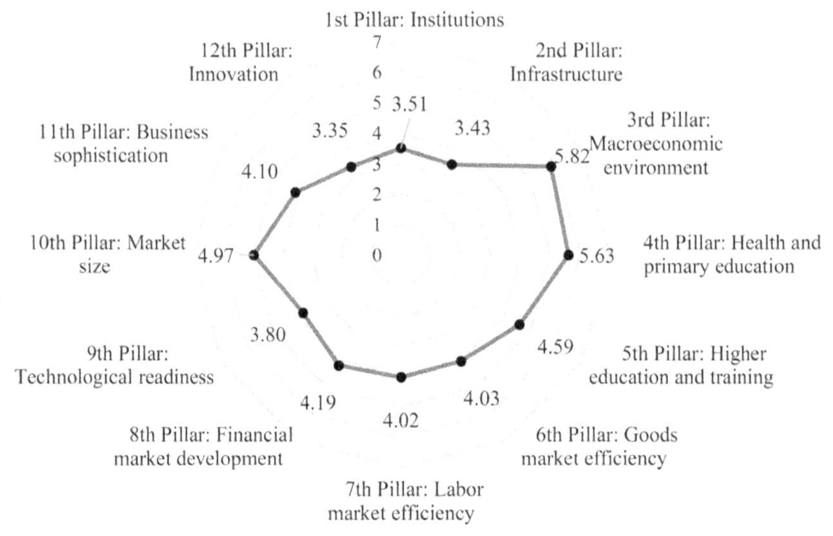

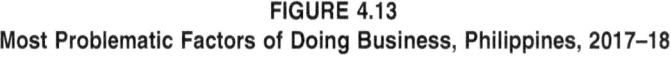

Sources: World Economic Forum (2018).

FIGURE 4.13
Most Problematic Factors of Doing Business, Philippines, 2017–18

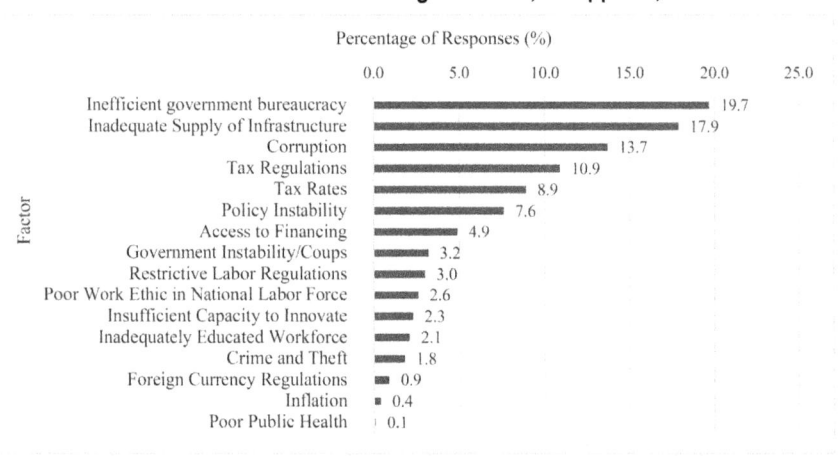

Sources: World Economic Forum (2018).

costs of production, efficient movement of goods and people and increased investment in the countryside, hence, more jobs and improved rural incomes.

No doubt, the B³P is a sizeable fiscal stimulus, but not without economic costs and risks. The economic costs include the increasing trade deficits due to the importation of capital equipment, as mentioned in the preceding section, and the worsening of the budget deficit in 2016 and 2017 (see Figure 4.14). From less than 1 per cent in 2015, the fiscal balance slipped to 2.4 per cent and 2.2 per cent in 2016 and 2017, respectively. The potential economic risks could arise from the ongoing disruptions in the economy. The increase in government expenditures could induce more inflation pressure, though Budget Secretary Benjamin Diokno, in his contribution to this volume, argues that 3.0 per cent of GDP is a sustainable deficit. The peso's depreciation and the interest rate increase could increase that part of the project cost funded by foreign borrowings. The B³P faced challenges as there were project implementation delays due to roadblocks in funding and other regulatory issues.

FIGURE 4.14
Fiscal Balance: Budget Surplus/Deficit and Ratio to GDP, Philippines, 2010–17 (PhP, %)

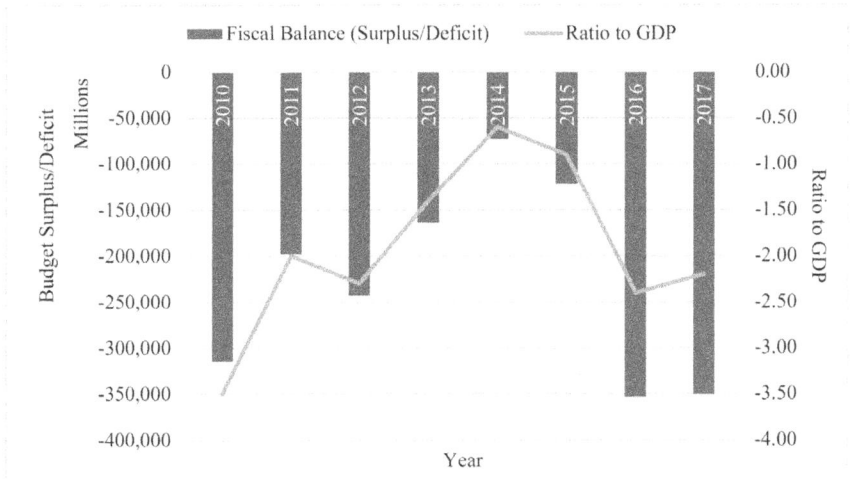

Source: Philippine Statistics Authority.

Tax Reform for Acceleration and Inclusion (TRAIN)

Tax regulations and tax rates were ranked 4th and 5th among the sixteen most problematic factors of doing business in the country (see Figure 4.13). To address the long-standing deficiencies of the tax system, the Duterte administration implemented, effective January 2018, the government's first package of the Comprehensive Tax Reform Program (CTRP), known as the TRAIN Act. The policy reform reduced the personal income taxes of 99 per cent of taxpayers after twenty years of not adjusting tax rates and brackets, gave cash transfers to the poorest ten million households, increased the excise tax on sweetened beverages, cigarettes, luxury items, sweetened beverages, among other things. The increase in tax revenues generated from the programme is planned to fund the government's B3P infrastructure and social programmes.

In only its first year of implementation, TRAIN became unpopular because of its inflationary effects, as discussed earlier. While the government argues that TRAIN's effects on inflation are minimal, the people's perception increases inflationary expectations. Because of this, the approval of the second package of TRAIN was delayed. Called the Tax Reform for Attracting Better and High-Quality Opportunities (TRABAHO)[5] bill, the proposed package targeted cuts in corporate income tax (CIT) and rationalization of tax incentives by giving more bias to investments outside the metro and urban areas. The reduction in CIT is expected to attract investments and create more job opportunities in rural areas.

Manufacturing Resurgence Program (MRP)

The implementation of MRP started with the Aquino administration and carried over with the Duterte administration. The programme aims to revive the country's manufacturing sector and enhance competitiveness. Before 2013, the sector's growth performance was weak, and its contribution to GDP low. Unlike its neighbours in the ASEAN region, the economy has not experienced structural transformation from agriculture to industry, despite the market-oriented policy reforms implemented by the government since the 1980s.

The government, therefore, embarked on the MRP as the new industrial strategy to promote the growth and development of the manufacturing sector. The goal is to develop globally competitive industries with strong forward and backward linkages, which are characterized by deep participation, particularly by micro, small and medium enterprises (MSMEs), in regional and global production networks and value chains. The MRP has three phases: Phase I, whose implementation was completed in 2014–17, involved the rebuilding of capacities of existing industries; Phase II, which covers the period 2018–21, involves shifting to high value-added activities and investment in upstream industries; and Phase III in 2022–25 will deepen linkage with regional and global production networks (DTI 2018; Raquiza, this volume).

Initially, thirty-seven industry roadmaps were prepared and implemented under the MRP (Aldaba 2017).[6] The strategy has been paying off, as shown by the record performance of the manufacturing sector of late, and has contributed to the ongoing structural transformation of the economy, as discussed above. Other industry roadmaps are being prepared, such as garments, textiles, processed fruits and nuts. If the current growth trajectory of the manufacturing sector continues until 2025, when the MRP completes its final phase, its contribution to generating inclusive economic growth for the country will be significant.

CHALLENGES AND UNCERTAINTIES: WHAT LIES AHEAD

Given the lower-than-expected growth rate during the second quarter of 2018, the elevated inflation rate and peso volatility, the international funding institutions slightly downgraded their GDP growth forecasts for the Philippines for 2018 and 2019. The Asian Development Bank lowered its growth projection from 6.8 per cent to 6.4 per cent for 2018 and from 6.9 per cent to 6.7 per cent for 2019 (ADB 2018a, 2018b; de Vera 2018c). On the other hand, the International Monetary Fund revised its earlier projection from 6.7 per cent to 6.5 per cent for 2018 but maintained its forecast for 2019 at 6.7 per cent (Tubayan 2018). The World Bank projection remained at 6.7 per cent for both years (World Bank 2018a).

Notwithstanding the cut in projected growth rate, the funding institutions underscored the favourable medium-term outlook for the country due to strong domestic demand driven by investments and the government's infrastructure spending. Likewise, BSP projected its inflation target to remain at 4.3 by the end of 2019, given the anticipated effects of its tight monetary policies.

Apart from domestic challenges, the country continues to face external risks and uncertainties that could slow down economic growth, as briefly discussed below.

   a. *Greater uncertainty in the global trade environment related to growing trade protectionism and ensuing trade wars among developed countries.* There has been uncertainty in the global environment since the 2008–9 financial crisis. Global economic growth has been sluggish. As a result, global demand has been weak, and investment flows have slowed down significantly (UN-ESCAP 2015, 2016). In response, exporting economies from the East have decoupled from their traditional markets in the West, particularly the United States and EU, by diversifying their exports and boosting domestic consumption and services. On the other hand, the growing discontent with globalization and trade liberalization due to rising income inequalities has generated populist and anti-trade sentiments globally, as shown by Brexit and the burgeoning trade war between China and the United States. The latter "poses a clear downside risk to the outlook of developing Asia" (ADB 2018a, p. 1). These developments could dampen the growth of the Philippines as the United States, EU and China are the country's major export markets and links to the global supply chain.[7]

   b. *Increase in the number of Asian FTAs with non-Asian partners*
   There is a rise in the number of Asian Free Trade Agreements (FTAs) with non-Asian partners (ADB 2017). FTAs are characterized by zero tariffs and other preferential arrangements which facilitate the movement of goods and services along global supply chains. Since all FTA partners of the Philippines are in Asia, the rise in the number of Asian FTAs with non-Asian partners may pose a threat to the country's exports and link to the regional and global supply chain.

   c. *Emergence of non-tariff measures (NTMs) as potential barriers to trade*
   The NTMs include compliance with environmental standards,

labour standards and testing requirements in FTAs. With compliance comes additional costs that may affect the export performance of the country's small and medium enterprises (SMEs). Compliance with environmental standards requires materials recovery facilities. Labour standards require compliance with working hours, working conditions and minimum wage. On the other hand, compliance with testing requirements requires testing machines, the cost of which could be prohibitive, as experienced by some of the country's SMEs in the food processing industry.

d. *Potential withdrawal of the GSP+ status of the Philippines by the EU*
The alleged and actual extra-judicial killings (EJKs) that have occurred since the start of the Duterte administration are putting pressure on the country's GSP+ (General System of Preferences) status with the European Union (EU).[8] Based on the recent assessment of the Philippines, there are increasing concerns about the country's failure to fully comply with most of GSP's conventions, particularly on human rights promotion (European Commission 2018; Curato and Franco, this volume). If GSP+ is withdrawn, some of the country's exporters may no longer be able to export to the EU's member states.

e. *Industry Revolution 4.0*
The Fourth Industry Revolution, called "Industry 4.0", is causing disruptions across virtually all industries.[9] It creates uncertainty as it will transform the entire production, distribution and consumption system. Based on the evaluation of one hundred countries for their readiness for future production, the Philippines belongs to the group of countries characterized by a strong production base today that are at risk for the future (World Economic Forum 2018). In contrast, China, South Korea, Malaysia and Singapore are classified among the leading countries with strong current production bases positioned well for the future.

Harnessing the potential of Industry 4.0 hinges on the country's readiness for innovation. But innovation is one area where the Philippines is currently weak, as shown by the Global Innovation Index for 2018 (Cornell University, INSEAD, and WIPO 2018). The country has been ranked low compared to some of its regional peers (see Figure 4.15). Among the pillars, the Philippines obtained the lowest scores in human capital and research, knowledge and technology and creative outputs (see Figure 4.16). To create its future today, the country needs to improve

The Philippine Economy 55

Figure 4.15
Global Innovation Index Rank, ASEAN-6, China and India, 2018

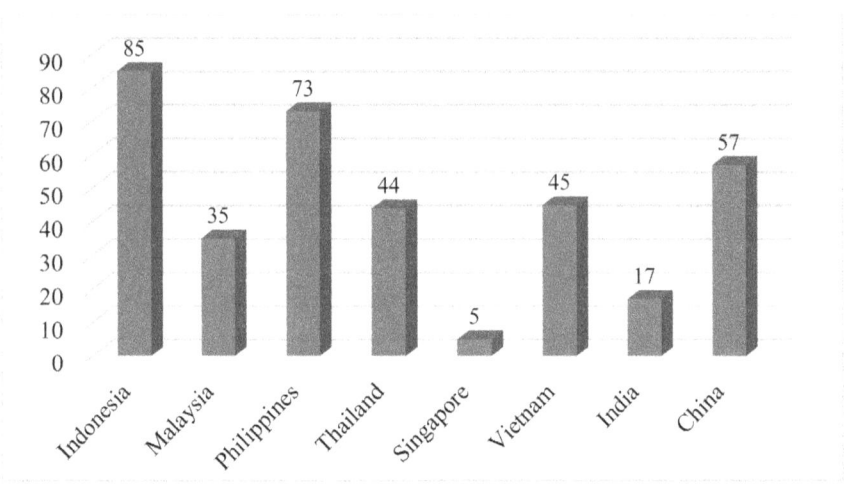

Source: Cornell University, INSEAD, and WIPO (2018).

Figure 4.16
Global Innovation Index, by Pillars, ASEAN-6, China and India, 2018

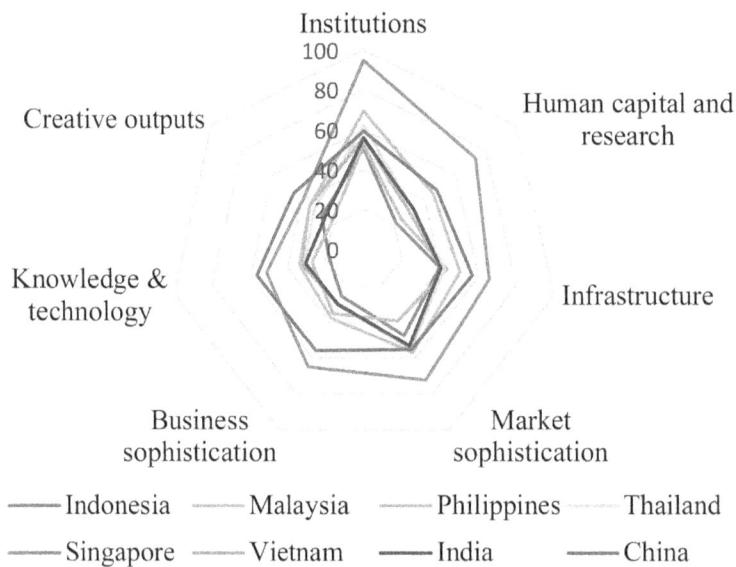

Source: Cornell University, INSEAD and WIPO (2018).

in these areas. Otherwise, remaining on its projected long-term growth path will be at risk.

SUMMARY AND CONCLUSION

Over the past few years, the Philippines has transitioned from its decades-long poor economic performance to an emerging economic tiger among its peers in Asia. The study by the World Bank (2018b) underscored the cumulative effects of structural reforms implemented by the different administrations in the past that are now finally creating a significant impact on the economy. The impacts are manifested in the increasing contribution of TFP to the growth of the economy and the structural transformation taking place, both of which are crucial to sustaining growth in the long term.

The Duterte administration addressed the long-standing constraints to growth through its massive infrastructure programme and comprehensive tax policy reforms. The reforms have economic costs, as shown by the increasing trade deficits and inflation rates, the effects of which are aggravated by external forces. The government is implementing tight monetary policies as countermeasures to meet the concerns head-on and safeguard the country's economic stability.

Amidst the uncertainties in the domestic as well as the global environment, the economic outlook for the country remains positive. The key is for the country to continue addressing longer-term constraints to its competitiveness.

Notes

1. The author would like to thank Ms Eva Marie Aragones for the excellent research assistance provided.
2. An investment grade is a seal of good housekeeping, as it signals to investors that it is safe to do business and encourages them to put huge capital in the country. An investment grade means the Philippines, as a borrowing country, has strong ability to pay its debt. This lowers its borrowing costs, generating savings, which may be spent for social services (e.g., education and health care).
3. Editors Note: The discussion in this chapter is as of August 2018.
4. See Figure 4.1.

5. Originally called TRAIN-2, the proposed packaged was renamed TRABAHO to disassociate it from TRAIN because the latter is partly blamed for the escalating inflation rate. "Trabaho" means "work" in Filipino. It was eventually passed in 2021 as the Corporate Recovery and Tax Incentives for Enterprise (CREATE) Act (RA 11534) (Villanueva 2022).
6. The thirty-seven roadmaps include automotive, automotive parts, biodiesel, cement, ceramic tiles, chemicals, copper and copper products, furniture, mass housing, motorcycle, petrochemicals, rubber products, tool and die manufacturing, electric vehicles, electronics, iron and steel, IT-BPM, metal casting, plastics, paper, natural health products, aerospace, retirement, shipbuilding, IC design, health care services, printing, book publishing, processed fruits-dried mango, processed shrimps/prawns, seaweeds, carrageenan, coco coir, bamboo, holiday décor, gifts and houseware.
7. This uncertainty, of course, continues into the current period as the Covid-19 pandemic disruption was followed by economic dislocations caused by the 2022 Russian invasion of Ukraine.
8. The Philippines is eligible for the European Union's (EU) GSP, which is a preferential tariff arrangement granted by the EU to selected exports of developing and least developed countries (LDCs). The unilateral grant is subject to certain terms and conditions including, but not limited to, rules of origin (ROO) and the compliance of beneficiary countries with certain labor and environmental standards, anti-discrimination standards, and human rights promotion.
9. "Industry 4.0" refers to the automation of data and data exchange. A product of the fusion of technologies and diffusion of innovation, it includes cyber-physical systems, robotics, data analytics, the internet of things, cloud computing, among other things.

References

ADB (Asian Development Bank). 2017. *Asian Economic Integration Report 2017*. Mandaluyong: Asian Development Bank.

———. 2018a. *Asian Development Outlook Supplement, July 2018: The Outlook Remains Stable*. Mandaluyong: Asian Development Bank.

———. 2018b. *Asian Development Outlook (ADO) 2018: How Technology Affects Jobs*. Mandaluyong: Asian Development Bank.

Aldaba, Rafaelita M. 2017. "PH Manufacturing Resurgence Program Journey towards Industrialization". Powerpoint presentation at the Manufacturing Summit 2017. https://industry.gov.ph/wp-content/uploads/2017/11/Presentation-by-Assistant-Secretary-Rafaelita-Aldaba-Department-of-Trade-and-Industry.pdf (accessed 2 March 2018).

Anand, Rahul, Kevin C. Cheng, Sida Rehman, and Longmei Zhang. 2014. "Potential Growth in Emerging Asia". IMF Working Paper, 2014/002, 13 January 2014. https://www.imf.org/en/Publications/WP/Issues/2016/12/31/Potential-Growth-in-Emerging-Asia-41198 (accessed 5 April 2018).

Blanchard, Olivier, and David R. Johnson. 2014. *Macroeconomics: Global Edition*. 6th ed. Singapore: Pearson Education Limited.

Cornell University, INSEAD, and WIPO. 2018. *The Global Innovation Index 2018: Energising the World with Innovation*. Ithaca, Fontainebleau, and Geneva.

De Vera, Ben O. 2018a. "Jica: Traffic Congestion Now Costs P3.5 Billion a Day". *Philippine Daily Inquirer*, 22 February 2018. https://newsinfo.inquirer.net/970553/jica-traffic-congestion-now-costs-p3-5-billion-a-day-metro-manila-traffic-jica-cost-of-traffic (accessed 28 February 2018).

———. 2018b. "Economic Prospects Still Bright, Govt Says". *Philippine Daily Inquirer*, 19 September 2018. https://business.inquirer.net/257511/economic-prospects-still-bright-govt-says (accessed 20 September 2018).

———. 2018c. "ADB Lowers PH Growth Forecasts". *Philippine Daily Inquirer*, 27 September 2018. https://business.inquirer.net/257970/adb-lowers-ph-growth-forecasts#ixzz5SGZHYpLy (accessed 27 September 2018).

DTI (Department of Trade and Industry). 2018. *Manufacturing Resurgence Program*. https://industry.gov.ph/manufacturing-resurgence-program/ (accessed 30 August 2018).

European Commission. 2018. *The Philippines GSP+ Assessment*. https://www.eeas.europa.eu/sites/default/files/10_en_2016_-_2017_gsp_swd_philippines.pdf (accessed 30 April 2018).

Glindro, Eloisa T., and Rosemarie A. Amodia. 2016. "Decomposing Sources of Potential Growth in the Philippines". *Bangko Sentral Review* 2015. https://www.bsp.gov.ph/Media_And_Research/Publications/BS2015_01.pdf (accessed 18 March 2018).

Llanto, Gilberto M. 2012. "Philippine Productivity Dynamics in the Last Five Decades and Determinants of Total Factor Productivity". *PIDS Discussion Paper Series No. 2012-11*, April 2012. Quezon City: Philippine Institute for Development Studies.

Lucas, Daxim. 2018. "Inflation Aggravated by Weak Peso but Yearend Relief Coming, Says BSP". *Philippine Daily Inquirer*, 18 September 2018. https://business.inquirer.net/257476/inflation-aggravated-weak-peso-yearend-relief-coming-says-bsp (accessed 18 September 2018).

Tubayan, Elijah Joseph C. 2018. "IMF Cuts Philippine Growth Forecast for 2018 Amid New Challenges". *BusinessWorld*, 28 September 2018. https://www.bworldonline.com/imf-cuts-philippine-growth-forecast-for-2018-amid-new-challenges/ (accessed 28 September 2018).

UN-ESCAP. 2015. *Asia-Pacific Trade and Investment Report 2015: Supporting Participation in Value Chains*. Thailand: United Nations.

⸺. 2016. *Asia-Pacific Trade and Investment Report 2016: Recent Trends and Developments*. Thailand: United Nations.

Villanueva, Joann. 2022. "Tax Reforms Boost PH's Position in Asia". Philippine News Agency, 7 April 2022. https://www.pna.gov.ph/articles/1171617 (accessed 11 March 2023).

World Bank. 2018a. *Philippines Economic Update: Investing in the Future*. Washington, D.C.: The World Bank.

⸺. 2018b. *Growth and Productivity in the Philippines: Winning the Future*. Washington, D.C.: The World Bank.

World Economic Forum. 2018. *Readiness for the Future of Production Report 2018*. Geneva: World Economic Forum.

5

The Philippine Services Export Economy and Prospects of Manufacturing

Antoinette R. Raquiza

Since the 2000s, the Philippine economy has been on a roll. From 2010 to 2019, it grew an annual average of 6.4 per cent, a jump from 4.5 per cent from 2000 to 2009 (World Bank 2022). Given the economy's rapid growth, the National Economic and Development Authority reported in 2018 that the country could achieve upper middle-income status, with a gross national income per capita of about US$4,000 by end-2019 (Cigaral 2018). The economy's strong performance is nothing less than stunning and tells of the sea change in the country as it moves on from being Asia's "sick man" to a "rising star".

This chapter examines the Philippines' economic rise, specifically focusing on the sources of rapid growth. Since the 2000s, international trade in services has played a central role in fast-tracking the country's growth. The share in gross domestic product (GDP) of remittances grew from 2.5 per cent in 1985 to 9.3 per cent in 2019 (World Bank

2021). Similarly, from its slow start in the 1990s, the business process outsourcing (BPO) industry has expanded dramatically since the second half of the 2000s; by 2019, its contribution to GDP was a high 9 per cent (Oxford Business Group n.d.). In this light, the migrant labour and BPO industries have been referred to as the "two legs" on which the Philippines' growth economy stands (ibid.). The increase in incomes of remittance-receiving households and the BPO talent pool has expanded the domestic market for services industries (e.g., retail trade and other commercial services) and manufacturing.

Whether this trend—which can potentially strengthen the manufacturing-services nexus in the country—will be sustained and lead to more profound structural transformation remains an open question, however. In this connection, the Philippine case provides an opportunity to interrogate services export as the driver of the economy.

This chapter is divided into four sections. The succeeding two sections briefly discuss the factors for the country's rapid growth and key features of and trends in the country's labour and services export industries. The third section will examine the resurgence of the manufacturing sector and provide the broad strokes of the country's "new industrial policy". The chapter concludes by highlighting the Philippine government's proactive role in effecting such diversification—an approach it adopted to grow service exports more than a decade ago.

THE RISE OF SERVICES EXPORTS

There is near unanimity among development analysts that the Philippines' rapid economic growth today has been fuelled by private consumption on the demand side and a booming service sector on the supply side (Dayoan and Cordero 2017, p. 20; ADB 2017). In 2019, for instance, household consumption contributed more than 73 per cent to growth, while the service sector's value added to GDP was 60.8 per cent (World Bank 2021). Yet, not too long ago, this same development pattern was seen as indicative of the country's shallow structural transformation—the reason for its failure to play catch-up with its industrializing neighbours up until the mid-2000s. In 1995, with the economy growing 4.7 per cent, household consumption spending accounted for 74 per cent of GDP while the service sector's value added to GDP was 46 per cent; ten years later, with GDP growing 4.8 per cent, the contribution of consumption spending and services contribution to growth was 75 per cent and 53.5 per cent, respectively. It is noteworthy that these figures did not translate into rapid growth (see Table 5.1). In this light, one can argue that high household consumption and a robust service sector cannot, by themselves, fully explain the country's economic turnaround.

TABLE 5.1
Philippine Growth Drivers

	GDP Growth	Private Consumption (% of GDP)	Services (% of GDP)
1995	4.7%	74%	46%
2005	4.8%	75%	53.5%
2015	6%	73.7%	58.8%
2019	6.1%	73.2%	60.8%

Source: World Bank (2021).

How can this development pattern, identified with middling economic performance in decades past, produce rapid growth today? Drawing on previous works, I will stress the critical role played by a combination of external and internal factors—specifically, the explosion of the global services industries since the late 1990s and the government's aggressive efforts to promote international trade in services that began in the mid-2000s.

Two trends in the global services industries have dramatically contributed to the country's booming trade in services. While labour has been one of the Philippines' key exports since the 1970s, this industry received a major boost in the 2000s with the explosion of the global care economy, defined as the "paid and unpaid labor related to caregiving such as childcare, elder care and domestic chores" (Barnes and Ramanarayanan 2022). The demand for personal care and household services grew in response to the ageing population, the decline of the welfare state system and changing gender roles and household arrangements in developed countries (Douglass 2012; ILO

2018). Following global trends, the feminization of Philippine labour migration became much more pronounced during this period. From 1995 to 2010, the number of women among newly hired contract workers grew from 55 to 72 per cent (POEA 1995, 2010). In 2016, of the 582,816 newly hired land-based workers, 275,073 were categorized as household service workers (POEA 2016).

The other trend has been the digital revolution that has transformed the service sector and, partly in consequence, global production and distribution systems (Bartels and Lederer 2009). That services today have gone beyond direct exchange and can be codified and traded across borders has seen global BPO players investing in developing countries with a skilled but low-cost labour force. Both global trends have created a massive demand for the Philippines' English-speaking, Western-oriented skilled workforce (Lee 2015), expanding the domestic consumer class and service sector.

But timely government action likewise proved critical in securing the country's position among the world's top services exporters. Since the mid-2000s, the government has worked to further institutionalize trade in services as a critical plank of the national development strategy. Toward this end, the national government has undertaken various programmes to rev up overseas labour deployment, including decentralizing Philippine Overseas Employment Agency operations to facilitate provincial labour recruitment and regular hosting of international labour trade fairs. As of October 2018, the government had also successfully negotiated forty-three bilateral labour agreements with twenty-seven key receiving countries (Mangulabnan and Daquio 2019).[1]

In response to the shift in government orientation towards labour migration—away from being a temporary option to ease domestic unemployment and currency shortfall to now being a key result area of government—agencies and units opened windows to facilitate and assist Filipino workers' deployment overseas. In light of such efforts, the number of overseas Filipino workers (OFWs) increased from 7.41 million in 2001 to 9.45 million in 2010, while remittances tripled from US$6.03 billion to US$18.70 billion (Nejar 2012b, pp. 2–3).[2]

Similarly, while the country's rich human capital has been credited for the success of its BPO industry, quick government action was also essential to attract the big industry players into the country. The passage in 1995 of Republic Act 7925, or the Public Telecom Policy Act, liberalized the telecommunication industry. In 2000, the Philippine Economic Zone Authority (PEZA) included information technology (IT) companies that derive 70 per cent of their revenues abroad and developers and operators of IT parks and buildings as among the business activities eligible for fiscal and nonfiscal incentives under the Special Economic Zone Act of 1995. The offer of incentives to locators and "facilities-providers" in what would be known as "cyberzones" was what the Department of Trade and Industry (DTI), PEZA and industry leaders presented to foreign investors in joint trade missions.[3]

Not long after the adoption of the cyberzone concept, Sykes Asia set up the first multinational call centre in the country; HSBC followed suit and established Cyber City in the former Clark Air Base in Pampanga (Oxford Business Group 2016). From 2004 to 2010, total export earnings of the industry—also called business process management (BPM)—skyrocketed from about US$1.5 billion to US$8.9 billion (Nejar 2012a, p. 6). Since then, the bulk of investments in the IT-BPM industry has come from foreign capital (BSP 2015).

The phenomenal growth of labour migration and the BPO/BPM industries has produced rich dividends for the country. Remittances and the BPO industry contribute 10 per cent and 9 per cent to the country's gross domestic product, respectively. The massive flow of foreign revenues due to these growth industries has contributed to current account surpluses and macroeconomic stability. These export industries have also contributed to the rapid expansion of domestic consumption. For instance, the Bangko Sentral ng Pilipinas found that OFW households used more than 90 per cent of the remittances they receive to meet their basic needs (BSP 2018)—a staggering amount when one considers that in 2017, remittances totalled US$31.3 billion. For its part, the IT-BPO industry has created relatively high-paying jobs for the country's professionals. In 2019, the sector had 1.3 million full-time employees and registered US$26.3 billion in revenues (Campos 2020).

All told the country's labour export and IT-BPM have contributed significantly to both the demand and supply side of the growth equation.

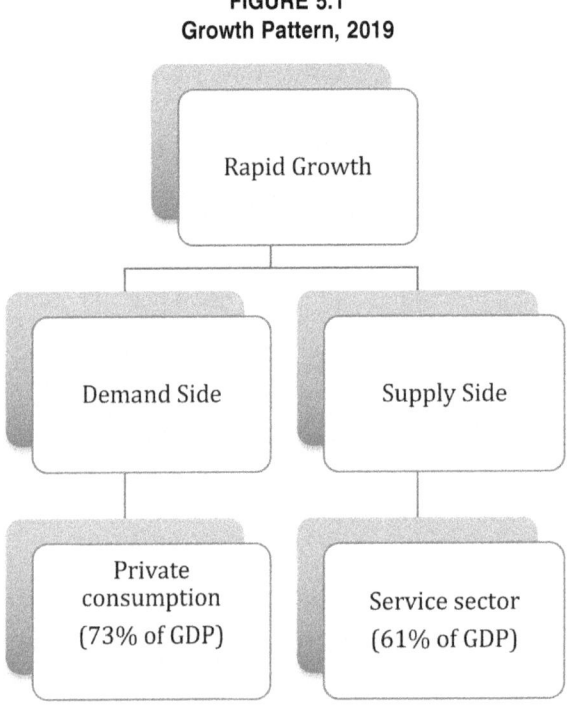

FIGURE 5.1
Growth Pattern, 2019

Source: World Bank (2022).

Labour migration and services export have translated into a robust domestic service sector. While a full-blown discussion on the causal mechanism between the two is beyond the scope of this chapter, suffice it to say that critical in this relationship is the growth of the purchasing power of the middle-class segment that directly participates in and benefits from these services export industries. The other winner and critical actor of this growth momentum are the commercial elites, especially those in banking and other financial institutions through which billions of dollars are remitted. Such elites also develop housing for OFW families, lease out IT-BPO offices primarily to multinational companies, diversify into the education and health industries, and open franchises or distribution outlets catering to the growing western-oriented consumer market (Raquiza 2014).

SPECIFIC PATTERN OF THE PHILIPPINE SERVICES EXPORT ECONOMY

In this chapter, I use the term "services export economy" to highlight a development pattern in which trade in services is front and centre of the country's growth. I qualify the country's service economy to distinguish it from the more traditional development pattern associated with northern post-industrial economies, where the service sector overtakes manufacturing as the driver of growth due to the rise of labour productivity and incomes in a maturing manufacturing sector (Rowthorn and Ramaswamy 1997; Dasgupta and Singh 2006). In the Philippines, as suggested earlier, the growth of the economy and, in particular, the service sector is directly and indirectly due to the massive flows of remittances that primarily go to consumption. Until recently, domestic and foreign direct investments have had minimal impact on the country's economic performance.

Will such a growth pattern elevate the Philippines to high middle-income status? The Philippine experience suggests that trade in services may jumpstart a low-middle-income economy towards rapid growth. Nevertheless, because trade in services mainly consists of linking Philippine labour to global markets, it has minimal linkages to the domestic economy and thus has not led to deep structural transformation. Moreover, as currently configured, the country's trade in services involves skills at the lower end of the value chain. The biggest population of newly hired contract workers since the 2000s has been domestic workers. While the government and industry have worked to attract higher-value business services into the country, contact centres continue to dominate the BPO sector. These two booming sectors' main contribution to the economy has been as consumers of services industries rather than suppliers to productive industries (Raquiza 2017).

In fact, among developing countries that rank the highest in trade in services, only the Philippines has no other sector to fall back on. In terms of trade in services, India is perhaps most similar to the Philippine case. Both countries belong to the world's top five remittance-receiving countries and vie with each other as the most preferred IT-BPO hub among developing countries. Yet India has an established (albeit struggling) manufacturing sector to build on, with its outsourcing industry also anchored on the strength of its domestic software industry.

GOING BACK TO BASICS?

The Philippine government seems to have awakened from what it sees as its "long hiatus" in promoting manufacturing (BOI 2014). In light of the country's lack of structural transformation, it has embarked on a sectorally-differentiated development programme to address obstacles to realizing its full growth potential. Concretely, the DTI has put forward the need to strengthen manufacturing as an answer to long-standing problems of declining total factor productivity, unemployment and decreasing gross domestic investment.

In 2012, the DTI tapped the Philippine Institute for Development Studies (PIDS) to work with it and the private sector to draw up, study and consolidate existing industry roadmaps.[4] This process produced more than thirty roadmaps. Out of these, the DTI identified twelve priority areas that were incorporated in the BOI Investment Priorities Plan (IPP) for 2014. The twelve priority areas are aerospace parts and aircraft maintenance, repair and overhaul (MRO); agribusiness; IT-BPM; construction, transport and logistics; tourism; shipbuilding; automotive and auto parts; electronic/semiconductors; chemicals; furniture, garments, creative industries; iron and steel; and tool and die.

The year 2014 saw the DTI engage in a flurry of activities aimed at reviving the country's manufacturing sector, whose value added to growth had gone down from about 24 per cent in 2005 to about 20.6 per cent in 2014 (World Bank 2021). In the 2014 IPP, the government made known its intention to promote manufacturing and thus reverse the sector's decline:

> With its strategic shift ... towards industry development ..., the DTI-BOI has now taken a proactive role in steering the country's industrialisation. ... With the updated [Philippine Development Plan] ... as its foundation, *the IPP espousing the new industrial policy* now serves both as a developmental tool for investment decisions of the private sector and a promotional tool for government to encourage first movers in new investment areas and to provide appropriate responses to the most

binding constraints that prevent the entry of investments or prevent industries from moving up the value chain. The new industrial policy aims to transform and upgrade the manufacturing industry with the long-term vision to develop globally competitive industries supported by strong *forward and backward linkages* (Domingo 2014, italics supplied).

That manufacturing has gained favour among the country's policymakers owed much to two factors. First is the fact that despite more than a decade of service-led rapid growth, manufacturing had been the top provider of quality employment and revenue earner. As the Annual Survey of Philippine Business and Industry (ASPBI) reveals, in 2013, even as there were only 25,197 manufacturing establishments (representing 11.1 per cent of the total number of establishments in the country), the sector employed 1,223,577 workers or one in every five workers in the country. The manufacturing sector was also the top revenue earner, generating PHP 4.6 trillion or 32.5 per cent of the country's total income and the most significant contributor to total value added, with 29.4 per cent of PHP 4 trillion (PSA 2017). As the above discussion shows, partly because of the booming trade in services' limited link to the domestic economy and the domestic services sector's relatively low productivity, manufacturing had had a more significant multiplier effect than those in services.

The second factor for the resurgence of domestic manufacturing is the country's growing consumer market, partly driven by OFW households' and BPO community's spending. This link may be gleaned from the dominance of the consumer goods industries in the sector. According to the Philippine Statistics Authority (PSA) data, factory output grew the fastest in eight years among the following industries: food (32.6 per cent), electrical machinery (30.3 per cent), beverages (24.1 per cent), petroleum products (23.4 per cent), other manufactures (20.5 per cent) and leather products (14.4 per cent) (Castañeda 2018). Illustrating the link between manufacturing activities and domestic demand is the rise in the food and beverage industries' share of investments, which went up from 27 per cent in the 1990s to 57 per cent from 2000–9 (Aldaba and Aldaba 2012, p. 5).

The lynchpin of the push towards industrial development was the Manufacturing Resurgence Plan (MRP), launched in 2014 with PHP

2.3 billion in funding from the national government. The MRP was part of the national development programme that sought to integrate small and medium-scale manufacturing enterprises into domestic and global production networks and agribusiness and services with manufacturing activities to raise these sectors' productivity. For the period 2014–17, the plan aimed to strengthen current industry efforts in the following industries:

- Manufacturing
  - Automotive, aerospace parts, electronics, garments, food and resource-based, chemicals, furniture, tool and die, shipbuilding
- Agribusiness
  - Rubber, coconut, mangoes, coffee, cacao, etc.
  - Agro-processing
- Services
  - Labour-intensive sectors, tourism, construction, shipbuilding
  - Infrastructure, engineering

In accordance with the plan, the government issued in 2015 Executive Order No. 182, which launched the Comprehensive Automotive Resurgence Strategy (CARS) Program. This period saw the automobile industry enjoying brisk sales, with 224,747 units sold in 2014 (Remo 2015). This robust domestic market provided a necessary condition for the success of any attempt to revive the auto manufacturing industry. Other conditions that came into consideration in the choice of the auto industry as a flagship programme included the presence of five big automakers already operating in the country, thus, presenting stock knowledge and expertise. The existing potential to undertake cluster development around the industry could, in turn, contribute to the promotion of the Philippines as a regional hub.[5]

The CARS is among the most comprehensive and boldest of the DTI's industry programmes. Under the programme, the government would provide "time-bound, output-based" fiscal incentives of up to PHP 27 billion over six years and other government assistance (Aldaba 2017). In turn, the two participating car manufacturers, Toyota Motors Philippines and Mitsubishi Motors Philippines, were each expected to produce 200,000 units of the approved car models in six years (*The Philippine Star* 2016). As designed, a distinct contribution of the programme would be the formation of value chains that would link these giant automakers with domestic manufacturers of parts and components—an arrangement that is envisioned to benefit chemical, metalworking, tool and die, plastics, electronics, rubber, glass and textile sectors, and directly and indirectly create 200,000 jobs (ibid.).

As a continuation and an updating of the MRP, DTI has since launched various programmes, some in connection with other departments. In 2016, with the change of administration, the DTI launched the "i^3S program" that highlighted the need for an inclusive and innovation-driven industrial policy. Among the new features of the policy was the inclusion of new programmes aimed at strengthening the micro, small and medium enterprises, especially those outside Metro Manila,[6] and closer collaboration with the Department of Science and Technology (DOST), which works with the country's research and development community under its "Filipinnovation" programme. Subsequently, the newly formed Department of Communications and Technology was tasked with facilitating the digital transformation of industry and society.

The general push to grow manufacturing had begun to show results by 2020. According to the DTI, the implementation of the MRP from 2014 to 2017 saw the sector's gross value added (GVA) grow at a rate of 7.4 per cent while its contribution to GDP went up to 23.3 per cent from 22.4 per cent registered in the pre-MRP period (2010–13) (DTI-BOI 2019, p. 3). Equally encouraging is the 2018 government census finding on the growth of manufacturing using the 2012 figure as the baseline: the number of establishments grew by 15.6 per cent to 28,968; total value added increased by 63.1 per cent to PHP 1.9 trillion; and total revenue grew by 26.5 per cent to PHP 5.8 trillion (PSA 2020, p. 3).

The DTI-BOI report also noted that while food manufacturing continued to be the most significant contributor to total manufacturing value added, many industries from 2011 to 2018 grew by double digits, specifically: "furniture and fixtures (26.09 per cent), chemical and chemical products (18.10 per cent), fabricated metal products (13.98 per cent), basic metals (12.58 per cent), publishing and printing (11.88

per cent), machinery and equipment except electrical (11.75 per cent), office, accounting and computing machines (11.04 per cent)" (DTI-BOI 2019, p. 4).

CONCLUSION

The Philippine development story is still unfolding. Since the mid-1980s, economic growth has proceeded in fits and starts, partly due to the impact of contentious politics on economic policy. The rise of the country's trade in services has provided a way to insulate the domestic economy from domestic politics, which would partly explain its rapid growth. Yet, as current developments suggest, hitching one's star to global markets without developing the country's real economy can only go so far. In this light, the government's move to more consciously promote industrialization by using the opportunity that an expanded domestic consumer market provides contributes to ensuring that the gains from trade in services are more evenly distributed.

Nevertheless, promoting structural transformation will be an uphill battle. As with the law of the market, the profitability of the service sector and high entry barriers to manufacturing will continue to skew investment decisions, including those of domestic business elites who are heavily vested in commercial activities (Raquiza 2014). More than 99 per cent of the formal economy is comprised of micro, small and medium enterprises and in 2020, about 46.7 per cent of these were in vehicle repairs, while only 11.6 per cent were in manufacturing (DTI 2021). As noted earlier, the shallow structural transformation has meant the country suffers from low labour productivity. In 2020, the Philippines' labour productivity, estimated at US$21,315, was lower than that of Thailand (US$31,193), Malaysia (US$55,776) and the average figure for East Asia and the Pacific (US$35,940) (*BusinessWorld* 2022).

Perhaps the biggest constraint confronting DTI, DOST and other implementing agencies is the lack of a budget to more thoroughly reverse the decline of manufacturing in the country. For instance, in 2019, the government budget for DTI and DOST was a little more than PHP 18.7 billion and PHP 20 billion, respectively, while that of the Department of National Defense amounted to PHP 186 billion, and the Department of Public Works and Highways was allotted PHP 454 billion (Rey 2019). The DOST also noted that the country's funding for research and development in the past decades had only been 0.14 per cent to 0.18 per cent of GDP (Cruz 2021). Such a budget distribution suggests the government's priorities and its market-driven approach to industrial development.[7]

There is also the question of how the country's current industrialization drive will fare in the global economy's rebalancing to developing Asia (Prasad 2009). Due to the phlegmatic consumer demand in advanced countries, multinational corporations are shifting their sights to the booming consumer markets of emerging markets. One implication of this rebalancing is the influx of imported goods that can overwhelm fledgling domestic industries hoping to capture a sizeable share of the domestic market. While trade in services has contributed to the country's positive balance of payment, this has not translated into a more favourable trade balance (Paderanga 2009). From 2014 to 2018, the country's trade deficit averaged 76.54 per cent (*Rappler* 2019).

Fortunately, the government, notably the DTI-BOI, seems aware of what domestic industries are up against. Noteworthy, there are indicators of the government's attempt to avoid the problems that befell the country's earlier experiences in industrial policy during the import-substitution phase in the 1950s to 1960s and, again, during the authoritarian rule in the 1970s to mid-1980s. One, the development of the current industrial policy has spanned three administrations, which is noteworthy in a country where the turnover of political leadership usually signals a change in development policy or programmes. Two, below the secretary levels, occupied by cabinet members, some of those directly working on industrial policy and thus have industry experience and expertise have stayed in place across administrations, thereby providing policymaking some autonomy from partisan politics.[8] Three, the general contours of government incentives and manufacturing assistance do not differ much from what was given to the labour and services export industries. This similarity minimizes the programme's vulnerability to rent-seeking charges and ensures that the country's history of trial and error informs policy. Finally, the current industrial policy is no longer exclusively focused on export manufacturing but also on domestic production. This domestic focus allows smaller players access to government assistance, thus better ensuring their viability.

In sum, it is argued that auspicious conditions have come together for a manufacturing revival. With a robust internal market, business confidence derived from a rapidly growing economy and government officials willing to do the hard work and take (calculated) risks, the Philippines today may very well be at a rare juncture. Much work lies ahead, but given the moment, there may be hope that the third time's a charm.

Notes

1. Examples of such agreements are the Japan-Philippines Economic Partnership Agreement (2008) that includes provisions to facilitate the migration of Filipino healthcare workers and the 2013 Agreement on Domestic Worker Recruitment between the Philippines and Saudi Arabia.
2. For more comprehensive analyses of the country's reliance on remittances, see Pernia (2011) and Medalla, Fabella, and De Dios (2014).
3. Interview with Gigi Virata, then senior executive director of the Information Technology and Business Process Association of the Philippines (IBPAP) on 4 April 2014 in Metro Manila.
4. Interview with Dr Rafaelita Aldaba, then DTI Assistant Secretary, on 24 May 2018 at her Board of Investment office in Makati. Aldaba was the researcher on the manufacturing industry at PIDS before she was recruited to the DTI.
5. Interview with Aldaba, 24 May 2018.
6. Such programmes include "Go Negosyo".
7. This market-driven approach, in fact, is stated in the country's Omnibus Investment Code of 1987, where the government identified the private sector as the prime mover of economic development.
8. This is true at DTI, for instance, with Aldaba, who has since been promoted as Undersecretary for the Competitiveness and Innovation Group and Dr Ceferino Rodolfo, Undersecretary for the Industry Development Group (IDG) and Board of Investments Vice Chairman and Managing Head.

References

ADB (Asian Development Bank). 2017. *Asian Development Outlook 2017: Transcending the Middle-Income Challenge*. Metro Manila: Asian Development Bank.

Aldaba, Rafaelita M. 2017. "PH Manufacturing Resurgence Program Journey towards Industrialization". Powerpoint presentation at the Manufacturing Summit 2017. https://industry.gov.ph/wp-content/uploads/2017/11/

Presentation-by-Assistant-Secretary-Rafaelita-Aldaba-Department-of-Trade-and-Industry.pdf (accessed 28 September 2018).

Aldaba, Rafaelita M., and Fernando T. Aldaba. 2012. "Do FDI Inflows Have Positive Spillover Effects? The Case of the Philippine Manufacturing Industry". *Philippine Institute for Development Studies (PIDS) Policy Notes* 2012-01, March 2012. https://pidswebs.pids.gov.ph/CDN/PUBLICATIONS/pidspn1201.pdf (accessed 5 March 2023).

Barnes, Sarah B., and Deekshita Ramanarayanan. 2022. "The Global Care Economy". *Global Health & Gender Policy Brief* 1 (April). https://www.wilsoncenter.org/sites/default/files/media/uploads/documents/The%20Care%20Economy%20-%20MHI%20Policy%20Brief%20Apr%202022.pdf (accessed 5 March 2023).

Bartels, Frank L., and Suman Lederer. 2009. *Outsourcing Markets in Services: International Business Trends, Patterns and Emerging Issues, and the Role of China and India.* Vienna: United Nations Industrial Development Organization.

BOI (Board of Investments). 2014. *The 2014 Investment Priority Plan: Industry Development for Inclusive Growth.* https://industry.gov.ph/investment-priorities-plan-ipp-2014-2016/ (accessed 5 March 2023).

BSP (Bangko Sentral ng Pilipinas). 2015. *Results of the 2013 Survey of Information Technology – Business Process Outsourcing (IT-BPO) Services.* https://www.bsp.gov.ph/Media_And_Research/Survey%20of%20IT-BPO%20Services%20Report/ICT_2013.pdf (accessed 5 March 2023).

―――. 2018. "Consumer Expectations Survey: Third Quarter 2018". https://www.bsp.gov.ph/Lists/Consumer%20Expectation%20Report/Attachments/15/CES_3qtr2018.pdf (accessed 5 March 2023).

BusinessWorld. 2022. "How the Philippines' Labor Productivity Compares with Its Neighbors in the Region". *BusinessWorld*, 31 August 2022. https://www.bworldonline.com/infographics/2022/08/31/471657/how-the-philippines-labor-productivity-compares-with-its-neighbors-in-the-region/ (accessed 5 March 2023).

Campos, Othel V. 2020. "BPO Sector Expects Recovery with Revenue of $29B by 2022". *Manila Standard*, 20 November 2020. https://manilastandard.net/business/it-telecom/340042/bpo-sector-expects-recovery-with-revenue-of-29b-by-2022.html (accessed 7 May 2023).

Castañeda, Christine J.S. 2018. "Feb. Factory Output Growth Fastest in Nearly 8 Years". *BusinessWorld*, 6 April 2018. https://www.bworldonline.com/editors-picks/2018/04/06/148452/feb-factory-output-growth-fastest-in-nearly-8-years/ (accessed 5 March 2023).

Cigaral, Ian Nicolas. 2018. "Philippines Can Be Upper Middle-Income Nation by 2019 — NEDA". *The Philippine Star*, 3 April 2018. https://www.philstar.

com/headlines/2018/04/03/1802419/philippines-can-be-upper-middle-income-nation-2019-neda (accessed 3 March 2023.)

Cruz, Kaithreen. 2021. "DoST Seeks Bigger Research Budget". *Manila Times*, 12 November 2021. https://www.manilatimes.net/2021/11/12/news/national/dost-seeks-bigger-research-budget/1821922 (accessed 3 March 2023).

Dasgupta, Sukti, and Ajit Singh. 2006. "Manufacturing, Services and Premature Deindustrialization in Developing Countries: A Kaldorian Analysis". Research Paper 2006/049. Helsinki: United Nations University–World Institute for Development Economics Research.

Dayoan, Sharon G., and Hadassah May R. Cordero. 2017. "Asia's Rising Star: Taking Stock and Looking Forward". In *Philippine Consumer Market Report: 2017 Investment Guide by KPMG in the Philippines*, pp. 8–27. Makati: KPMG R.G. Manabat & Co. and the Institute for Development and Econometric Analysis.

Domingo, Gregory L. 2014. "Foreword". In *The 2014 Investment Priorities Plan: Industry Development for Inclusive Growth*. https://industry.gov.ph/investment-priorities-plan-ipp-2014-2016/ (accessed 5 March 2023).

Douglass, Mike. 2012. "Global Householding and Social Reproduction: Migration Research, Dynamics and Public Policy in East and Southeast Asia". Asia Research Institute Working Paper Series No. 188, August 2012. Singapore: Asia Research Institute.

DTI (Department of Trade and Industry). 2021. "2020 MSME Statistics". 8 May 2022. https://www.dti.gov.ph/resources/msme-statistics/ (accessed 3 March 2023).

DTI-BOI (Department of Trade and Industry-Board of Investments). 2019. "Manufacturing Resurgence Program (MRP) Accomplishment Report (As of April 2019)". Unpublished.

ILO (International Labour Organization). 2018. *Care Work and Care Jobs for the Future of Decent Work*. Geneva: International Labour Organization.

Lee, Don. 2015. "The Philippines Has Become the Call-Center Capital of the World". *Los Angeles Times*, 1 February 2015. https://www.latimes.com/business/la-fi-philippines-economy-20150202-story.html (accessed 7 April 2023).

Mangulabnan, Bernard Paul M., and Carl Rookie O. Daquio. 2019. "A Review of Bilateral Labor Agreements Concluded by the Philippines with Countries of Destination: Toward a Framework for Monitoring and Evaluation". *Philippine Journal of Labor Studies* 1, no. 1: 1–39.

Medalla, Felipe M., Raul V. Fabella, and Emmanuel S. de Dios. 2014. "Beyond the Remittances-driven Economy: Notes as if the Long Run Mattered". University of the Philippines School of Economics Discussion Papers 2014-11, August 2014.

Nejar, Eva Marie T. 2012a. "Taxation and Fiscal Incentives of the Philippine BPO Industry". *NTRC Tax Research Journal* 24, no. 1: 1–33.

———. 2012b. "Profile and Taxation of the Philippine Overseas Remittance Industry". *NTRC Tax Research Journal* 24, no. 3: 1–19.

Oxford Business Group. 2016. "The Philippines' Business Process Outsourcing Sector Expands into High-Value Services". https://oxfordbusinessgroup.com/overview/strength-strength-sector-continues-expand-higher-value-services (accessed 5 March 2023).

———. N.d. "What Does the Covid-19 Outbreak Mean for the Philippines' BPO Industry?" https://oxfordbusinessgroup.com/articles-interviews/what-does-the-covid-19-outbreak-mean-for-the-philippines-bpo-industry (accessed 5 March 2023).

Paderanga, Cayetano Jr. 2009. "The Macroeconomic Impact of Remittances in the Philippines". University of the Philippines School of Economics Discussion Paper No. 0903, June 2009.

Pernia, Ernesto M. 2011. "Is Labor Export Good Development Policy?" *The Philippine Review of Economics* 48, no. 1: 13–34.

Philippine Star, The. 2016. "Toyota, Mitsubishi Investing P8 B to Roll Out New Models under CARS". *The Philippine Star*, 16 June 2016. https://www.philstar.com/business/2016/06/16/1593279/toyota-mitsubishi-investing-p8-b-roll-out-new-models-under-cars (accessed 10 September 2018).

POEA (Philippine Overseas Employment Administration). 1995. "Deployment Per Skill for the Year 1995 (New Hires)". https://www.dmw.gov.ph/archives/ofwstat/depperskill/1995.pdf (accessed 5 March 2023).

———. 2010. "OFW Deployment Per Skill and Country - New Hires for the Year 2010". https://www.dmw.gov.ph/archives/ofwstat/depperskill/2010.pdf (accessed 5 March 2023).

———. 2016. "Overseas Employment Statistics: Deployed Overseas Filipino Workers 2016 vs 2015". https://www.dmw.gov.ph/archives/ofwstat/compendium/2015-2016%20OES%201.pdf (accessed 5 March 2023).

PSA (Philippine Statistical Authority). "2014 Annual Survey of Philippine Business and Industry – Economy Wide All Establishments: Final Results". https://psa.gov.ph/content/2014-annual-survey-philippine-business-and-industry-economy-wide-all-establishments-final (accessed 20 September 2018).

———. 2018. "2015 Annual Survey of Philippine Business and Industry (ASPBI) – Business Process Management (BPM) Industries for All Employment Sizes: Final Results". https://psa.gov.ph/content/2015-annual-survey-philippine-business-and-industry-aspbi-business-process-management-bpm (accessed 5 September 2018).

———. 2020. "2018 Census of Philippine Business and Industry: Manufacturing". https://psa.gov.ph/content/2018-census-philippine-business-and-industry-manufacturing (accessed 5 March 2023).

Prasad, Eswar. 2009. "Rebalancing Growth in Asia". *Finance & Development* 46, no. 4: 19–22. https://www.imf.org/external/pubs/ft/fandd/2009/12/pdf/prasad.pdf (accessed 10 September 2018).

Rappler. 2019. "PH Trade Deficit 'Alarming,' Says BOI Official". 27 December 2019. https://r3.rappler.com/business/248045-philippine-trade-deficit-alarming (accessed 5 March 2023).

Raquiza, Antoinette R. 2014. "Changing Configuration of Philippine Capitalism". *Philippine Political Science Journal* 35, no. 2: 225–50.

———. 2017. "Philippine Services Sector, Politics, and Governance Issues". In *Southeast Asia beyond Crises and Traps: Economic Growth and Upgrading*, edited by Khoo Boo Teak, Keiichi Tsunekawa, and Motoko Kawano, pp. 225–49. London and New York: Palgrave Macmillan.

Remo, Amy R. 2015. "Vehicle Sales Zoomed 30% to 234K Units in 2014". *Philippine Daily Inquirer*, 13 January 2015. https://business.inquirer.net/184985/vehicle-sales-zoomed-30-to-234k-units-in-2014#ixzz80EfmA790 (accessed 1 March 2023).

Rey, Aika. 2019. "Winners and Losers under Duterte's 2019 Budget". *Rappler*, 19 May 2019. https://www.rappler.com/newsbreak/in-depth/229539-winners-losers-national-budget-philippines-2019/ (accessed 1 March 2023).

Rowthorn, Robert, and Ramana Ramaswamy. 1997. "Deindustrialisation: Causes and Implications". Working Paper of the International Monetary Fund, April 1997. https://www.imf.org/external/pubs/ft/wp/wp9742.pdf (accessed 5 March 2021).

World Bank. 2021. *World Development Indicators*. https://databank.worldbank.org/source/world-development-indicators (accessed 2 February 2021).

———. 2022. "The World Bank in the Philippines". 21 March 2022. https://www.worldbank.org/en/country/philippines (accessed 5 March 2023).

6

The Philippine Climate Change Commitments and the Energy Transition to a Low-Carbon Future[1]

Manuel P.S. Solis

INTRODUCTION

As the global energy demand soars to drive economic growth, high fossil fuel prices and increasing greenhouse gas (GHG) emissions are prompting the search for low-carbon solutions. With climate change looming large on the horizon, countries have signed, accepted, approved and/or ratified an international climate change legal regime where a global energy transition to climate-friendly sources, technologies and systems is inevitable. While there is no single pathway to achieve global energy transition, there are guiding principles, focus areas and recommended actions to tackle the challenge of the energy trilemma in terms of security, sustainability and equity. These are concretized on the national level, where context largely defines the energy transition.

In recent years, the Philippines has seen an economic renaissance that contributes to a robust outlook and makes it one of the fastest growing economies in Southeast Asia. The Philippine Development Plan 2017–2022 targeted an inclusive economic growth rate of 7 to 8 per cent (NEDA 2017). This, coupled with population growth, is driving increased energy demand that is projected to grow by 80 per cent between 2017 and 2040 (Department of Energy 2017a). The parallel rise in consumption for all fuels brings energy security to the fore. However, being one of the three countries that are most vulnerable to climate change (Flores 2018), the Philippines' economic aspirations and energy choices are also influenced by climate change and environmental considerations. For example, the United Nations (UN) Sustainable Development Goal (SDG) 7 aims to ensure access to affordable, reliable, sustainable and modern energy for all by 2030. Similarly, UN SDG 13 highlights the need for climate action around the world. This is highly relevant if the country is to achieve economic growth with equity and sustainability, where it is reported that 11 million Filipinos still do not have access to electricity and 61 million are still reliant on the traditional use of biomass for cooking, particularly in remote rural areas (International Energy Agency 2017).

For purposes of complying with the historic 2015 Paris Agreement, the country's Intended Nationally Determined Contribution (INDC) seeks a 70 per cent reduction of GHG emissions by 2030 from the business-as-usual scenario in energy, transport, forestry, industry and waste, albeit conditioned on the provision of the means of implementation that the country will receive in the form of technical capacity and financial assistance (UNFCCC 2015). Much earlier, the Philippines ratified the UN Framework Convention on Climate Change (UNFCCC) with a shared commitment with the rest of the world (196 other countries) to stabilize "greenhouse gas concentrations in the atmosphere at a level that would prevent dangerous anthropogenic interference with the climate system" (United Nations 1992). For the first time in its Fifth Assessment Report, the Intergovernmental Panel on Climate Change (IPCC) introduced the concept of a carbon budget considering the 2015 Paris Agreement goal of limiting average global warming to well below 2°C and pursuing efforts to limit the global mean temperature increase to 1.5°C above pre-industrial levels. According to the IPCC (2014), a greenhouse gas emissions budget of 840 Gigatons of Carbon (GtC) is allocated for the world to have a 50 per cent chance of staying below 2°C of warming by 2100 to significantly reduce the risks and impacts of climate change. Alarmingly, more than half of that, or over 531 GtC, has already been emitted into the atmosphere. At current emission rates (around 10 GtC per year), the carbon budget will be used up in just thirty years.

Against this backdrop, in December 2017, the Duterte administration signed a comprehensive tax reform package into law (the Tax Reform for Acceleration and Inclusion Act 2017 [TRAIN]) that imposes, among others, a higher tax on coal, which for decades has been the fossil fuel of choice for power generation in the Philippines. Initially, renewable energy development is hampered by "very high start-up cost, immature technology and competitive prices of fossil fuels" (Agaton 2018). However, as renewable energy technology matures and costs fall globally, the contribution of renewable energy to the Philippine energy mix by fuel type, which currently stands at 37 per cent, is expected to increase. Despite criticism that the initial implementation of Feed-in-Tariffs (FIT) for renewable energy, particularly solar, has resulted in additional costs to consumers (La Viña et al. 2018), renewable energy is expected to eventually address the problem of affordability of electricity in the Philippines, which has one of the most expensive rates in Asia and the world (Verzola, Logarta and Maniego 2017). Are we seeing the advent of the much-anticipated energy transition to a 2015 Paris Agreement-compliant low-carbon future in the Philippines?

This chapter seeks to describe the challenges and opportunities associated with the global energy transition, as driven by the 2015 Paris Agreement. It then focuses on the Philippine energy transition by describing and analysing the trend/trajectory of the Philippine energy sector, the legal and policy instruments in place, and the challenges and opportunities that lie ahead for the country as the world's energy systems transition to a low-carbon one. In addition, it examines the pitfalls and opportunities that lie ahead, especially when the trilemma of energy security, energy equity and environmental sustainability inevitably intersect. At the end, the chapter encapsulates the findings to situate the Philippine energy transition landscape and submits several recommendations to ensure compliance with the 2015 Paris Agreement.

THE CHALLENGE OF THE ENERGY TRILEMMA

In a carbon-constrained world, the Philippine energy sector is at a crossroads. Globally, the energy sector is in transition, accelerated by a global consensus, as mentioned earlier, to limit global warming between 1.5 and 2°C above pre-industrial levels under the 2015 Paris Agreement. This entails the rapid reduction of GHG emissions everywhere, particularly decarbonizing the energy sector in pursuit of cleaner growth. With 40 per cent of global GHG emissions coming from the energy sector alone (World Bank 2013), the goals of the international climate change accord will not be met without implementing changes to existing energy policy, market design and infrastructure in a given jurisdiction. But this represents only one part of the challenge of the energy trilemma—environmental sustainability, which the World Energy Council (WEC) defines as the "achievement of supply- and demand-side energy efficiencies and development of energy supply from renewable and other low-carbon sources" (WEC 2016, p. 12). Two other dimensions, however, are equally important: (1) energy security or the "effective management of primary energy supply from domestic and external sources, reliability of energy infrastructure, and ability of energy providers to meet current and future demand"; and (2) energy equity, which encompasses "accessibility and affordability of energy supply across population" (ibid., p. 12).

Energy transition in any country is not possible without addressing the energy trilemma according to national circumstances and capabilities. There is also no single or fit-all transition pathway. While energy transition is challenging, the International Renewable Energy Agency (IRENA) points out in its recent report that this is "technically feasible and economically beneficial" but "it will not happen by itself" (IRENA 2018, p,. 14). This means that proactive, innovative and forward-looking regulatory and policy tools and levers are necessary to steer a fossil fuel-dependent energy system to a low-carbon pathway that addresses energy security, energy equity and environmental sustainability together. Neglecting one of the dimensions or focusing too much on one can create unintended and costly consequences (WEC 2016). The right timing or "temporal dynamics" (Sovacool 2016, p. 202) are also important, as are finding the optimal combination of policies and setting clear procedure, enabling regulatory frameworks to overcome the barriers associated with, and to make progress on, the energy trilemma.

According to Kern and Rogge (2016), the transition of the existing global energy system to a low-carbon one will occur more swiftly than what research on historical transitions suggests. There are three reasons for this. First, the momentum generated through the years by the variety of actors across different levels of governance—international, regional, national and local involving policymakers, businesses and civil society—is accelerating the transition towards low-carbon energy systems. Second, a highly interconnected world economy is significantly shaping national developments and "creating a dynamic feedback mechanism" (ibid., p. 13) that can quicken the pace of the transition to low-carbon energy systems. Third, as mentioned before, the 2015 Paris Agreement unequivocally enunciates the need for a paradigm shift towards reducing energy-related GHG emissions, among others, to mitigate and adapt to climate change. In short, those who delay their energy transition will be confronted with greater challenges to escape what Unruh (2002, p. 317) calls the "carbon lock-in".

This carbon lock-in culminates in a "techno-institutional complex" that traps economies into carbon-intensive energy systems through path-dependent technological and institutional co-evolution processes (ibid.). Even if they are economically obsolete, vested interests and incumbent industries that benefit from current carbon-intensive energy systems are likely to resist change, and this only makes the energy transition more difficult to traverse (Rogge, Kern and Howlett 2017). For this reason, strategic, mixed and coordinated policy approaches are needed.

Regulation plays an important role in encouraging and supporting behaviour change (IRENA 2018). Thus, it is either a transformation tool or a rampart of the old order. As the World Energy Council (2016, p. 24) emphasizes, ultimately, "policymaker choice is a key discriminating factor of energy performance.". For example, increasing the share of renewable energy in the energy mix will not only reduce GHG emissions but also offer technology solutions "that are safe, reliable, affordable, and widely available" (IRENA 2018, p. 9).

THE LAWS AND POLICIES ON ENERGY

Globally, the 2015 Paris Agreement is accelerating the energy transition, albeit national circumstances are highly relevant for this transition to occur. A recent study on navigating the energy transition in the Philippine context observes that a country typically starts with a vision of its energy future (La Viña et al. 2018, p. 37). This vision invites planning for the energy transition, which is then translated through laws and policies to govern the process and meet the challenges of the energy trilemma. Heffron, McCauley and Sovacool (2015) assert that effective energy law and policy lie at the heart of balancing the objectives reflected in the energy trilemma to deliver the best results for the energy transition.

According to IRENA (2018, p. 68), "planning for the energy transition requires fundamental shifts in policies, investments, planning processes, attitudes and behaviour." These, in turn, raise several key questions. For example: "Is the Energy Transition at the centre of government policies? Which sectoral policies could be enhanced to strengthen the Energy Transition? Within the energy sector, are policies and regulations focused on delivering the Energy Transition?" (ibid.).

The country context is very significant in considering the trade-offs and spillovers that the energy trilemma framework brings to the discourse (WEC 2016). Moreover, the regulatory framework for the energy sector is indicative of the existence of path dependency or carbon lock-in conditions. For this purpose, this part of the chapter elucidates further the Philippine climate change commitments under the 2015 Paris Agreement. Then, the four principal legal and policy instruments relevant to the energy trilemma and the 2015 Paris Agreement for the Philippine energy sector are reviewed—namely, (1) the Electric Power Industry Reform Act 2001, (2) the Renewable Energy Act 2008, (3) the Energy Efficiency and Conservation Act 2019, and (4) the Climate Change Act 2009.

The 2015 Paris Agreement

The Philippines is a party and one of 189 countries that have ratified the 2015 Paris Agreement, which came into force on 4 November 2016. Prior to this, the global community had been struggling for a while since the 1997 Kyoto Protocol to reach a new international pact to implement the UNFCCC as the founding treaty. The 2015 Paris Agreement represents a monumental breakthrough and paradigm shift in approach from a mitigation-centric view to one that also emphasizes adaptation and support. Thus, it builds on three conceptual pillars for its "acceptability and effectiveness": (1) ambition, (2) differentiation, and (3) support (Rajamani and Guerin 2017).

The 2015 Paris Agreement sets an ambitious temperature limit as articulated in Article 2, which Rajamani and Guerin (2017) describe as the global pact's "centrepiece". The goal to limit the global average temperature increase "to well below 2°C above pre-industrial levels" and to pursue "efforts to limit the temperature increase to 1.5°C above pre-industrial levels" is a shared global ambition, but implemented to reflect equity and the principle of common but differentiated responsibilities and respective capabilities, in the light of different national circumstances. To reach this limit with a better chance of success, country parties to the 2015 Paris Agreement—the Philippines included—are expected to pursue mitigation and adaptation actions with support, particularly developing countries.

The 2015 Paris Agreement frames each country's commitments to achieve the international pact's objectives through an instrument called "nationally determined contribution (NDC)". As Winkler (2017) amplifies, the NDCs are, essentially, starting points with a legal expectation for progression over time to reflect a country's highest possible ambition. It will be noted that Article 3 of the Paris Agreement on the NDCs providing for "all Parties ... to undertake and communicate ambitious efforts" applies across mitigation, adaptation and support to developing countries. More importantly, it "creates a substantive new obligation—progression across mitigation, adaptation and support" (Rajamani 2017, p. 140). This progression is captured through a mandatory, comprehensive and collective implementation assessment of the 2015 Paris Agreement called "global stocktake" in Article 14, which has a five-year cycle, with the first one to be undertaken in 2023.

Friedrich (2017, p. 337) describes the global stocktake as "the central vehicle to create a dynamic towards enhanced ambition" and to assist country parties to overcome "purely domestic perspectives and adjust their actions ... to reach their common objectives". In effect, country parties are expected to reflect a progression of both mitigation and adaptation commitments, including support to developing countries, in their NDCs for purposes of achieving the long-term goals of the 2015 Paris Agreement. This is the broad context and normative expectation that serves as a key consideration in mapping the road ahead for the Philippines' energy transition to be compliant with the 2015 Paris Agreement.

The Electric Power Industry Reform Act 2001

Due to prolonged power shortages and unstable power supplies in the late 1990s, the Philippines restructured and reformed its energy sector with the enactment of Republic Act (RA) 9136 or the Electric Power Industry Reform Act 2001 (EPIRA). It sought the privatization of the assets of the state-owned National Power Corporation (NPC), a national monopoly, consistent with the liberalization policies enunciated in the law. EPIRA broke up the once vertically integrated energy sector into generation, transmission, distribution and supply. Notably, EPIRA declares as a matter of policy the quality, reliability, security and affordability of the supply of electric power. To achieve this, it is important to provide new capacity requirements in a free and fair competition regime. Other key reform features introduced by EPIRA include the creation of an independent quasi-judicial regulatory body—the Energy Regulatory Commission—to promote competition, encourage market development, ensure customer choice and penalize abuse of market power in the restructured electricity industry. Also, it establishes a Wholesale Electricity Spot Market (WESM) as a market-based competitive bidding mechanism to attract new power generators and to create additional capacity by "matching" supply and demand in the market. This works by driving competition among power generators, which sell electricity to off-takers at a market price during peak and off-peak demand times. The simple notion is that utility companies will not take the more expensive electricity if a cheaper one is available in the spot market.

Another important EPIRA reform provision is the entry of qualified third parties into remote and unviable villages to provide electric service or participate in rural electrification if a franchized utility is unable to do so for whatever reasons.[2] Also, missionary electrification or the delivery of basic electricity service to unviable areas remains a service domain of the NPC-Small Power Utilities Group (NPC-SPUG) in order to provide power and associated power delivery systems in areas that are not connected to the main transmission grid and cannot be serviced by distribution utilities or qualified third parties. NPC-SPUG generates power using diesel and bunker-fuelled generators, that is, carbon-emission intensive, and notably admits that small islands and isolated grids are expensive to operate and maintain despite being heavily subsidized (Ahmed 2018).

From an institutional standpoint, EPIRA gave the Department of Energy (DoE) the mandate not only to oversee the restructuring of the electric power industry but also to undertake the formulation of policies towards the efficient supply and economical use of energy consistent with the policies on environmental protection and conservation and maintenance of ecological balance. Also, EPIRA tasked the DoE to prepare the Philippine Energy Plan (PEP), which contains a roadmap for both electricity supply and demand side management, among others. The PEP 2017–2040 offers an interesting insight into the current Philippine energy landscape and where it will be by 2040. By fuel type, coal at 22 per cent and oil at 34.9 per cent constitute the bulk of the energy mix, with renewable energy contributing 37 per cent in 2016. By 2040, the Philippines will be using more coal (41.6 per cent) but a little less oil (32.2 per cent), which means that fossil fuel-based sources will increase in total from 56.9 per cent in 2016 to 73.8 per cent in 2040 (Department of Energy 2017b). Effectively, the share of renewable energy in the energy mix will decrease in the long term. Notably, the baseload demand in the Philippines is mostly met by coal-fired power plants, with 80 per cent of the coal stock imported from abroad (Ahmed and Logarta 2017). With the automatic pass-through provisions of fuel, operating and maintenance costs in power supply contracts, the risk of global coal price and exchange rate shocks are passed onto consumers (ibid.). In a recent report (ibid.), 10,423 MW of coal-fired power plants worth close to US$21 billion are in the pipeline to meet present and future energy supply and demand requirements. In this scenario, the Philippines is placing its bet on coal in the long run.

The Renewable Energy Act 2008

While the EPIRA reforms were still underway, the Philippines passed RA 9513 or the Renewable Energy Act 2008 (REA), to provide a national framework for the promotion, development, utilization and commercialization of renewable energy sources in the country. It declares as a matter of state policy the need to accelerate the exploration and development of renewable energy resources. Also, the law sets out the institutional arrangements, fiscal incentives and structural policies available for on-grid and off-grid renewable energy development, including various schemes and mechanisms to support renewable energy development, utilization and commercialization. Fiscal incentives include FIT, income tax holidays, tax credits and cash incentives. On the other hand, structural policies include the Renewable Portfolio Standard (RPS), Renewable Energy Market (REM), net-metering and Green Energy Option Program (GEOP).

The FIT scheme applies to electricity from emerging renewable energy sources such as wind, solar, ocean, run-of-river hydro and biomass. The FIT obligates electricity power industry participants to source electricity from emerging renewable energy sources at a guaranteed fixed price for a stipulated period under the rules. In addition, it provides for priority connection to the grid for electricity generated from emerging renewable sources as well as priority purchase and transmission of such electricity by grid system operators. The RPS obligates electricity industry participants such as generators, distribution utilities or suppliers to source or produce a minimum percentage of their power requirements from eligible renewable energy resources on a sector and per-grid basis. This is intended to diversify the supply of energy while at the same time reducing greenhouse gas emissions in the country.

To facilitate compliance with the RPS, the DoE is authorized to create a REM and to supervise the establishment of a Renewable Energy Registrar (RER) through the Philippine Electricity Market Corporation (PEMC). The RER can issue Renewable Energy Certificates (REC) as proof of compliance with the RPS, which can then be traded in the REM.

The RECs can also form part of an international trading emission and compliance scheme. The GEOP allows end-users to choose renewable energy as their source of power. Subject to the determination of the DoE, end-users may directly contract from renewable energy facilities their energy requirements through the relevant distribution utilities. Net-metering is adopted as a consumer-based renewable energy incentive scheme wherein distribution end-users generate electricity from an eligible on-site renewable energy facility that is delivered to the local distribution grid. The electricity generated can then be used by distribution end-users to offset electricity consumed from the distribution utility or gain credit in case of electricity delivered to the grid from the on-site renewable energy facility exceeds what is consumed therefrom. The distribution utility is required to enter into a net-metering agreement upon request of a distribution end-user wishing to install an on-site renewable energy facility, subject to the distribution utility's technical standards, including economic considerations, for the renewable energy facility. To make the scheme more attractive to the distribution utility, it will be entitled to any RECs issued under the arrangement, which in turn can be counted towards its compliance with the RPS. In terms of institutional arrangements, the DoE has been designated as the lead agency for the implementation of the provisions of REA. To support the DoE, the Renewable Energy Management Bureau (REMB) is created as a staff and support bureau to implement policies, plans, and programmes to accelerate the development, utilization and commercialization of RE resources and technologies.

Aside from the REMB, the National Renewable Energy Board (NREB) was established, consisting of multi-sectoral representatives from different government line agencies, government-owned or controlled corporations and financial institutions, renewable energy developers, private distribution utilities, electric cooperatives, electric suppliers, and non-governmental organizations. The NREB is tasked to evaluate and recommend to the DoE the RPS and minimum renewable energy generation capacities in off-grid areas. It is also empowered to recommend specific actions and monitor and review the implementation of the National Renewable Energy Program (NREP), which seeks to attain consistency and preclude functional overlaps among the different government agencies involved in renewable energy development. Insofar as the renewable energy outlook is concerned, the NREP 2011–2030 aims to increase the installed capacity from renewable energy to at least 20,000 MW by 2040 from 7,082 MW in 2016 (Department of Energy n.d.). However, the NREP 2011–2030 is being updated, and thus, it is identified as a major policy gap until a new one is issued. Per the RE Roadmap 2017–2040, the NREP 2017–2040 update is a deliverable in the medium term (2019–22) and should contribute to the overall objective by 2040 of increasing RE installed capacity to at least 20,000 MW (Department of Energy n.d.).

The Energy Efficiency and Conservation Act 2019

In 2019, the Philippines enacted RA 11285, or the Energy Efficiency and Conservation Act (EECA), to "institutionalise energy efficiency and conservation as national way of life". It also seeks to "promote and encourage the development and utilisation of efficient renewable energy technologies and systems to ensure optimal use and sustainability of the country's energy sources". Moreover, EECA aims to reinforce related laws such as the EPIRA and REA. Similar to EPIRA and REA, the DoE is the lead agency in the implementation of the EECA, including the creation and update of the National Energy Efficiency and Conservation Plan (NEECP). The NEECP provides "the national comprehensive framework, governance structure, and programs for energy efficiency and conservation with defined national targets, feasible strategies and regular monitoring and evaluation" (Section 49 [z], RA 11285). Notably, however, other government agencies, particularly the Climate Change Commission (CCC), are required to collaborate with the DoE in establishing targets and determining strategies that are aligned with the NEECP, including monitoring and recording all GHG reductions resulting from energy efficiency and conservation projects.

Prior to the enactment of the EECA, the Philippines Energy Efficiency and Conservation Roadmap 2017–2040, which is based on the pre-existing NEECP, provided the national framework for building an energy-efficient country and incorporates the priority goals of the Duterte administration (2017–22). It is supportive of the Philippine commitments enunciated at the UNFCCC Conference of the Parties (COP), particularly at "COP21 and COP22 by providing a consistent and holistic approach for implementing energy efficiency measures in the short, medium and long term" (Department of Energy 2017a, p. 10). If utilized as the basis for the NEECP under the EECA, it has the potential to reduce energy intensity by 3 per cent across economic sectors (Department of Energy 2017a) and avoid the equivalent of 10 per cent of GHG emissions from current policy projections assuming the full implementation of the targets under NREP 2011–2030, if carried over in its updated version (Climate Action Tracker n.d.).

As the DoE implements the EPIRA, REA and EECA, these pieces of legislation are seen as providing a consistent and harmonized approach to energy planning in the Philippines with the salient elements of the NREP and NCEEP incorporated or feeding into the PEP.

The Climate Change Act 2009

The Philippines is one of the most vulnerable countries to climate change, especially in the last two decades (Eckstein, Kunzel and Schafer 2017). In response, the country enacted RA 9729 or The Climate Change Act 2009[3] (CCA), in recognition of the need to ensure that national and subnational policies, plans and programmes are founded upon sound environmental considerations and the principles of sustainable development. The CCA declares that the Philippines, as a party to the UNFCCC, adopts the ultimate objective of the Convention to stabilize the GHG concentrations in the atmosphere "at a level that would prevent dangerous anthropogenic interference with the climate system within a time frame that is sufficient to allow ecosystems to adapt naturally to climate change, to ensure that food production is not threatened, and to enable economic development to proceed in a sustainable manner" (Section 2, RA 9729). The CCA calls for the integration of the concept of climate change in various phases of policy formulation, development plans, poverty reduction strategies and other government development tools and techniques. To align initiatives as a national undertaking, the CCA encourages the participation of local governments, businesses, non-government organizations and local communities and the public to mitigate the adverse effects of climate change.

The CCA established the CCC as an independent, autonomous and sole policymaking and science-based body attached to the Office of the President. It is primarily tasked to coordinate, monitor and evaluate programmes and action plans of the Philippine government on climate change. The CCC has an Advisory Board consisting of representatives from government agencies, local government units, the academe, the business sector and non-governmental organizations. It is significant that the DoE sits as a member of the Advisory Board. Also, the CCC is supported by the National Panel of Experts, composed of the country's leading climate scientists and the Intergovernmental Panel on Climate Change lead authors.

The CCA mandates the formulation of the National Framework Strategy on Climate Change (NFSCC), which serves as the basis for a programme on climate change planning, research and development, extension and monitoring of activities to protect vulnerable communities from the adverse impacts of climate change. Interestingly, the NFSCC is formulated considering climate change vulnerabilities, specific adaptation needs and mitigation potential consistent with multilateral environmental agreements, specifically the UN Framework Convention on Climate Change. The CCC promulgated the NFSCC for 2012–22 and identified key result areas (KRAs) for mitigation and adaptation in climate-sensitive sectors. These include energy, agriculture, biodiversity, infrastructure, population, health and demography.

The KRAs for mitigation enunciate a long-term objective that aims to facilitate the transition of the Philippines towards a low-carbon economy. Targets include the development and enhancement of clean energy sources and other efficiency measures and the realization of the full potential of the country's renewable energy capacity to contribute to energy security and promote low-carbon growth in the energy sector. On the other hand, KRAs for adaptation seek to build the adaptive capacity of communities and increase the resilience of natural ecosystems to climate change in the long run. Also, cross-cutting strategies are identified, which involve capacity building, knowledge management and information, education and communication, research and development and technology transfer.

In accordance with the NFSCC, the National Climate Change Action Plan (NCCAP) 2011–2028 was prepared to assess the national impact of climate change, identify the most vulnerable communities and areas, identify the differential impact of climate change, assess and manage risk and vulnerability, identify GHG mitigation potential and determine appropriate adaptation measures. The NCCAP sets the road map for the Philippine government in implementing short, medium and long-term climate actions in seven priority areas: (1) food security, (2) water sufficiency, (3) ecosystem and environmental stability, (4) human security, (5) climate-smart industries and services, (6) sustainable energy, and (7) knowledge and capacity development. The NCCAP is being updated to articulate the country's Nationally Determined Contribution (NDC), which, in turn, replaces the submitted INDC under the 2015 Paris Agreement. The CCC has conducted consultations, validation meetings and workshops on the NDC, which provides a road map on the energy transition to a low-carbon pathway, including mitigation and adaptation targets and options for the agriculture, waste, industry, transportation, forestry, and energy sectors. The NDC is supposed to be issued in 2018 (CCC 2018), which must be submitted for purposes of complying with the 2015 Paris Agreement. It will be noted that pending the completion and submission of the NDC, the INDC's target of a 70 per cent reduction of GHG emissions by 2030 across sectors compared to a business-as-usual pathway, which according to experts is feasible (Verzola, Logarta and Maniego 2017), will stand (World Resources Institute n.d.). The Climate Action Tracker has rated the Philippine INDC as 2°C compatible, but the current policies that are in place do not meet the target articulated in the INDC, albeit it is still undergoing revision.

Consistent with the provisions of the Local Government Code, the NFSCC and NCCAP, local governments are mandated to formulate, plan and implement Local Climate Change Action Plans (LCCAP) in their respective areas, which shall be regularly updated to reflect changing social, economic and environmental conditions and emerging issues (Section 14). Notably, inter-local government unit collaboration shall be maximized in the conduct of climate-related activities. For example, the *barangay*s shall be directly involved with municipal and city governments in prioritizing climate change issues and in identifying and implementing best practices and other solutions. Also, municipal and city governments shall consider climate change adaptation as one of their regular functions. In addition, provincial governments shall provide technical assistance, enforcement and information management in support of municipal and city climate change action plans. However, it shall be the responsibility of the national government to extend technical and financial assistance to local governments for the accomplishment of their LCCAPs. It must be emphasized that the LCCAPs are expected to provide robust local contexts and contributions to implementing the NCCAP.

MIND THE GAPS: THE LEGAL AND POLICY CONCERNS

While the regulatory and policy framework to address the energy trilemma and drive the energy transition have been in place for quite some time, there are three major concerns that emerge from the existing legal and policy instruments. These are (1) the lack of consistency, coherence and certainty of regulations and policies; (2) the risk of stranded coal power assets; and (3) the unfinished business of rural electrification.

Lack of consistency, coherence and certainty of regulations and policies

The EPIRA, REA, EECA and CCA are designed to complement one another to address energy security, energy equity and environmental sustainability. In theory, this makes the Philippines a global leader when it comes to regulatory and policy enactment (La Viña and Guiao 2013) on addressing the energy trilemma. But implementation has proven difficult and demonstrates the constraints of balancing the "differing, overlapping and sometimes contradicting objectives of the energy trilemma of security, equity, and sustainability" (La Viña et al. 2018, p. 40). This is reflected in two contrasting and inconsistent scenarios that the DoE and the CCC are pursuing—one is on a high-carbon emission pathway under the PEP, and the other on the low-carbon side under the NREP, NCEEP, NCCAP and INDC. Disturbingly, the high-carbon emission approach in the existing PEP will not meet the 70 per cent GHG emission reduction target in the INDC (Verzola, Logarta and Maniego 2017). Brown and Chandler (2008, p. 474) point out that "fluctuating ... policies ... can forestall commitments to clean energy or accelerate investments in carbon-intensive energy options.".

Between the DoE, a line agency, and the CCC, a policymaking body, the implementation of laws and prioritization of programmes essentially repose with the DoE. La Viña et al. (2018) illustrate the discretionary power exercised by the DoE that lends itself to policy inconsistency and incoherence. In 2014, the DoE adopted an optimal energy mix policy in the energy sector. After the national elections in 2016, however, the Duterte administration, through the Energy Secretary, shifted the focus away from an optimal energy mix policy to that of meeting the country's capacity requirements with a strong emphasis on energy security (ibid.). As La Viña et al. (2018, p. 41) lament,

> The changing priorities of each administration are also reflected in the country's numerous, varying energy plans, and accentuated by the lack of a single, coherent, long-term plan that different government administrations are bound to.

There is another serious concern in navigating the energy trilemma through the existing regulations and policies in the Philippines. As the country's national framework for the promotion, development, utilization and commercialization of renewable energy sources, the REA incorporates time-bound, complementary and interlinked schemes, mechanisms and programmes that are designed to achieve the legislative objective of increasing the deployment of renewable energy to grid and off-grid areas in the Philippines. A decade since its passage into law, REA is still hampered by delays punctuated by a piecemeal approach to its implementation. The DoE has issued the FIT, net-metering, RPS, REM and GEOP rules at different times beyond the target dates for implementation. Interestingly, the RPS, REM and GEOP rules have been issued only in 2018 and 2019 against the backdrop of legal action before the courts and audit queries from the Commission on Audit—an independent constitutional commission empowered to audit all accounts pertaining to all government revenues and expenditures/uses of government resources—that are attributed to the REA's delayed implementation since its enactment in 2008.

Even when the relevant rules are issued, there is a need to ensure that these are fully operational rather than conditional; that is, the necessary elements or components for implementation are in place. Also, design flaws have emerged in the process of implementation. For example, the FIT has spurred investments in renewable energy, specifically solar. However, it also resulted in additional cost burden to consumers, who ultimately shoulder the mandatory payments of the FIT allowance that are no longer needed due to falling global solar prices (La Viña et al. 2018). The inability of regulations and policies to keep in step with drastic changes to a disruptive and quickly evolving technology landscape exemplifies the difficulty in transitioning to low-carbon energy systems such as RE. In addition, there is consistent reference to the lack of national and local government capacity, coordination and harmonization of permitting/approval rules between the two levels of government as major concerns. As Marquardt (2017, p. 5) points out, the "lack of coordination across jurisdictional levels", including "a dearth of capacities", are impeding the full and effective implementation of REA. Furthermore, the NREP 2011–2030 is being updated, and thus, it is identified as a major policy gap until a new one is issued. Effectively, the absence of an updated NREP makes it difficult to predict the energy landscape and anchor medium and long-term expectations, particularly for stakeholders. Lastly, there is no policy instrument that links RE targets and deployment to the policy objective of the REA to reduce harmful emissions and capture socio-economic impacts such as job creation or employment.

Any semblance of implementation delay or lack of decisive action on the part of the government to fully operationalize REA sends the wrong signal to the public and the investing community. Alarmingly, it has been reported that the implementation delays have stymied more than US$2.5 billion worth of potential RE investments in the country (WWF International 2013). Worse, there is an apprehension that the second package of TRAIN will remove or reduce the incentives for RE development, even before these are fully implemented (Rivera 2018). The implementation deficit and the news surrounding the REA incentives project weakened political support for RE development and an impression to preserve the status quo as long as possible—that is, keeping RE "marginalised by distortions in the world's electricity markets created by decades of massive financial, political and structural support to conventional power technologies" (European Renewable Energy Council and Greenpeace International 2009, p. 21). As Katz (2012, p. 144) further observes, "[t]here may not be sufficient political will to persevere with the renewable energy policy", especially when confronted with the politics surrounding the push for RE development.

Risk of stranded coal power assets

It will be difficult to achieve carbon emission cuts, stay within the carbon budget and limit the rise in global mean temperatures to 1.5 to 2°C without phasing out coal (IRENA 2017). Thus, the potential risk of power asset stranding in the energy sector—particularly of coal-fired energy plants—to realize global decarbonization objectives is immense (ibid.). In its energy directions discussion paper, the World Bank (2013, p. 25) adopted, as a guiding principle, that financial support for new greenfield coal power generation projects will be provided "only in rare circumstances" such as "meeting basic energy needs in countries with no feasible alternatives". Several international banks, such as the Standard Chartered Bank, Société Générale and Deutsche Bank, have gone further ahead by deciding to stop funding for coal power projects (Hicks 2018). This sends a signal to the market that financial institutions are taking seriously the risk of asset stranding from coal-fired power plants. In addition, the Government of Canada's Department of Environment and Climate Change, the French Development Agency (AFD), Germany's Federal Ministry for the Environment, Nature Conservation and Nuclear Safety (BMU), the United Kingdom's Department for Business, Energy and Industrial Strategy (BEIS), in partnership with global philanthropies, are offering financial resources and technical assistance to Southeast Asian countries, such as the Philippines, to accelerate the energy transition and meet the Paris commitments (European Climate Foundation 2018).

For the Philippines to succeed in its energy transition, the share of RE in the energy mix needs to reach up to 40 per cent by 2030 (Marquardt, Steinbacher and Schreurs 2016). Unfortunately, the Philippines is moving in the opposite direction by betting big on coal, as enunciated under the existing PEP. This not only perpetuates the existing fossil fuel-based energy systems but also poses "a growing material and inevitable [asset stranding] risk to the Philippines" (Ahmed and Logarta 2017, p. 1). That risk includes missing out on the Philippine commitment under the Paris Agreement on a 70 per cent GHG emission reduction by 2030 per the INDC. The preference for coal, as proponents argue, is meant to secure the baseload power from a stable and reliable source, which is needed to drive a growing economy and meet energy security requirements. But this has dire, costly consequences with an economy-wide effect. As Ahmed and Logarta (2017, p. 10) observe,

> The coal-dependent strategy playing out now in the Philippines will inevitably create stranded assets, which are damaging to the unlucky investor who puts money into them or—in the case of the Philippines—damaging to the ratepayers who end up paying for them in the long run.

As mentioned earlier, the Philippines already has one of the highest electricity costs in Asia and the world. Adding more imported coal-fired power capacity with large sunk costs in the technology infrastructure amid a coal tax hike under TRAIN will further aggravate the price volatility in the energy sector with an accelerated risk of asset stranding. Even though TRAIN taxes coal that can boost RE cost competitiveness, it is argued that TRAIN "is unlikely to incentivise a shift away from coal-fired power generation as major distributors can still pass the higher generation costs on to end consumers" (Climate Action Tracker n.d.). This means that escaping the carbon lock-in and meeting the affordability aspect of the energy trilemma remain ongoing concerns.

Unfinished business of rural electrification

The rapid deployment of RE technologies is ushering in technological changes in the energy landscape and bringing solutions to development goals that were previously beyond reach (Ban 2011). In this vein, the energy equity pillar of the energy trilemma can be realized by utilizing grid, mini-grid and off-grid electrification approaches. Considering that energy poverty is prevalent in the countryside, RE technologies offer an opportunity to complete the business of rural electrification and facilitate universal access to modern energy services in remote and off-grid areas of developing countries such as an archipelagic country like the Philippines. However, the privatization and liberalization approach espoused under EPIRA and the promotion of off-grid RE systems under REA have revealed difficulties in addressing the environmental sustainability and energy equity pillars of the energy trilemma.

The market-oriented framework under EPIRA has shifted the treatment of electricity as a form of social service to one described by Byrne and Mun (2003, p. 49) as "a commodity in need of optimal allocation". In effect, market dynamics, positive marginal costs and dispatchability of power (Blazquez et al. 2018), rather than socio-political considerations, dictated the structural changes to be introduced in the energy sector. The underlying ideology of power liberalization lies in the claim that improvements in resource allocation, market regulation, consumer choice and environmental quality can be achieved through economic efficiency (Byrne and Mun 2003). It includes attaining universal access to electricity as a key success indicator of the reforms in developing countries. However, Wamukonya (2003, p. 24) notes that "there is emerging evidence that reform has been designed to mainly address economic and, in particular, financial concerns, with insufficient consideration for social and environmental issues." In effect, universal access to electricity will unlikely be achieved through the private sector unless the government undertakes this by itself, or provides the corresponding policy support and incentives to the private sector in order to address the unattractiveness of, and discrimination against, the rural segment of electrification. As Besant-Jones (2006, p. 93) emphasizes:

> [A] well-conceived reform program ... offers the opportunity to introduce new ways for expanding access to electricity supply by the poor, and it also helps target subsidies efficiently on the poor in place of current approaches that largely favor the better-off consumers.

Another negative aspect of power liberalization is its environmental impact. Although it promised to deliver an enhanced environmental quality by driving out old technologies and investing in new ones, the EPIRA reforms did not only "leave existing environmental problems unaddressed [but created] new challenges in meeting sustainability goals" (Byrne and Mun 2003, p. 59). The promotion of a short-term, profit-driven electricity system neglects sustainable alternatives such as RE technologies and demand-side efficiency because "electricity as a commodity drives economic actors to focus on selling more kWhs [kilowatt-hours]—rather than providing more services with fewer kWhs" (ibid., p. 59). As a result, there is a considerably reduced interest in capital-intensive RE projects and a preference for cheaper fossil fuel plants due to shortened time horizons, increased borrowing costs and heightened demand for higher rates of return under a liberalized and privatized set-up (Agbemabiese, Byrne and Bouille 2003).

Moreover, power liberalization has fostered centralization instead of decentralization of the energy system "in the form of utility mergers and acquisitions, and in the operation of transmission and distribution networks" (Byrne and Mun 2003, p. 53). Byrne and Mun (2003, p. 54) also explain that "the transmission system is operated mostly as sophisticated technocratic institutions that enable the transfer of large volumes of electrons (and private gains) among a small number of sizable companies". With the commodification of electricity, it makes sense for such companies to merge and increase the scale of power generation to compete in a less restrictive electricity market for "the delivery of large volumes of electricity to large, interconnected grids" (ibid., p. 55). Apart from being considered disruptive in nature to incumbents with large sunk costs in existing technology infrastructure (Fuentes-Bracamontes 2016), decentralized electricity systems will not likely thrive in a market-oriented environment unless various support mechanisms are extended to encourage deployment of RE technologies and distributed generation alongside power liberalization initiatives (Martinot 2003). This is problematic with the non-operationalization of the necessary fiscal and non-fiscal incentive rules for off-grid RE development in the Philippines to the detriment of the 11 million Filipinos still without access to electricity.

CONCLUSION AND MOVING FORWARD

The 2015 Paris Agreement, technology and innovation are paving the way to an energy transition and a development path that allows developing countries to leapfrog environmentally into a low-carbon future. Global deployment of RE technologies indicates the realization of such a promise, as demonstrated by the increasing share of RE in the energy mix worldwide to achieve the mitigation and adaptation goals of the 2015 Paris Agreement. This is enabled and sustained by a suite of international and national regulatory and policy instruments that are deemed 2015 Paris Agreement-compliant while addressing the energy security, energy equity and environmental sustainability pillars of the energy trilemma simultaneously.

Despite a national regulatory and policy framework that seeks to tackle the energy trilemma, the case of the Philippines exemplifies that much work needs to be done to balance the concerns on energy security, energy equity and environmental sustainability and overcome the barriers to a low-carbon future. A review of the existing regulatory and policy framework in the country reveals the gaps, constraints and risks that the country confronts in moving to a low-carbon future and meeting its 2015 Paris Agreement commitments, including the difficulty in escaping the carbon lock-in. In addition, it is proving to be very challenging to achieve consistency, coherence and certainty in the sphere of regulations and policies to govern the energy transition. Accordingly, there are four main recommendations that can be teased out from the chapter in moving forward.

First, there is a need to align all the related energy plans in the country, considering that one prominent line department, the DoE, has the authority and opportunity under the existing legal and policy framework to implement a national energy policy, plan and strategy that are in accordance with the country's 2015 Paris Agreement commitments. Second, the remaining policy gaps need to be filled. For example, the updated NREP has to be issued to anchor medium and long-term expectations and provide predictability on the RE landscape in the country. In the updating process, the NREP also offers an opportunity to link RE targets and deployment to the policy objective of reducing harmful emissions and meeting adaptation targets. The opportunity for such a linkage can be quantified by undertaking a regulatory impact analysis or assessment of the NREP. Third, all the issued rules and regulations must be functional, operational and implementable in their entirety, ensuring consistency and coherence across energy sector-related pieces of legislation. This will require an implementation review or study of the related rules and regulations, including an institutional capacity assessment to analyse the issues, resources and opportunities associated with full implementation. Finally, the NDC must be completed and submitted soon in lieu of the INDC articulating in sufficient detail an evidence and science-based mitigation and adaptation target across the energy, transport, forestry, industry and waste sectors, especially if the Philippines is to access the support required for the implementation of its 2015 Paris Agreement commitments, while mindful of the first global stocktake in 2023.

Decisions are still being made in the face of heightened climate change hazards that a climate-vulnerable developing country such as the Philippines is confronting. There is still an opportunity to make the right ones, but time is of the essence.

Notes

1. Reprinted with permission from "The Philippine Climate Change Commitments and the Energy Transition to a Low-Carbon Future", in *Promoting Energy Security in the Philippines:ASEP-CELLs Project Research Compendium*, edited by Josef T. Yap (Ateneo School of Government, 2022), https://asepcells.ph/2022/05/16/asep-cells-research-compendium/ (accessed 4 February 2023).
2. "Unviable areas" refer to a geographical area within the Franchise Area of a Distribution Utility where immediate extension of distribution line is not feasible.
3. The CCA was amended in 2011 to create the People's Survival Fund (PSF). The PSF is established to finance adaptation programmes and projects planned under the NFSCC.

References

Agaton, Casper. 2018. "To Import Coal or Invest in Renewables? A Real Options Approach to Energy Investments in the Philippines". In *Transition Towards 100% Renewable Energy*, edited by Ali Sayigh, pp. 1–10. New York: Springer International Publishing.

Agbemabiese, Lawrence, John Byrne, and Daniel Bouille. 2003. "Stakeholder Roles in Promoting Equity and Environmental Protection". In *Electricity Reform: Social and Environmental Challenges*, edited by Nijeri Wamukonya, pp. 227–56. Roskilde: UNEP.

Ahmed, Sara Jane. 2018. "Electricity in the Philippines Does Not Need to Be So Expensive—Or Dirty". *Eco-Business*, 16 May 2018. https://www.eco-business.com/opinion/electricity-in-the-philippines-does-not-need-to-be-so-expensiveor-dirty/ (accessed 12 February 2023).

Ahmed, Sara Jane, and Jose Logarta Jr. 2017. *Carving Out Coal in the Philippines: Stranded Coal Plant Assets and the Energy Transition*. Institute for Energy Economics and Financial Analysis and Institute for Climate and Sustainable Cities https://ieefa.org/wp-content/uploads/2017/10/Carving-out-Coal-in-the-Philippines_IEEFAICSC_ONLINE_12Oct2017.pdf (accessed 12 February 2023).

Ban Ki-Moon. 2011. Sustainable Energy for All: A Vision Statement by Ban Ki-Moon, Secretary General of the United Nations. New York: United Nations. https://www.seforall.org/sites/default/files/l/2014/02/SG_Sustainable_Energy_for_All_vision.pdf (accessed 12 February 2023).

Besant-Jones, John E. 2006. "Reforming Power Markets in Developing Countries: What Have We Learned?" *Energy and Mining Sector Board Discussion Paper No. 19*. Washington: The World Bank.

Blazquez, Jorge, Rolando Fuentes-Bracamontes, Carlo Andrea Bollino, and Nora Nezamuddin. 2018. "The Renewable Energy Policy Paradox". *Renewable and Sustainable Energy Reviews* 82 (February): 1–5. https://doi.org/10.1016/j.rser.2017.09.002 (accessed 12 February 2023).

Brown, Marilyn, and Sharon Chandler. 2008. "Governing Confusion: How Statutes, Fiscal Policy, and Regulations Impede Clean Energy Technologies". *Stanford Law and Policy Review* 19: 472–509.

Bureau of Internal Revenue. 2017. "Republic Act No. 10963: Tax Reform for Acceleration and Inclusion Act 2017". https://www.bir.gov.ph/images/bir_files/internal_communications_1/TRAIN%20matters/RA-10963-RRD.pdf (accessed 25 February 2023).

Byrne, John, and Yu-Mi Mun. 2003. "Power Liberalisation or Energy Transformation?" In *Electricity Reform: Social and Environmental Challenges*, edited by Nijeri Wamukonya, pp. 48–76. Roskilde: UNEP.

CCC (Climate Change Commission). Climate Change and the Philippines: Executive Brief. Manila: Climate Change Commission.

Climate Action Tracker. N.d. *Philippines*. https://climateactiontracker.org/countries/philippines/ (accessed 13 September 2020).

Department of Energy. 2001. "Republic Act No. 9136: Electric Power Industry Reform Act 2001". https://www.doe.gov.ph/sites/default/files/pdf/issuances/20010608-ra-09136-gma.pdf (accessed 25 February 2023).

———. 2008. "Republic Act No. 9513: Renewable Energy Act 2008". https://www.doe.gov.ph/sites/default/files/pdf/issuances/20081216-ra-09513-gma.pdf (accessed 25 February 2023).

———. 2017a. *The Philippines Energy Efficiency and Conservation Roadmap 2017–2040*. https://www.doe.gov.ph/sites/default/files/pdf/energy_efficiency/ee_roadmap_book_2017-2040.pdf (accessed 13 September 2020).

———. 2017b. *Philippine Energy Plan 2017–2040*. https://www.doe.gov.ph/sites/default/files/pdf/announcements/acd_15_phil_energy_plan_2017-2040.pdf (accessed 13 September 2020).

———. n.d. *Renewable Energy Roadmap 2017–2040*. https://www.doe.gov.ph/pep/renewable-energy-roadmap-2017-2040 (accessed 13 September 2020).

Eckstein, David, Vera Kunzel, and Laura Schafer. 2017. *Global Climate Risk Index 2018: Who Suffers Most from Extreme Weather Events? Weather-Related Loss Events in 2016 and 1997 to 2016*. Bonn: Germanwatch.

European Climate Foundation. 2018. "Government and Philanthropies Announce Southeast Asian Energy Transition Partnership". 27 September 2018. https://www.linkedin.com/pulse/governments-philanthropies-announce-south-east-asia-energy-collyer/ (accessed 18 March 2023).

European Renewable Energy Council and Greenpeace International. 2009. *Energy Revolution: A Sustainable World Energy Outlook*. https://www.greenpeace.org/usa/wp-content/uploads/legacy/Global/usa/report/2009/4/energy-r-evolution-a-sustain.pdf (accessed 20 April 2022).

Flores, Helen. 2018. "Climate Change Vulnerability: Philippines Ranks 3rd". *The Philippine Star*, 21 March 2018. https://www.philstar.com/headlines/2018/03/21/1798866/climate-change-vulnerability-philippines-ranks-3rd (accessed 13 September 2020).

Friedrich, Jurgen. 2017. "Global Stocktake (Article 14)". In *The Paris Agreement on Climate Change: Analysis and Commentary*, edited by Daniel Klein, María Pía Carazo, Meinhard Doelle, Jane Bulmer, and Andrew Higham, pp. 319–37. Oxford: Oxford University Press.

Fuentes-Bracamontes, Rolando. 2016. "Is Unbundling Electricity Services the Way Forward for the Power Sector?" *The Electricity Journal* 29, no. 9: 16–20. https://doi.org/10.1016/j.tej.2016.10.006 (accessed 25 February 2023).

Heffron, Raphael J., Darren McCauley, and Benjamin K. Sovacool. 2015. "Resolving Society's Energy Trilemma through the Energy Justice Metric". *Energy Policy* 87 (December): 168–76. https://doi.org/10.1016/j.enpol.2015.08.033 (accessed 25 February 2023).

Hicks, Robin. 2018. "Standard Chartered Bank Quits Coal". *Eco-Business*, 25 September 2015. https://www.eco-business.com/news/standard-chartered-bank-quits-coal/ (accessed 13 September 2020).

International Energy Agency. 2017. *Southeast Asia Energy Outlook 2017*. https://www.iea.org/reports/southeast-asia-energy-outlook-2017 (accessed 25 February 2023).

IPCC (Intergovernmental Panel on Climate Change). 2014. "Climate Change 2014: Synthesis Report. Contribution of Working Groups I, II and III to the Fifth Assessment Report of the Intergovernmental Panel on Climate Change". Geneva: IPCC. https://www.ipcc.ch/site/assets/uploads/2018/02/AR5_SYR_FINAL_SPM.pdf (accessed 25 February 2023).

IRENA (International Renewable Energy Agency). *Stranded Assets and Renewables: How the Energy Transition Affects the Value of Energy Reserves, Buildings and Capital Stock.* Abu Dhabi: IRENA.

———. 2018. *Global Energy Transformation: A Roadmap to 2050.* Abu Dhabi: IRENA.

Katz, Linda C. 2012. "Promoting Renewable Energies in the Philippines: Policies and Challenges". *Renewable Energy Law and Policy Review* 3, no. 2: 140–45. https://www.jstor.org/stable/24324742 (accessed 25 February 2023).

Kern, Florian, and Karoline S. Rogge. 2016. "The Pace of Governed Energy Transitions: Agency, International Dynamics and the Global Paris Agreement Accelerating Decarbonisation Processes?" *Energy Research & Social Science* 22 (December): 13–17. https://doi.org/10.1016/j.erss.2016.08.016 (accessed 25 February 2023).

La Viña, Antonio G.M., and Cecilia Guiao. 2013. "Climate Change and the Law: Issues and Challenges in the Philippines". *Ateneo Law Journal* 58, no. 3: 612–36.

La Viña, Antonio G.M., Joyce Melcar Tan, Teresa Ira Maris Guanzon, Mary Jean Caleda, and Lawrence Ang. 2018. "Navigating a Trilemma: Energy Security, Equity, and Sustainability in the Philippines' Low-Carbon Transition". *Energy Research & Social Science* 35 (January): 37–47. https://doi.org/10.1016/j.erss.2017.10.039 (accessed 25 February 2023).

Marquardt, Jens. 2017. "How Power Affects Policy Implementation: Lessons from the Philippines". *Journal of Current Southeast Asian Affairs* 36, no. 1: 3–27. https://doi.org/10.1177/186810341703600101 (accessed 25 February 2023).

Marquardt, Jens, Karoline Steinbacher, and Miranda Schreurs. 2016. "Driving Force or Forced Transition? The Role of Development Cooperation in Promoting Energy Transitions in the Philippines and Morocco". *Journal of Cleaner Production* 128 (August): 22–33. https://doi.org/10.1016/j.jclepro.2015.06.080 (accessed 25 February 2023).

Martinot, Eric. 2003. "Power Sector Restructuring and the Environment: Trends, Policies, and GEF Experience". In *Electricity Reform: Social and Environmental Challenges*, edited by Nijeri Wamukonya, pp. 200–26. Roskilde: UNEP.

NEDA (National Economic Development Authority). 2017. *Philippine Development Plan 2017–2022.* Manila: NEDA.

Rajamani, Lavanya. 2017. "Guiding Principles and General Obligations (Article 2.2 and 3)". In *The Paris Agreement on Climate Change: Analysis and Commentary*, edited by Daniel Klein, María Pía Carazo, Meinhard Doelle, Jane Bulmer, and Andrew Higham. Oxford: Oxford University Press.

Rajamani, Lavanya, and Emmanuel Guerin. 2017. "Central Concepts in the Paris Agreement and How They Evolved". In *The Paris Agreement on Climate Change: Analysis and Commentary*, edited by Daniel Klein, María

Pía Carazo, Meinhard Doelle, Jane Bulmer, and Andrew Higham. Oxford: Oxford University Press.
Rivera, Danessa. 2018. "Clean Energy Program at Risk from TRAIN 2". *The Philippine Star*, 5 August 2018. https://www.philstar.com/business/2018/08/05/1839655/clean-energy-program-risk-train-2 (accessed 13 September 2020).
Rogge, Karoline S., Florian Kern, and Michael Howlett. 2017. "Conceptual and Empirical Advances in Analysing Policy Mixes for Energy Transitions". *Energy Research & Social Science* 33 (November): 1–10. https://doi.org/10.1016/j.erss.2017.09.025 (accessed 25 February 2023).
Sovacool, Benjamin K. 2016. "How Long Will It Take? Conceptualising the Temporal Dynamics of Energy Transitions". *Energy Research & Social Science* 13 (March): 202–15. https://doi.org/10.1016/j.erss.2015.12.020 (accessed 25 February 2023).
UNFCCC (United Nations Framework Convention on Climate Change). 2015. "Republic of the Philippines Intended Nationally Determined Contributions". https://www4.unfccc.int/sites/submissions/INDC/Published%20Documents/Philippines/1/Philippines%20-%20Final%20INDC%20submission.pdf (accessed 20 April 2022).
United Nations. 1992. "United Nations Framework Convention on Climate Change". https://unfccc.int/files/essential_background/background_publications_htmlpdf/application/pdf/conveng.pdf (accessed 27 February 2023).
Unruh, Gregory C. 2002. "Escaping Carbon Lock-In". *Energy Policy* 30, no. 4: 317–25. https://doi.org/10.1016/S0301-4215(01)00098-2 (accessed 25 February 2023).
Verzola, Roberto S., Jose D. Logarta Jr., and Pedro H. Maniego Jr. 2017. *Towards a Just Transition in the Philippine Electricity Sector*. Pasig City: Friedrich Ebert Stiftung. https://library.fes.de/pdf-files/bueros/philippinen/14215.pdf (accessed 25 February 2023).
Wamukonya, Nijeri. 2003. "Power Sector Reform in Developing Countries: Mismatched Agendas". In *Electricity Reform: Social and Environmental Challenges*, edited by Nijeri Wamukonya, pp. 7–46. Roskilde: UNEP.
WEC (World Energy Council). *World Energy Trilemma*. London: World Energy Council.
Winkler, Harald. 2017. "Mitigation (Article 4)". In *The Paris Agreement on Climate Change: Analysis and Commentary*, edited by Daniel Klein, María Pía Carazo, Meinhard Doelle, Jane Bulmer, and Andrew Higham. Oxford: Oxford University Press.
World Bank. 2013. *Toward a Sustainable Energy Future for All: Directions for the World Bank Groups Energy Sector*. http://documents.worldbank.org/curated/

en/745601468160524040/pdf/795970SST0SecM00box377380B00PUBLIC0.pdf (accessed 30 September 2018).

———. 2014. *Understanding CO_2 Emissions from the Global Energy Sector.* http://documents.worldbank.org/curated/en/873091468155720710/pdf/851260BRI0Live00Box382147B00PUBLIC0.pdf (accessed 13 September 2020).

World Resources Institute. N.d. "What is an INDC?" https://www.wri.org/indc-definition (accessed 13 September 2020).

WWF International. 2013. *Meeting Renewable Energy Targets: Global Lessons from the Road to Implementation.* Gland: WWF International. https://awsassets.panda.org/downloads/meeting_renewable_energy_targets__low_res_.pdf (accessed 25 February 2023).

7

Hey Big Spender: Filipino Migrants, Consumption and Social Change, 1980–2018[1]

Mina Roces

In his fictionalized autobiographical account of Filipino male undocumented workers in Japan, Rey Ventura (2007, pp. 101–2) shares the story of the eighteenth birthday celebration of Dante's daughter, Laura.

> The party was held at a five-star hotel in Manila. There were around a hundred guests. There were eighteen boys who presented her with eighteen roses. She danced with them plus a few old men. She was like a princess in her pink gown. She looked innocent and virginal. She also starred in a fashion show in which she was the only model: as the evening wore on, she sashayed in several dresses especially made for her. As the youngest of three children and the only one left in school and not married, she was special.
>
> While her escorts took turns dancing with Laura, Dante rang from Japan; his call was hooked up to the public address system. This was the climax of the party—a father-daughter long-distance dialogue.

Everybody froze to attention and listened to a private conversation. Around Laura were gathered her elder sister, her brother and her fat mother:

"Hello! Daddy!"
"Hello, my daughter. Happy Birthday!"
"Thank you, Daddy. I miss you!" "I miss you, too. I love you! I miss you!"
"I love you, Daddy. I miss you." "I love you! I miss you."

Dante's voice was cracking and the members of his family were all teary-eyed. Their relatives and friends, too, were on the verge of tears. The line was taken off the PA system and Laura passed the phone to her elder sister. She wiped her tears.

For this two-hour party, Dante had set aside US$7,000—a year's savings.

This poignant, fictionalized tale of conspicuous consumption underscores the proportion of their savings that Filipino migrants are prepared to spend in order to experience one day of a luxurious upper-class lifestyle. Dante hoped to taste what it felt like, and even for a moment, to be a middle-class family on show and the envy of all his guests. In this story, the irony of Dante being unable to enjoy the party he paid for, or to bask in the high social status of the venue, seems to be lost on all the participants. The climax of the celebration—Dante's international phone call where father and daughter's intimate conversation about their love for each other was broadcasted publicly to the guests—also highlights the connection between a father's material gift of a grand party and his love for his daughter while being physically absent. Dante's story demonstrates a new cultural norm born out of the great Filipino labour migration of the post-1980s, where material gifts were interpreted as signs of love.

The US$7,000 that Dante spent that night would have allowed him to finally return home. A forty-six-year-old grandfather of three who worked as a scaffold builder for twelve years, Dante suffers lingering back pain. He laments that if he only had savings of US$5,000, he would go home. More than a decade later, he has still not fulfilled his dreams for return. Instead, in this story, his daughter—whom he hoped would work in a hospital—follows him to Japan to work in the "pleasure districts" as a bar hostess (Ventura 2007, pp. 103–4).

Dante's decision to have an extravagant celebration for his daughter's debutante ball has tragic consequences for him and his family. While Ventura's account does not discuss the effect of Dante's splurge on his finances, migrant debt has been identified as an important issue in a study conducted by the Filipino Women's Council among Filipinos in Italy (Basa, de Guzman and Marchetti 2012).

This chapter analyses the way migration from the Philippines has altered the social values, attitudes and norms associated with reciprocity in Philippine society since the 1980s. Changing long-held cultural beliefs takes time. A historical perspective enables us to identify the transformations that forty years of labour migration have made to the practices of gift-giving and the meanings associated with this custom in the Philippines. Today it seems to be a normal practice or a "tradition" for migrants all over the world to ship *Balikbayan* boxes (huge cartons full of gifts and food) to the family and the village in the Philippines. But this is an invented tradition that dates from as recently as the 1980s.

Which cultural norms of gift-giving and reciprocity have been dramatically altered? First, the belief that migrants *must* send gifts back in *Balikbayan* boxes to the homeland in regular shipments throughout the year has become entrenched. That this gift-giving is in only one direction—that is, those who benefit are not expected to reciprocate—is a revolutionary change to the Filipino value of reciprocity, normally seen as the cornerstone of Filipino culture (Hollsteiner 1961; Lynch 1973; Kaut 1961). Traditionally recipients are obliged to reciprocate gifts and favours, with interest, in keeping with the values of *utang ng loob* (debt of gratitude), but this is no longer the case. The social perception that migrants are wealthy because their salaries, when converted to pesos, are much higher than local wages encourages a sense of entitlement to some of their earnings by those who remain in the Philippines. Hence, while migrants are now expected to give gifts, the recipients are no longer expected to give anything back. These new rules of etiquette are today seen as "normal", but they actually shake one of the foundations of Filipino cultural values.

Second, migrants' gifts are now seen to be the barometer for the giver's love and affection for the receiver. Because of this semiotic connection, migrants feel enormous pressure to give away their hard-earned money to family, relatives and the village, even when they cannot afford it. Third, the need to demonstrate that the migration was a success motivates migrants to show off their new status as middle class by purchasing real estate or branded goods and becoming patrons of the community by paying for relatives' education and donating to the village church. A fourth issue is that all these demands prevent migrants from saving for their future. This has public policy consequences. Remittances by overseas workers to the Philippines reached US$28 billion, or 10 per cent of the GDP (gross domestic product) in 2017. Fear of losing future remittance revenue is one reason why the Philippine government, Philippine banks and NGOs (non-government organizations) have, since about 2015, offered free financial literacy seminars to try to direct migrants away from spending and towards saving and investing. It is still too soon to evaluate the impact of these seminars, but my first-hand observation is that they propose revolutionary changes in Filipino norms and attitudes. Not only do the seminars advise migrants to think about their retirement, investments and their financial future, they also encourage participants to say no to financial requests from the family, the kin group and the village. The consequence of denying the many pleas for money and gifts is social ostracism. Thus, while the advice itself is financially prudent, there is a question about whether it may increase the anxieties that migrants already experience in their position as breadwinners and patrons of the family and village left behind.

Consumption itself is an important value for migrants. For many, it is the reward for all the hard work they endured overseas (Villanueva 2012; Lamvik 2002, pp. 128–33, 185–90). Those experiences are varied and cannot be homogenized, but one common denominator is that consumption symbolizes the success of the migration "project" and affirms the migrant's new status as middle class. A lifestyle that now includes eating out in trendy restaurants, and buying the latest electronic gadgets and travel tourism has become an intrinsic part of the migrant's new identities as a cosmopolitan subject and local patron.

Sources for this chapter include primary sources produced by migrants including memoirs, autobiographies, migrant magazines and newsletters such as *Filipinas Magazine* (San Francisco, 1992–2010),

Planet Philippines (London issues), *Tinig ng Marino* (the newsletter of the union of Filipino seafarers), author interviews with businesses selling products to migrants (including air-cargo services) and Filipino migrants in the United States, Singapore, Padova, and in Santa Rosa and San Roque, Laguna. I combined these printed and oral sources with ethnographic work in Santa Rosa, Laguna, and Padova, Italy, as well as Lucky Plaza, Singapore. I also attended a financial literacy seminar run by PinoyWISE (a subsidiary of ATIKHA) in Singapore on 16 July 2017 and two debutante parties in Padova, Italy, in 2018 (one of which cost over EUR5,000).

LIVING IN A MATERIAL WORLD: CONSUMPTION AS LOVE

Filipino migrants' remittances are mainly used by recipients for housing (including maintenance); education of their children, family members or relatives; health bills; and the day-to-day grocery bills. Remittances are also used to purchase land or set up businesses.

Migrants make these payments either through cash advances or through sending *Balikbayan* boxes. Budgets were also set aside for phone calls and communication equipment such as mobile phones, iPads, smartphones and computers, including laptops (author interviews with Filipino domestic workers 2015; Verma Villanueva, author interview, 2014; Planet Philippines 2007, p. 36). Children left behind by migrant parents are sent to private schools, so tuition fees become a major expense for families but are also seen as an investment for the children's future employment. Remittances also cover the health care expenses of elderly parents (Zontini 2010). My focus here is on consumer practices rather than on remittances, although the lines between remittances and consumption are often blurred when remittances are sent in the form of goods.

Consumption connects the migrant to the homeland and enables them to fulfil the social expectations of contributing to the family and the village/community. Door-to-door courier businesses make it possible for them to send gifts to the Philippines on a regular basis. These shipments, the invented tradition of the *balikbayan* boxes, have become a regular practice. The origins of the practice could be traced to the custom of buying *pasalubongs* (souvenirs and gifts) that a traveller brought back to family and friends in the Philippines. The original significance was a token to mean that the traveller had thought about them while they were away and to share their overseas experience with them. But the *pasalubong* was meant to be a small, inexpensive, one-off gift. The *balikbayan* box has magnified the *pasalubong* tradition into an expensive, time-consuming exercise, with senders filling up gigantic boxes with gifts and shipping them several times a year. For example, Alsomavic Cargo Ltd.'s super jumbo box from the United Kingdom measures 34 by 27 inches according to the company's website, or nearly a metre square. The goods that fill the boxes range from daily grocery items such as canned goods (e.g., spam and sardines), laundry detergent, beauty products (e.g., shampoo and soap), chocolates and clothing (new, branded or second hand) to secondhand appliances (including air conditioners) and even an entire kitchen (Camposano 2012, p. 16; De Guzman Jr. 2012, p. 170; Jocelyn Averion Ebora, author interview, 2015). Boxes sent vary in size, but larger boxes are the most popular (Noeline Rivera, author interview, 2017). According to courier LBC, Filipina domestic workers in Singapore send boxes all year round but particularly during Christmas, New Year, Chinese New Year (since employers give their helpers cash and secondhand items as part of the "spring cleaning" for the New Year) and the start of the school year in the Philippines (to send school supplies that include notebooks, shoes and socks) (Noeline Rivera, author interview, 2017). Ventura's (2007, p. 68) autobiographical account of the lives of undocumented Filipino workers in Japan describes the dwellings of construction workers as crowded with items destined for their families in the Philippines—from secondhand clothing to knick-knacks picked up at outdoor markets. The undocumented Filipinos in London also cluttered their houses with toys and canned goods—many of them regularly bought from weekend car-boot sales (*karbut*) (McKay 2016, p. 101).

Sending these boxes is an expensive enterprise. In Singapore, it cost S$100 to send a large box of 24 by 24 by 30 inches to Manila (or S$115 to Mindanao) in 2017 (Sharon Tordesillas, author interview, 2017). The steep freight prices also endow the sender with the status of generous benefactor or patron, especially if the gifts are distributed beyond the family to the rest of the community (Camposano 2012, pp. 1–28). Since some of these goods are actually available in the Philippines, the popularity of this custom defies economic logic.

The practice may be not so much about the tightly packed contents but about the meaning of the contents that have been so carefully chosen for each family member. Hence, Filipino journalists labelled it "love in a box", concluding that "Albeit materialistic in nature, it's living proof of our thoughtfulness, a tangible expression of care and concern across the miles" (Rimban and Mercado-Obias, quoted in Camposano 2012, p. 2). Anthropologist Deirdre McKay (2012, p. 103) argues that through the sending of groceries and household items, "Migrants remind their households of their long-distance affections and demonstrate, in a material way, how they continue to participate in these households." Another reason migrants are prepared to send these items is because they want to have some control over the household expenses (Camposano 2012; Alburo 2005).

Migrant memoirs claim that these boxes are symbolic of the love and sacrifices they make for their children. A male nurse in Kuwait described the *Balikbayan* box as "the symbol of an overseas Filipino worker's love for his/her family" [*Iyan daw ang sumisimbolo sa pagmamahal ng isang OFW sa kaniyang pamilya*] (De Guzman 2012, p. 170). Sherald Salamat's story remembers how much he looked forward to the big boxes that accompanied his father's return because he was sure to receive several gifts that included expensive toys, electronic robots, remote control toy cars, new clothes and chocolate (Salamat 2012, p. 189). Another confided: "You have your love in that box for people back home because you purchased something for them [...] It symbolizes [...] love for people back home" (Dahlia 1999, quoted in Alburo 2005, p. 148). Mothers working abroad confess that they deprived themselves of luxuries in order to send expensive items, including chocolates that they themselves have never tasted: *Ako nga 'di kumakain ng Ferrero Roche [sic] dito pero pinapadala ko iyan sa Pilipinas* ["I don't even eat Ferrero Roche [sic] here, but I send them to the Philippines"] (Camposano 2012, p. 18). McKay's (2016, pp. 101–7) informants lived a life of austerity and abstained from health care, haircuts, new clothes and vacations just to be able to afford to send gifts and fulfil their filial as well as community expectations.

The recipients of the imported gifts interpreted these as a sign that they were in the thoughts and memories of their kin, despite the physical separation.

Entrepreneurs responsible for shipping the gifts further endorsed the view that "what is inside the boxes would not be as important as the idea of them: keeping the family close even over great distances" (quoted in Maas 2008, p. 139). Advertisements perpetuate this constructed connection between the material gift and the abstract affection the migrant felt for family and friends. For example, an advertisement for LBC International Freight Company at Lucky Plaza Singapore in August 2017 included handwritten (imaginary) letters from a mother to her child:

> Hello *Anak*,
> *Sana maramdaman mo lalo ang pagmamahal ko habang binubuksan mo ang padala ko. Wala naman ako dyan sa Kaaraawan mo alam mong nandito lang ako parati para sa 'yo. Nanay (surrounded by heart emojis).* [Dear Son/Daughter, I wish that you would feel my love while you open the presents I have sent you. I may not be there for your birthday, but you know that I am always here for you. Mom]

Another one (also in August 2017) stated,

> *Dear Baby Chloe, Your favourite toy is inside na. Mahal na mahal ka ni Mommy. Mommy Olga (with emoji love hearts).* [Dear Baby Chloe, Your favourite toy is inside this box. Mommy loves you very much. Mommy Olga]

If indeed the sending of gifts is a symbolic gesture of one's love, no wonder the custom has become so entrenched. The mother who feels guilty about leaving her child, the seaman father who feels obliged to provide for his community or the dutiful eldest daughter who feels responsible for her younger siblings keep this "tradition" going, despite its negative effect on migrant savings. Add to this mix is the family and community's perception that all migrants are wealthy, and this pressures many to agree to hand out cash gifts and loans that they could not afford. There is a story of a seafarer's astute wife who forbids him from seeing anybody in the village when he returns home for vacations for fear that he would be inundated with requests for loans from the neighbourhood—hoping to protect his hard-earned salary from disappearing rapidly (Tan 2008, p. 36).

This example reveals the extreme measures that may be required to challenge this well-established expectation that migrants must share their earnings with the family and the community left behind. In its current iteration, however, this sharing is supposed to go only one way—from the migrant to those who remained behind.

If sending a *balikbayan* box is a symbol of love, its opposite—not sending one—implies that the migrant has forgotten his obligations. Gunnar Lamvik's interviews with seafarers explained that not giving anything caused a deterioration of friendships: "Sometimes they who did not receive a gift from you have a hard feeling for you" or "If you do not give them, they have a hard feeling, they do not love you anymore" (Lamvik 2002, p. 141). A column written by Frederick Arceo, a Saudi-based overseas Filipino worker (OFW), complained that the consequence of forgetting to give one person a gift was social ostracism since the offended party would sulk and then ruin the migrant's reputation (presumably through spreading gossip that the migrant was "shameless" (*walang hiya*)) (Arceo 2011, p. 7; Tadios 2015). Lamvik also noted that gift-giving enabled seafarers to perform *pakikisama*, or the Filipino social value of "getting along with the group" (Lamvik 2002, p. 141). If the buying and sending of gifts is a symbol of love, this makes the sending of gift boxes compulsory. McKay (2016, p. 101), writing on Filipino undocumented migrants from the Cordillera who work in London, observes,

> Sending goods was such a fundamental obligation for Kankanaey migrants that locating, selecting and acquiring these goods formed a big part of their leisure activity in London ... Making up these boxes diverted value, time and space from their United Kingdom-based activities and relationships, crowding non-Filipino partners and visitors out.

At the same time, *not* sending gifts also sends the tragic message that the migration project has been a failure. Divine Villanueva, an overseas domestic worker in Jordan, titled her life story *Bagahe* ("Baggage"), confessing that her migration narrative was one of "bad luck" because she returned home without gifts for her family (Villanueva 2012, pp. 187–88).

Migrants hope that their thoughtful gift-giving will be cherished. A domestic worker in Hong Kong wrote a poem about door-to-door boxes, ending it with the hope that the recipients would acknowledge the hardship she endured (Aryo 2009, p. 31). Raquel Delfin, who has compiled at least two anthologies of migrants' stories, complains that the "abusive family" is one that takes these presents for granted:

> Some family members do not think that the expensive gadgets they are using are the result of the OFW's frugal lifestyle adopted in order to give the family their desire for luxurious items. The older sister is now popular with her branded clothes, bags and shoes. The elder brother has a car now. The younger sibling has the latest expensive gadgets. The mother has become a gambler and the father now has lots of friends because he goes drinking with them and treats them ... What can she do if she [overseas worker] has already spoken of her hardship but her family takes it for granted? (Padilla 2012, pp. 30–31). [Author's translation from the original Tagalog]

Not all recipients appreciate the acts of self-denial that make the shipments possible.

CONTESTING SPENDING AND DIRECTING SAVING

The story of Dante's debutante party for his daughter that opened this chapter was a grim reminder of how spending could sabotage the overseas worker's dream of returning to the Philippines to retire or build a nest egg for the family. It is echoed in the all-too-familiar story of Eloina Reyes Rebollos, whose earnings over nine years as a domestic worker in Riyadh and Kuwait single-handedly paid for the education of countless nieces and nephews, who owed their careers of engineer, nurse and social worker to this one selfless relative. Her remittances also enabled them to build their own homes. But when she returned to the Philippines, not only was there no one to meet her at the airport, but also she had no money at all and had to be housed temporarily by activists of KAKAMMPI, an NGO dedicated to overseas workers' rights (Sison 2003, p. 55). The mother of a returning entertainer from Japan coined the term "one-day millionaires" in an effort to warn her daughter from spending all her hard-earned money from her six-month stint in Tokyo. Unfortunately, even before the daughter started unpacking after her return, her siblings had begun asking for iPods and new clothes. Relatives begged for money for investment in low-cost housing, to start businesses and demanded to be treated to restaurants, while two of them joked about asking for a loan. Despite her plans to go back to school to give her own daughter a better life, a few months later she was dead broke, with her PHP 250,000 savings all gone (Tan 2008, p. 36). This is not a unique story. Other "one-day millionaires" checked into five-star hotels and spent their money shopping and eating at bars and restaurants (ibid.).

The conspicuous consumption indulged in by overseas Filipino workers has been criticized by some observers who are concerned that the inability to save money is a barrier to ending the cycle of migration, especially for those who want to reunite with their families left behind (Battistella and Asis 2013, p. 117). Their anxiety was connected to the fear that such profligate spending did not foster development in the home country and encouraged a culture of dependence (Añonuevo 2002, p. 131). The positive impact of remittance spending (improving the quality of life of many families, including investment in the education of children) has been acknowledged (Battistella and Asis 2013, p. 117). However, studies reveal that many migrants are unable to save enough money to return home permanently. The lavish spending on birthdays, graduations and fiestas—as well as the money given to relatives for health care and emergencies—constantly drains disposable income, preventing them from saving and driving them into debt (Añonuevo 2002, pp. 130–31; Basa, de Guzman and Marchett 2012, p. 12). Non-government organization ATIKHA's interviews with Filipino migrant women in Rome made the startling discovery that even after many years working overseas and despite their relatively high salaries, 80 per cent of them were unable to save and invest their hard-earned money for their future return to the homeland—or for their eventual retirement (Melgar and Dizon-Añonuevo 2002, p. 173). In a study conducted by Arcinas (1991, pp. 137–38) with Filipino migrants in the Gulf states, few invested in productive assets (7 per cent on machinery and 18 per cent on vehicles for transportation), with only 10 per cent of respondents making business investments, 40 per cent of which were in small-scale retail (*sari sari*) stores. Habits of conspicuous consumption were partly to blame for this inability to accumulate sufficient savings, especially among those who had children left behind because migrant mothers pampered their loved ones with expensive gifts, and were afraid to deny them anything they asked for to assuage the guilt feelings engendered by their prolonged physical absence (Mai Añonuevo, author interview,

2014; Añonuevo 2002, p. 131). In addition, in places such as Hong Kong, for example, it is relatively easy for Filipino women to acquire loans (Tadios 2015). Half of those interviewed by Joy Tadios (ibid., p. 249) in her pioneering study on migrants and loans had borrowed money to buy technological gadgets, such as a laptop or smartphone, for themselves or their children—items identified by others as luxury products rather than essential goods.

Since the mid-2000s, the government (through the Overseas Welfare and Workers Administration [OWWA] and the Commission of Filipinos Overseas, for example), banks and migrant-focused NGOs embraced the task of encouraging migrants to save and invest their money in projects perceived to be more "development oriented" (Battistella and Asis 2013, p. 117). These actors produced the mantra: "We must force overseas Filipinos and their families to learn financial education" (Ang et al. 2014), an attitude which scholar Kathleen Weekley argued was yet another one of "disciplining" migrant workers "for the greater good" (defined in the literature as an investment for development) (Weekley 2006, p. 205). Banks and NGOs launched initiatives to direct migrants away from spending towards investing and saving. For example, they taught short courses on financial literacy to help families budget their disposable income and invest their savings. The Bangko Sentral ng Pilipinas (Central Bank of the Philippines) started the Financial Literacy Campaign (FLC) in 2005 in collaboration with OWWA (Gonzaga 2007, pp. 24–29). It extended its partnerships to include government agencies, NGOs and private entities running half-day activities (ibid., p. 25). The FLC aimed to

> [C]ultivate financial education among OFs [overseas Filipinos] and their families by informing them of alternative opportunities for the use of remittances, such as savings, investments in financial instruments and other microbusiness ventures. The thrust towards promoting financial literacy is to promote a culture of savings and investments among OFs and their beneficiaries. (ibid., p. 25)

These initiatives were radical moves that challenged Filipino families to resist the urge to express social status through conspicuous consumption and to reverse the view that material goods—including gifts posted to the family—were the only way to measure family love or migrant success.

One NGO that embraced this challenge was ATIKHA Overseas Workers and Communities Initiative Inc. ATIKHA's target group was the Filipino overseas contract workers who left their immediate family in the Philippines and viewed migration as only a temporary labour strategy. In 1995, a study by a Women's Resource Centre found that many migrant women returned without savings, coming home to a situation no different from when they first migrated. Mai Dizon-Añonuevo, together with other migrant returnees from Hong Kong and the Middle East and some religious leaders from Laguna, founded ATIKHA Inc. as an NGO aimed at addressing the issues of migrant returns by conducting seminars and skills training for alternative livelihoods (Melgar and Dizon-Añonuevo 2002, pp. 170–71). Eventually, ATIKHA focused on the social problems faced by children and families of overseas migrants in the CALABARZON area (an acronym referring to the provinces of Calamba, Laguna, Batangas, Rizal and Quezon provinces in Luzon) with offices in San Pablo City, Laguna and Mabini, Batangas. In 1998, they formed Balikabayani, an organization of OFWs focusing on the socio-economic component of reintegration with a focus on financial planning and investment (ibid., p. 173). They developed financial education modules aimed at teaching migrants how to save and invest their money. In 2012, they launched the PinoyWISE (Worldwide Initiative for Investment Savings and Entrepreneurship) International movement. This initiative was a financial education and investment mobilization programme whose objectives are "to provide financial education and encourage the overseas Filipinos and their families in sending province and receiving country to save and invest to enable successful integration" and

> to link overseas Filipinos (OFs) and families to business opportunities, business advisor services and concrete savings and investment programs of selected cooperatives, microfinance institutions, social enterprises, banks and other financial institutions in their provinces of origin (PinoyWISE International n.d.-b).

ATIKHA and Balikabayani conducted financial literacy seminars and provided financial counselling to families. Members in Hong Kong were offered concrete packages ranging from time deposits or trust funds to real estate investments (Melgar and Dizon-Añonuevo 2002, pp. 174–75). PinoyWISE ran forums to promote agribusiness and investment opportunities in goat raising, organic farming, rice and corn production, hog raising, cassava production and processing and linked the migrants to farm business schools, agriculture training institutes and private corporations or cooperatives involved in the business (PinoyWISE International n.d.-a). ATIKHA and Balikabayani also formed Koop Balikabayani International to focus on "consumers cooperatives for migrants' families in the Philippines, savings and credit cooperatives for the migrants abroad, housing cooperatives, and business development services for its members" (Melgar and Dizon-Añonuevo 2002, p. 182). These NGOs ran education modules in places where there were huge concentrations of Filipino overseas workers such as Italy, Hong Kong, Singapore and Dubai.

I attended one PinoyWISE Family and Income Management Training Module held in 2017 at St. Bernadette's Parish Church, Singapore. There were around fourteen to sixteen Filipina participants, as well as a larger number of PinoyWISE trainers (composed of both men and women). The lectures delivered in Tagalog informed participants about the need to have health insurance. They recommended investing their savings at a rate higher than inflation (4 per cent) and suggested that all of them keep an emergency fund of six times more than their monthly expenses. The second half of the programme focused on "borrowing and getting out of debt".

In the seminar I attended, an entire module was devoted to "how to say 'no'" to repeated financial requests from relatives for financial support or material gifts because "no one was abroad forever" (*walang forever sa abroad*). Lectures at that seminar alerted participants to rethink the way two emotions—guilt and pride—manipulated them into spending more money. Instead, participants were encouraged to involve their families in making a budget. This way, any requests that were not in the budget should be declined. Some strategies for saying no to requests from relatives for money for birthday celebrations and treats (including eating out at restaurants) included letting them know that they could not afford to exceed their predetermined budget.

ATIKHA's Mai Añonuevo was also aware that the intimate connection between conspicuous consumption and "love" had to be dismantled because it drained savings and sabotaged the migrant's future plans to return home (Añonuevo, author interview, 2014). To address this, ATIKHA ran "family interventions seminars" in the Philippines to replace the meaning of "consumption = love" with an alternative one that stressed that "love = family reunification". Instead of according symbolic capital to the material goods they received from the parent working overseas, children left behind were told that they needed to work together towards the migrant's eventual return, suggesting that "love" meant bringing the family together after years of separation (Añonuevo, author interview, 2014). ATIKHA included a "values formation component" where families were told to change the meanings and importance assigned to material goods and to shift their priority towards the future of the family instead of the usual "instant gratification" (Añonuevo, author interview and field notes, 2014; author's notes, PinoyWISE seminar, 2017).

This advocacy was revolutionary for several reasons. Firstly, it was going to be extremely difficult to say "no" because, in traditional culture, this results in a loss of face for the person making the request and may result in social ostracism for the refuser. Secondly, such advocacy went against the migrants' need to spend to express their rise in status as middle class (what ATIKHA referred to as "pride").

My interviews with those who have completed these seminars in 2015 and 2017 revealed that some of them had become successful and assertive investors, buying apartments in the Philippines and homes in Europe. "Jesme", a single domestic worker in Singapore, admitted that before she joined PinoyWISE, she paid for the debut celebration of her niece in the Philippines, funded the roast pig and cake/sweets for various birthday celebrations in the village and never thought of rejecting requests for gifts. These gifts were in addition to the weekly cash remittances she sent to her parents and the hospital bills of her siblings. Jesme acceded to all the requests because she felt she had a salary coming in every month and so she should share this with her family. She did not think about saving for her future retirement or an emergency. "Lisa", another domestic worker, also confided that she sent money for the funeral expenses of many people in her village. Both women claimed that after they completed the PinoyWISE modules, they no longer sent money for luxuries and focused on saving and investing for their future retirement. The Filipinos I interviewed in Padova who completed the ATIKHA seminars run in Milan used the skills they learned to invest in properties in the Philippines and in Italy. These examples may illustrate the success of the ATIKHA interventions, but they may also show that there are a good number of judicious consumers who have now become successful investors.

CONCLUSION

Consumption has proven to be a double-edged sword for Filipino migrants since the 1970s. On the one hand, it proclaimed their new status as members of the growing middle classes in the Philippines and gave them enormous satisfaction as benefactors if they helped their family build or remodel a house and fill it with white goods and furniture or if they sent siblings and relatives to school and university. Sending goods and presents to the Philippines regularly also maintained their emotional connections to the family and the village and gave them some control over the daily grocery budget. On the other hand, the family's relentless demands for goods and money undermined the migrant's own capacity to save for their retirement and often landed them in serious debt.

To curb the tendency towards conspicuous consumption, the Bangko Sentral ng Pilipinas and NGOs like ATIKHA have tried to alter the semiotics of spending by dismantling the imagined link between consumption and "love". Migrants were also advised to discipline spending practices by adhering strictly to a family budget and to resist the urge to splurge. These are challenging tasks. They also go against the fashioning of the migrant's identities as middle class and against the social values of *pakikisama* that pressured migrants to share their new wealth with everybody.

What do these new changes and new pressures faced by migrants mean for social cohesion in the homeland? Because 10 million Filipinos, or 10 per cent of the population, are working overseas, changes brought about by the migration context are likely to have an impact on society and cultural attitudes and practices there. This chapter shows that consumption is critical to social relationships in the family, kinship group and the community—since all three are beneficiaries of migrant spending and patronage. But the migration context also introduces new meanings to consumption, some of which are detrimental to a migrant's financial situation. If gift-giving is increasingly interpreted as a material expression of a migrant's affection for those left behind, migrants are pressured to buy presents in order to fulfil their duties as good parents, filial children and good citizens, even if they cannot afford it. Those left behind may be oblivious to the migrants' real financial situation, or the hardship migrants endured while making a living overseas. Perhaps this ignorance of the work migrants do may partially explain why family members absolve themselves from appreciating or reciprocating, even in a small way, the gifts and material goods that they have been given, often at great sacrifice. Banks and NGOs advise migrants through financial education seminars to say "no" to repeated requests for things that would sabotage their ability to save for their retirement. Yet the consequences for denying these requests are social ostracism, an outcome that causes profound emotional pain for many migrants.

Note

1. Material from *The Filipino Migration Experience: Global Agents of Change*, by Mina Roces (Ithaca, NY: Cornell University Press, 2021). Used with permission of the publisher.

References

Alburo, Jade. 2005. "Boxed In or Out? Balikbayan Boxes as Metaphors for Filipino American (Dis)Location". *Ethnologies* 27, no. 2: 137–57.

Ang, Alvin, Jeremiah Opiniano, Andrew C. Lacsina, Reynolph G. Ladon, and Charlotte G. Lizardo. 2014. "Remittance Investment Climate Analysis in Rural Hometowns (RICARCT): Results and Policy Implications". Powerpoint presentation sent to author by Rodrigo Garcia, Commission of Filipinos Overseas.

Añonuevo, Augustus T. 2002. "Reintegration, An Elusive Dream?" In *Women, Migration & Reintegration*, edited by Estella Dizon-Añonuevo and Augustus T. Añonuevo, pp. 127–36. Manila: Balikabayani Foundation and Atikha Overseas Workers and Communities Initiatives.

Arceo, Frederick. 2011. "Iba Pa Rin Sa. Pinas". *Planet Philippines*, January 2011.

Arcinas, Fe R. 1991. "Asian Migration to the Gulf Region: The Philippines Case". In *Migration to the Arab World: Experience of Returning Migrants*, edited by Godfrey Gunatilleke, pp. 103–49. Tokyo: United Nations University Press.

Aryo, Analyn D. 2009. "Door-to-Door Boxes". In *Nanny Tales: Voices from the Diary of an Overseas Filipina Worker*, pp. 31–32. Benguet: Research Mate Inc.

Basa, Charito, Violeta de Guzman, and Sabina Marchetti. 2012. "International Migration and Over-Indebtedness: The Case of Filipino Workers in Italy". Human Settlements Working Paper No. 36, October 2012. London: International Institute for Environment and Development.

Battistella, Graziano, and Maruja M.B. Asis. 2013. *Country Migration Report: The Philippines 2013*. Makati City and Quezon City: International Organization for Migration and Scalabrini Migration Center.

Camposano, Clement C. 2012. "Enacting Embeddedness through the Transnational Traffic in Goods: The Case of Ilonggo OFWs in Hong Kong". *Review of Women's Studies* 21, no. 2: 1–28.

De Guzman, Robert Jr. 2012. "Balikbayan Box". In *Sindi ng Lampara (OFW Stories)*, edited by Raquel Delfin Padilla and Jovelyn Bayubay Revilla, pp. 165–71. Philippines: Allibratore Enterprises.

Gonzaga, Ruth C. 2007. "The BSP Financial Literacy Campaign (FLC): Providing Overseas Filipinos and Their Beneficiaries Practical Tools for Financial Freedom". *Bangko Sentral Review* (January): 24–29. https://www.bsp.gov.ph/Media_And_Research/BS%20Review/BSR2007_02.pdf (accessed 25 March 2023).

Hollsteiner, Mary R. 1961. "Reciprocity in the Lowland Philippines". *Philippine Studies* 9, no. 3 (July): 387–413.

Kaut, Charles. 1961. "Utang na Loob: A System of Contractual Obligation among Tagalogs". *Southwestern Journal of Anthropology* 17, no. 3 (Autumn): 256–72.

Lamvik, Gunnar. 2002. "The Filipino Seafarer: A Life between Sacrifice and Shopping". PhD dissertation, Norwegian University of Science and Technology.

Lynch, Frank. 1973. "Social Acceptance Reconsidered". In *Four Readings in Philippine Values (IPC Papers No. 2)*, edited by Frank Lynch and Alfonso de Guzman II, pp. 1–68. Quezon City: Ateneo de Manila University Press.

Maas, Marisha. 2008. "Door-to-Door Cargo Agents: Cultivating and Expanding Filipino Transnational Space". In *Tales of Development: People, Power and Space*, edited by Paulus Gerardus Maria Hebinck, Sef Slootweg, and Lothar Smith, pp. 135–46. Assen: Royal Van Gorum B.V.

McKay, Deirdre. 2012. *Global Filipinos: Migrants' Lives in the Virtual Village*. Bloomington: Indiana University Press.

———. 2016. *An Archipelago of Care: Filipino Migrants and Global Networks*. Bloomington: Indiana University Press.

Melgar, Gina Alunan, and Mai Dizon-Añonuevo. 2002. "Mag-Atikha Para Maka-Balikbayani: Planting the Seeds of a Comprehensive Reintegration Program for OFWs". In *Women, Migration & Reintegration*, edited by Estella Dizon-

Añonuevo and Augustus T. Añonuevo, pp. 169–83. Manila: Balikabayani Foundation and Atikha Overseas Workers and Communities Initiatives.

Padilla, Raquel Delfin. 2012. "Si OFW at ang Mapang-Abusong Pamilya". In *Sindi ng Lampara (OFW Stories)*, edited by Raquel Delfin Padilla and Jovelyn Bayubay Revilla, pp. 30–31. Philippines: Allibratore Enterprises.

PinoyWISE International. n.d.-a. "Investment and Business Opportunities—PinoyWISE Market Place Events". https://www.pinoywiseinternational.org/what-we-do/investment-and-business-opportunities-pinoy-wise-market-place-events/ (accessed 19 March 2023).

──────. n.d.-b. "Who We Are: PinoyWISE Movement". http://www.pinoywiseinternational.org/who-we-are (accessed 29 August 2016).

Planet Philippines. 2007. "Not Enough Money to Save". November 2007, p. 36.

Salamat, Sherald. 2012. "Isang Malaking Kahon ang Pasalubong ni Papa". In *Sindi ng Lampara (OFW Stories)*, by Raquel Delfin Padilla and Jovelyn Bayubay Revilla, pp. 189–92. Philippines: Allibratore Enterprises.

Sison, Marites N. 2003. "Diaspora Dreams". *Filipinas*, May 2003, p. 55.

Tadios, Arenas Felma Joy. 2015. "Managing Transnational Families: Emotional Labour and Entrepreneurial Agency Among Filipino Migrant Domestics in Hong Kong". PhD dissertation, City University of Hong Kong.

Tan, Michael. 2008. "One Day Millionaires". *Planet Philippines*, January 2008, p. 36.

Ventura, Rey. 2007. *Into the Country of Standing Men*. Quezon City: Ateneo de Manila University Press.

Villanueva, Divine. 2012. "Bagahe". In *Sindi ng Lampara (OFW Stories)*, by Raquel Delfin Padilla and Jovelyn Bayubay Revilla, pp. 187–88. Philippines: Allibratore Enterprises.

Weekley, Kathleen. 2006. "From Wage Labourers to Investors? Filipina Migrant Domestic Workers and Popular Capitalism". In *Transnational Migration and Work in Asia*, edited by Kevin Hewison and Ken Young, pp. 193–212. London: Routledge.

Zontini, Elisabetta. 2010. *Transnational Families, Migration and Gender: Moroccan and Filipino Women in Bologna and Barcelona*. New York: Berghahn Books.

PART II

Waging Lawfare in the Philippines

8

Impeachment under Duterte: Liberal Tool or Illiberal Weapon?

Cristina Regina Bonoan and Björn Dressel

Liberal democratic institutions in the Philippines have been under attack. Under the Duterte administration (2016–22), Asia's oldest democracy saw abrupt reversals into authoritarian practices not experienced since the regime of Ferdinand Marcos Sr. (1965–86). These included extra-judicial killings as part of an ever-expanding war on drugs, the removal of the Supreme Court Chief Justice and legal threats against other high-ranking officials.

The use of impeachment procedures to threaten public officials is particularly noteworthy. When politicized, such threats can amount to a broad attack on liberal democracy, undermining the careful use of institutional checks and balances.

The use of impeachment as a political weapon is certainly not new, nor is it limited to the Philippines (Neumann 2007; Kim 2014; Hinojosa and Pérez- Liñán 2006). What is unprecedented, even by

Philippine standards, was its prevalent use as a threat to remove officials critical of the administration. Within one year, former President Rodrigo Duterte and his allies within and outside Congress moved to impeach four high-ranking officials: former Vice-President Maria Leonor Robredo, former Commission on Elections (COMELEC) Chair Andres Bautista, former Supreme Court Chief Justice Maria Lourdes Sereno and former Ombudsman Conchita Carpio Morales. The eventual ouster of Sereno was widely seen as a serious setback for the rule of law (International Commission of Jurists 2018), while the concerted use of impeachment against other high-ranking officials and critical oversight institutions raised further concerns about a general illiberal turn in the Philippines (Bonoan and Dressel 2018; Thompson 2016).

The use of impeachment to undermine liberal institutions is somewhat paradoxical. Impeachment is the procedure by which selected high-ranking public officials can be removed from office if they are guilty of "culpable violation of the Constitution, treason, bribery, or other high crimes and misdemeanors, or betrayal of public trust" (Const., (1987), art. XI, § 2 (Phil.)).

Impeachment was originally established to ensure accountability—to check the powers of the monarchy or a strong executive—and only later applied to other high-ranking officials (Bernas 2011; Ellis 2005). Although inherently political (Broderick 1974), impeachment is entrusted to the legislature as an exceptional means to mitigate abuse of power. Impeachment requires high legal and procedural standards to counter destabilizing side effects (Kim 2014). It is, therefore, somewhat surprising to see how easily this extraordinary measure has been resorted to in the Philippines under Duterte.

What has enabled the growing use of impeachment against public officials in the Philippines? And what are its implications for the state of liberal democracy in the country? These questions became ever more urgent as the Duterte administration used not only impeachment but also other legal proceedings against critics, such as laying criminal charges against former Senator Leila De Lima and the revocation of amnesty for former Senator Antonio Trillanes.

Despite the growing literature on Duterte's personality and presidency (Miller 2018; Heydarian 2018) and academic reflections on his rise, continuing appeal and the political dynamics of his administration (Curato 2017), few have so far drawn explicit attention to how Duterte has wielded law and legal procedures as a weapon (Gatmaytan 2018; Tiojanco 2018). Even fewer have explicitly scrutinized these legal developments in light of continuing efforts to reshape the Philippine political landscape, with the use of impeachment as part of a broader illiberal agenda, including repetitive attempts at constitutional change.

The basic argument we advance here is that impeachment in the Philippines is facilitated by the power of the presidency, which an authoritarian leader may use for his or her own illiberal purposes. Despite being an exclusively legislative power anchored in both chambers of the Philippine Congress, Philippine presidents have a significant—perhaps even undue—influence over the impeachment process for two reasons: the country's long tradition of a strong presidency and its weak, patronage-infested political parties (Dressel 2011; Hutchcroft 2008; Landé 1965). Creating the conditions for a hyper-presidential political system (Rose-Ackerman, Desierto and Volosin 2011), the president regularly controls majorities in Congress due to party switching (Mendoza, Cruz and Yap 2014). In this situation, impeachment proceedings can be used to attack political opponents rather than serving to promote accountability. Thus used by an illiberal populist leader, impeachment then becomes a device for undermining liberal democratic institutions.

To illustrate this argument, first, we review the requirements and process of impeachment as laid down by the 1987 Constitution. Second, we discuss past impeachment efforts under the same Constitution and contrast those with the Duterte administration's efforts. Third, we examine how the legal standards for impeachment were lowered under the Duterte administration to illustrate that its use is qualitatively different in nature and, more importantly, in intent. Through the case of Sereno, which culminated in her ouster, we illustrate how the judicial process circumvented the constitutional requirements for impeachment. Our chapter concludes that impeachment procedures can be easily abused in a hyper-presidential political system like the Philippines with weak political party institutionalization. In particular, when wielded by a populist president with little regard for constitutional checks and balances, abuse of impeachment poses severe risks for liberal constitutional practice.

THE 1987 CONSTITUTION: ESTABLISHING A LIBERAL DEMOCRATIC ARCHITECTURE

Coming out of a dictatorship, the 1987 Constitution of the Republic of the Philippines ("the Constitution") is a post-Martial Law document that was designed to provide stronger checks and balances. It provides for a tripartite system that limits presidential powers and, in particular, sought to strengthen judicial independence through a unique and ideally depoliticized appointment process (art. VIII, § 8), fiscal autonomy (art. VIII, § 3), and express powers of judicial review (art. VIII, § 1). The Constitution also provided for independent Constitutional Commissions (art. IX) and created the Office of the Ombudsman (art. XI, § 5).

As a further accountability mechanism, the Constitution provides for impeachment as a means to remove high-ranking officials. The Constitution provides that the president, the vice president, members of the Supreme Court, members of Constitutional Commissions and the Ombudsman may be removed by impeachment while all other public officers may be removed as otherwise provided by law (art. XI, § 2). Legal experts and constitutional law scholars, including drafters of the 1987 charter, have interpreted this provision to mean that impeachment is the sole means of removing impeachable officers (Bernas 2009; Patag 2018).

As we noted above, the Constitution also limits the grounds for impeachment to culpable violation of the Constitution, treason, bribery, graft and corruption, other high crimes and betrayal of public trust (art. XI, § 2).

Apart from the substantial legal requirements, the Constitution also provides for a high procedural bar to carry out an impeachment. Under art. XI, § 3, an impeachment complaint may be filed by a member of the House of Representatives or any citizen with an endorsement of a member of the House of Representatives. The Constitution prohibits the initiation of impeachment proceedings against the same official more than once within a period of one year. The complaint will be referred for hearings with the House Committee on Justice unless the complaint is filed by at least one-third of the members of the House of Representatives, which means that it shall constitute the Articles of Impeachment. Otherwise, the complaint will go through hearings by the Justice Committee and its resolution would need to be approved by at least one-third of the members of the House of Representatives before the Articles of Impeachment are transmitted to the Senate. The Senate shall convene as an impeachment court. In such a case, the House of Representatives will elect its prosecutors for the Senate impeachment trial, where a vote of at least two-thirds of senators is needed to convict.

The 1987 Constitution made it relatively easier to impeach with lower voting thresholds for both chambers of Congress, compared to previous constitutions through which no one had ever been successfully impeached (Panganiban 2017; Quezon 2017). While the Constitution provides for legal and procedural requirements, it does not obscure the fact that impeachment is inherently political, as illustrated by its purpose and the fact that the task of initiating, prosecuting and trying an impeachment is given to the legislature—or politicians—and not to the courts (Bernas 2011).

IMPEACHMENTS IN THE PHILIPPINES UNDER THE 1987 CONSTITUTION

The use of impeachment is nothing new in the post-1986 Philippines. Before the Duterte presidency, several impeachment complaints were filed against different officials in every administration between 1987 and 2016. In that period, three officials were successfully impeached by the House of Representatives (Panganiban 2017). The lower chamber voted to impeach former President Joseph Estrada in 2000, but his Senate trial was cut short; later he was deemed to have resigned after a popular revolt. In 2011, the House of Representatives voted to impeach former Ombudsman Merceditas Gutierrez and Chief Justice Renato Corona. Gutierrez resigned before the Senate impeachment court was convened. Meanwhile, Corona was successfully convicted for betrayal of public trust. To date, this is the only impeachment that has resulted in a finding of guilt by the Senate (ibid.).

In addition, various unsuccessful impeachment complaints were filed between 1987 and 2016 against six other high-ranking officials, some with multiple complaints being filed against them, such as former President Gloria Macapagal-Arroyo (Reuters 2008). However, as we see in Table 8.1, all complaints were either dismissed or not acted upon by the House of Representatives.

While less stringent than under previous constitutions, the history of limited successful impeachments from 1987 to 2016 illuminates the extraordinary nature of impeachment. Its primary function is to prevent power holders from abusing the constitutional order. Still, because it seeks to overturn electoral and appointive procedures by which the highest officials achieve power, the criteria for successful prosecution are also deliberately set high (Quezon 2017). And while the 1987 Constitution may have made it easier to impeach officials, the requirement of adherence to some legal and procedural standards has at least prevented, or short-circuited, many past impeachment efforts. However, as we see in Table 8.2, from 2017 to 2018, or within only one year under Duterte, there were increased efforts to impeach four high-ranking officials deemed critical of the Duterte administration.

In 2017, former Vice President Robredo, allied with the opposition, faced impeachment threats. The charges, filed by Duterte allies outside Congress, alleged that Robredo committed betrayal of public trust and culpable violation of the Constitution based primarily on her video message to the United Nations criticizing the administration's war on drugs, particularly the extra-judicial killings. However, the impeachment complaints were not acted upon for failure to garner any endorsement from members of the House of Representatives (Cepeda 2017).

Former COMELEC Chair Bautista was successfully impeached by the House of Representatives in 2017. The Duterte-allied Volunteers Against Crime and Corruption (VACC) accused Bautista of failing to declare certain properties in his statements of assets and to prevent the 2016 hacking of the COMELEC website. The House Committee on Justice dismissed the complaint, finding it insufficient in form. Despite Bautista announcing his resignation, the House plenary nevertheless voted to overturn the dismissal and impeached Bautista. However, the Articles of Impeachment were not transmitted by the House of Representatives to the Senate for trial (Cupin 2017b).

There were also impeachment threats against former Ombudsman Morales after her office announced it was investigating the Duterte family's alleged multi-billion-peso wealth. President Duterte accused Morales of selective justice and the use of falsified documents. The VACC submitted a complaint against Morales in December 2017 but

TABLE 8.1
Impeachments in the Philippines, 1987–2016[5]

NAME	POSITION	YEAR	
SUCCESSFUL IMPEACHMENTS			
1. Joseph Estrada	President	2000	Lower House voted to impeach but trial in the Senate aborted. Deemed resigned
2. Merceditas Gutierrez	Ombudsman	2011	Lower House voted to impeach but she resigned before Senate trial.
3. Renato Corona	Chief Justice	2012	Lower House voted to impeach and he was removed and disqualified after a Senate trial.
FAILED IMPEACHMENT COMPLAINTS			
1. Corazon Aquino	President	1988	Complaint dismissed for lack of substance.
2. Gloria Macapagal-Arroyo	President	2005, 2007 and 2008	Not acted upon
3. Benigno Aquino III	President	2014	Complaints rejected by the Congressional Justice Committee for lack of substance.
4. Hilario Davide	Chief Justice	June 2003 and October 2003	House Committee on Justice dismissed the June 2003 complaint in October. A second complaint was filed the next day. The second complaint ruled unconstitutional.
5. Benjamin Abalos	COMELEC Chair	2001	Resigned three days after the impeachment complaint was endorsed by three Members of the House.
6. Luzviminda Tangcangco	COMELEC Commissioner	2002	Dismissed for lack of substance
7. Aniano Desierto	Ombudsman	2001	Complaint rejected by the Congressional Justice Committee for lack of substance.

TABLE 8.2
Impeachments in the Philippines, 2017–18

NAME	POSITION	YEAR	
1. Maria Leonor Robredo	Vice President	2017	Complaint has not been endorsed by any Member of Congress.
2. Andres Bautista	COMELEC Chair	2017	Lower House voted to impeach him but he resigned before a Senate trial.
3. Conchita Carpio Morales	Ombudsman	2017	Complaint has not been endorsed by any Member of Congress. Finished her term
4. Maria Lourdes Sereno	Chief Justice	2017–18	Case was pending with the House Justice Committee. Removed when the *quo warranto* case filed against her was granted by the Supreme Court.

failed to garner an endorsement from any lawmaker (Buan 2017) until Morales's term as Ombudsman ended in July 2018.

These cases illustrate an apparent increase in the use of impeachment complaints against critics of the current administration. Moreover, we saw an increasingly politicized process with a deliberate lowering of legal standards. Nowhere is this more apparent than in the fourth impeachment complaint and subsequent *quo warranto* case against former Chief Justice Sereno.

LOWERING LEGAL STANDARDS? IMPEACHING A CHIEF JUSTICE, THEN AND NOW

Before her ouster, former President Duterte publicly threatened Sereno with impeachment, claiming that the Chief Justice was part of a plot to oust him and urged Congress to fast-track her impeachment (Lorena 2018; Ranada 2018). In August 2017, the House Committee on Justice accepted a complaint filed by a Duterte-allied lawyer alleging that Sereno committed culpable violation of the Constitution, corruption and other high crimes (Cupin 2017a).

Sereno was accused of failing to disclose income earned before her appointment, delaying and manipulating actions on petitions before the Supreme Court, purchasing a luxury vehicle for her official use and overspending for official trips, among other acts. Charges included betrayal of public trust by criticizing Duterte's imposition of martial law across a third of the country, practising favouritism with judicial personnel, making public statements in reply to the president's accusations of judges being involved in the drug trade and, in an effort to separate the co-equal branches of government, preventing justices of the Court of Appeals from making courtesy calls to the president.

In October 2017, the House Committee on Justice declared that the complaint alleged sufficient grounds for impeachment despite an answer filed by Sereno's lawyers asserting that the charges were baseless and did not constitute impeachable offences. Sereno's lawyers were barred from attending the months-long congressional hearings (Cupin 2017c), and the House Committee on Justice recommended Sereno's impeachment for a House plenary vote.

Comparing the impeachment case against Sereno and the impeachment complaints against two former chief justices—Chief Justice Hilario Davide and Chief Justice Renato Corona—it is apparent that there are significant legal and procedural differences. While Chief Justice Davide was not removed from office, both Corona and Sereno were removed from office, albeit through different legal remedies. The most glaring difference is how the Chief Justices were eventually removed and the Supreme Court's corresponding role in each case (Gatmaytan 2017).

In the case of Davide, two impeachment complaints were filed against him in 2003. The first impeachment complaint was filed by former President Joseph Estrada against Davide and seven other justices in June 2003 for their alleged role in helping oust Estrada from the presidency in 2001. Estrada's complaint was dismissed by the House Committee on Justice in October of that year. The day after the dismissal of the first impeachment complaint, a second complaint was filed by Congressman Felix William Fuentebella, charging Davide with alleged anomalies in the disbursement and expenditures of the Judiciary Development Fund, despite a finding by the Commission on Audit that the disbursements were aboveboard. Notwithstanding criticisms against the impeachment complaint from the Integrated Bar of the Philippines, the Philippine Bar Association, associations of law deans and professors, and various law student councils, the second complaint garnered the required one-third vote from the House of Representatives (Sy 2003).

Nevertheless, the Articles of Impeachment were never transmitted to the Senate for trial after a case was filed with the Supreme Court (Felongco 2003). In the case of *Francisco v. House of Representatives*,[1] the Supreme Court ruled that the second impeachment complaint was unconstitutional for having been initiated against the same official within the one-year period prohibited by the Constitution. While the 1987 Constitution does not grant the Supreme Court any powers of judicial review over an impeachment—which is political in nature—the court ruled that it had the power to review whether an impeachment conforms to the requirements and procedures provided under the Constitution.

Many see parallels between the case of Sereno and the impeachment of her predecessor, Chief Justice Corona. Both Sereno and Corona were accused of failing to make truthful declarations in their respective statements of assets and liabilities. Corona, however, was charged with—and later admitted to—failing to declare assets worth millions of dollars in unexplained wealth during his incumbency. On the other hand, Sereno was charged with failure to declare income that she earned prior to her appointment to the court.

In a controversial appointment, then President Gloria Macapagal-Arroyo appointed Corona as Chief Justice days after Benigno Aquino III won the 2010 presidential election and within the "midnight appointment ban" under the 1987 Constitution (Mercado and Rood 2012). President Aquino broke tradition by refusing to take his oath of office before Corona and expressed support for Corona's removal, claiming it was part of his administration's bid to eradicate corruption (Hookway 2012). Corona was impeached by the House of Representatives, with the complaint going directly to the Senate after it was signed by 188 members or more than the required one-third of the members of the House of Representatives. At the months-long televised trial by the Senate, Corona testified and admitted to failing to declare millions of dollars in bank deposits. During Corona's trial, the Supreme Court ruled in his favour in several related cases (Gatmaytan 2017). In the first case on the production of Court records and documents, the Supreme Court refused to provide documents and records requested by the House of Representatives impeachment prosecution panel with a subsequent subpoena issued by the Senate Impeachment Court.[2] The Supreme Court cited the principle of separation of powers and ruled that the documents and testimonies requested were confidential and covered by privileged communications. In the *Philippine Savings Bank v. Senate Impeachment Court*,[3] the Supreme Court—voting eight to five—again decided in favour of Corona when it ruled against the subpoena issued by the Senate against the bank to produce documents related to Corona's foreign currency deposits (Gatmaytan 2012).

Years after Corona's conviction, allegations surfaced about the disbursement of special allotments to legislators supposedly used as incentives to vote to impeach Corona. An audit report showed that at least forty-six former lawmakers received a total of PHP 229.6 million from the Disbursement Acceleration Program (DAP) days after the House of Representatives impeached Corona (Cayabyab 2014), even as the administration denied that the special allotments were granted in exchange for favourable votes.

In the case of Sereno, the House Committee on Justice conducted several hearings on the Sereno impeachment complaint. In these proceedings, four fellow justices and several employees of the Supreme Court attended and testified against her. Sereno's impeachment was aborted when she was removed through the decision of fellow members of the Supreme Court granting a *quo warranto* petition—a type of legal action to challenge a person's right or authority over an office.

Sereno is the first impeachable officer to be removed by the Supreme Court rather than through conviction by the Senate in an impeachment trial. Voting eight to six, the court ruled that Sereno's appointment was invalid from the start for her failure to comply with the requirement of submitting statements of assets back when she was a law professor at the University of the Philippines.[4] Seen as a substitute for a weak impeachment case and recognition that the Duterte administration allies lacked the two-thirds vote required in the Senate to convict Sereno, the *quo warranto* was criticized as a circumvention of the more stringent constitutional requirements on impeachment (La Viña 2018; Gavilan 2018).

The court's decision was heavily criticized by the members of the legal community—including the Integrated Bar of the Philippines (Buan 2018), several law deans, professors from top law schools and constitutional law experts, and drafters of the 1987 Constitution—on several grounds (La Viña 2018). First, the decision is seen as circumventing the constitutional provision that impeachable officers may be removed only by impeachment and subsequent conviction, thereby usurping Congress's exclusive constitutional power to remove them. Second, the petition was filed beyond the one-year prescriptive period provided under the Rules of Court for the remedy of *quo warranto*. Finally, objections were raised against the failure of the Supreme Court's six justices to inhibit in the decision despite having testified against Sereno in the congressional hearings on the impeachment case.

The majority decision ruled that impeachment and *quo warranto* are distinct remedies comprising different grounds, procedures and jurisdictional requirements. Therefore, a *quo warranto* case may proceed independently from an impeachment complaint. The court ruled that Sereno's failure to consistently submit her statements of assets as required by law shows her lack of integrity, a requirement for the Office of the Chief Justice under the 1987 Constitution. Thus, she was deemed unqualified to be appointed for the position. Moreover, the court brushed aside questions on the partiality of the six justices who testified against Sereno in Congress, considering that their participation in the hearings was a show of deference to the House of Representatives and its constitutional duty to investigate impeachment complaints.

In June 2018, the Supreme Court denied Sereno's motion for reconsideration and affirmed its earlier ruling in the *quo warranto* case invalidating her appointment as chief justice (Torres-Tupas 2018).

WEAPONIZING IMPEACHMENTS

On 23 August 2018, four House of Representatives opposition members filed impeachment complaints against the seven Supreme Court justices who voted to grant the *quo warranto* petition ousting Sereno, notwithstanding the fact that the opposition clearly did not have the numbers to support the impeachment in the Duterte-dominated House of Representatives. The justices were accused of culpable violation of the Constitution and betrayal of public trust. The impeachment complaint alleged that the justices violated the 1987 Constitution in granting the *quo warranto* even though impeachment was the recognized mode to remove impeachable officials, thus usurping the exclusive power of Congress (Cepeda 2018). The lawmakers further allege that the justices used *quo warranto* as a legal tool to wage their vendetta against Sereno. The House Committee on Justice dismissed the complaints for lack of evidence (Santos 2018).

Although not begun by this administration, it is clear that the indiscriminate filing and targeting of critics through impeachment opened the floodgates for what ought to be an extraordinary measure. With the ever-increasing frequency of its use, legal standards have been lowered, disregarded, and even circumvented, particularly in the case of Sereno's *quo warranto*. These illustrate not just the lowering of the legal bar but also the increasing politicization of the process. Impeachment and *quo warranto* have become the new weapons in escalated political warfare.

Neither has the Supreme Court been spared from politicization. It is clear that despite not having a defined constitutional role concerning the impeachment process, the Supreme Court has played a pivotal role in past impeachment cases and their outcomes (Gatmaytan 2018). This has also further politicized the court and, in some cases, may have contributed to lowering legal standards. With all sides emboldened to resort to these extraordinary legal remedies, threats of impeachment and *quo warranto* pose risks to the security of tenure of justices and the possible independence of the Supreme Court.

Even with the checks and balances under a tripartite system, the Philippine president wields powers that may undermine other government institutions. While impeachment was designed as a check on the executive and other officials, its current use and abuse indicate a subversion of the process. It has proven particularly problematic in the context of hyper-presidentialism in the Philippines. Paradoxically, these excessive presidential powers also allowed Duterte to subvert the impeachment process to undermine horizontal accountability.

Excessive presidential powers rely on weak party politics, where party switching ("turncoatism") before and especially after elections is common (Teehankee 2015). For example, in the 2016 national elections, out of the 238 district representative seats for the House of Representatives, only three congressional seats were won by the PDP-Laban, the party of Duterte. However, within a month of the elections, elected representatives bolted their parties to join PDP-Laban. The administration enjoyed a "supermajority" in the House of Representatives, effectively obliterating any real opposition (Cabacungan 2016).

In the Senate, a similar shift in alliances after elections ensured that the Duterte administration also controlled a clear majority needed for votes, such as a conviction in an impeachment case.

After the 2019 midterm elections, Duterte further consolidated his influence over the legislature. No opposition senator was elected that year and Duterte's allies secured well over 85 per cent of the seats in both houses (Dressel and Susilo 2023).

Considering that the 1987 Constitution grants both chambers of Congress exclusive powers over impeachment, turncoatism allowed Duterte significant influence over all impeachments through his allies in Congress, thereby ensuring that the president and his allies are safe from impeachment while using the threat of impeachment against his critics.

CONCLUSION

The increasing frequency in the use of impeachment has emboldened the resort to this extraordinary remedy and lowered legal standards. While impeachment was designed as a check on the executive and other officials, its current use and abuse indicate a subversion of the process to silence critics and tamper with horizontal accountability mechanisms that could check hyper-presidentialism in Philippine politics. Paradoxically, it is also these excessive presidential powers that allowed Duterte to subvert the impeachment process to undermine horizontal accountability.

Operating as they do at the juncture of law and politics, the impeachment and *quo warranto* cases expose the vulnerabilities of Philippine democracy. Under a hyper-presidential system such as the Philippines, the excessive powers of the executive allow any president to wield significant influence over the impeachment process. Under

Duterte, resort to threats of impeachment and other remedies such as *quo warranto* played a part in the efforts to reorder the post-1986 liberal architecture in the Philippines. Seen in their entirety, the cases reveal a calculated and strategic effort to use impeachment and other legal remedies as political weapons to silence dissent by high officials and demolish institutional veto gates.

Despite the long-established democratic structures and accountability mechanisms that the country adopted from the United States, the Duterte period showed that Philippine democratic institutions are vulnerable to attack from within. With his influence over both chambers of Congress, Duterte used impeachment to attack political opponents and critical voices within the government. While this may not be new in the Philippine context, the explicit intent of these legal manoeuvrings should give us pause for concern. Similar to the authoritarian rule under Marcos—who was a trained lawyer like Duterte—it appears that a distinctly illiberal agenda was pursued that was directed at dismantling the post-1987 liberal constitutional order under the veil of legal processes and rhetoric.

Understanding the politics of impeachment in the Philippines can tell us much about the state of Asia's oldest democracy. As impeachment is used increasingly as a weapon to quash dissent and undermine liberal democratic institutions, such developments expose continuing weakness in Philippine democratic practice. It seems that the country that once led the wave of democratization in the region has been at the forefront of regional illiberal reversal. While similar impeachment proceedings in Korea that removed a corrupt president in the public interest suggest that the process is not necessarily unfolding uniformly (Shin and Moon 2017), it is clear that how citizens resist temptations by populist leaders in the region to tinker with the legal order will be critical to how democratic practice in the region will evolve in the years to come. In that respect, the Philippines, once more, has much to teach.

Notes

1. Francisco v. House of Representatives, G.R. No. 160261 (10 November 2003) (Phil.), https://elibrary.judiciary.gov.ph/thebookshelf/showdocs/1/47018 (accessed 28 December 2022).

2. *In re* Production of Court Records and Documents and the Attendance of Court officials and employees as witnesses under the subpoenas of 10 February 2012 and the various letters for the Impeachment Prosecution Panel dated 19 and 25 January 2012 (14 February 2012) (Phil.), https://www.officialgazette.gov.ph/downloads/2012/02feb/20120214-Notice-of-Resolution.pdf (accessed 15 January 2021).
3 Philippine Savings Bank v. Senate Impeachment Court, G.R. No. 200238 (9 February 2012) (Phil.), https://elibrary.judiciary.gov.ph/thebookshelf/showdocs/1/55379 (accessed 28 December 2022).
4 Republic of the Philippines v. Sereno, G.R. No. 237428 (11 May 2018) (Phil.), https://elibrary.judiciary.gov.ph/thebookshelf/showdocs/1/64003 (accessed 28 December 2022).
5 "Impeachment: A Political and Historical Guide", Official Gazette, https://www.officialgazette.gov.ph/interactive-a-primer-on-impeachment/ (accessed 11 December 2022).

References

Bernas, Joaquin G. 2009. *The 1987 Constitution of the Republic of the Philippines: A Commentary*. Quezon City: REX Book Store.

———. 2011. "Eyes on the Impeachment Process". *Philippine Daily Inquirer*, 21 March 2011. https://opinion.inquirer.net/4087/eyes-on-the-impeachment-process (accessed 15 January 2021).

Bonoan, Cristina Regina, and Björn Dressel. 2018. "Dismantling a Liberal Constitution, One Institution at a Time". *New Mandala*, 24 May 2018. https://www.newmandala.org/dismantling-liberal-constitution-one-institution-time (accessed 15 January 2021).

Broderick, Albert. 1974. "The Politics of Impeachment". *American Bar Association Journal* 60, no. 5: 554–62.

Buan, Lian. 2017. "VACC Submits Morales Impeach Complaint, but without an Endorsement". *Rappler*, 13 December 2017. https://www.rappler.com/nation/191214-morales-impeachment-vacc-endorsement (accessed 17 December 2022).

———. 2018. "IBP to Appeal Sereno Ouster; Lawyers Called to Rise Up". *Rappler*, 11 May 2018. https://www.rappler.com/nation/202289-ibp-appeal-sereno-ouster (accessed 17 December 2022).

Cabacungan, Gil. 2016. "From 3 to 300, PDP-Laban Forms 'Supermajority' in House". *Philippine Daily Inquirer*, 26 May 2016. https://newsinfo.inquirer.net/787547/from-3-to-300-pdp-laban-forms-supermajority-in-house (accessed 15 January 2021).

Cayabyab, Marc Jayson. 2014. "46 Former, Incumbent Solons Got DAP after Corona Impeachment". *INQUIRER.net*, 18 August 2014. https://newsinfo.inquirer.net/630398/46-former-incumbent-solons-got-dap-after-corona-impeachment (accessed 25 June 2021).

Cepeda, Mara. 2017. "Still No Endorsers for Robredo Impeachment Complaint". *Rappler*, 3 May 2017. https://www.rappler.com/nation/168726-impeach-leni-movement-still-no-endorsers-robredo-impeachment-complaint (accessed 17 December 2022).

―――. 2018. "After Sereno Ouster, 7 SC Justices Slapped With Impeachment". *Rappler*, 23 August 2018. https://www.rappler.com/nation/210193-impeachment-complaints-supreme-court-justices (accessed 17 December 2022).

Cupin, Bea. 2017a. "25 Lawmakers Endorse Impeachment Complaint vs. Sereno". *Rappler*, 30 August 2017. https://www.rappler.com/nation/180651-lawmakers-endorse-impeachment-complaint-chief-justice-sereno (accessed 17 December 2022).

―――. 2017b. "House Impeaches Comelec Chairman Andres Bautista". *Rappler*, 11 October 2017. https://www.rappler.com/nation/184940-house-representatives-impeaches-comelec-chairman-andres-bautista (accessed 17 December 2022).

―――. 2017c. "House Panel: 'Sufficient Grounds' in Sereno Impeachment Complaint". *Rappler*, 5 October 2017. https://www.rappler.com/nation/184357-sereno-impeachment-sufficient-grounds (accessed 17 December 2022).

Curato, Nicole, ed. 2017. *A Duterte Reader: Critical Essays on Rodrigo Duterte's Early Presidency*. Quezon City: Ateneo de Manila University Press.

Dressel, Björn. 2011. "The Philippines: How Much Real Democracy?" *International Political Science Review* 32, no. 5: 529–45.

Dressel, Björn, and Fakhridho Susilo. 2023. "Presidential Democracies". In *Routledge Handbook of Asian Parliaments*, edited by Rehan Abeyratne and Po Jen Yap, pp. 82–100. London: Routledge.

Ellis, Richard E. 2005. "Impeachment". In *The Oxford Companion to the Supreme Court of the United States*, edited by Kermit L. Hall, pp. 488–89. Oxford: Oxford University Press.

Felongco, Gilbert. 2003. "House Vote Puts an End to Davide Impeachment". *Gulf News*, 12 November 2003. https://gulfnews.com/uae/house-vote-puts-an-end-to-davide-impeachment-1.369933 (accessed 15 January 2021).

Gatmaytan, Dante. 2012. "Impeachment as a Popular Check on Official Misconduct". *IBP JOURNAL* 37, nos. 3 and 4 (July–December 2012): 146–58.

―――. 2017. *More Equal Than Others: Constitutional Law and Politics*. Quezon City: University of the Philippines, College of Law.

———. 2018. "Philippines: The State of Liberal Democracy". *The I·CONnect-Clough Center 2017 Global Review of Constitutional Law*, I-CONnect-Clough Center: 220–24. https://dx.doi.org/10.2139/ssrn.3215613 (accessed 11 December 2022).

Gavilan, Jodesz. 2018. "CHR: Granting of Quo Warranto Petition vs Sereno 'Erodes Rule of Law'". *Rappler*, 15 May 2018. https://www.rappler.com/nation/202591-chr-quo-warranto-supreme-court-sereno-rule-of-law-democracy (accessed 17 December 2022).

Heydarian, Richard J. 2018. *The Rise of Duterte: A Populist Revolt against Elite Democracy*. London: Palgrave.

Hinojosa, Victor J., and Aníbal S. Pérez-Liñán. 2006. "Presidential Survival and the Impeachment Process: The United States and Colombia". *Political Science Quarterly* 121, no. 4: 653–75.

Hookway, James. 2012. "Philippines Senate Ousts Supreme Court Chief". *The Wall Street Journal*, 1 June 2012. https://www.wsj.com/articles/SB10001424052702303395604577433900439033094 (accessed 25 June 2021).

Hutchcroft, Paul D. 2008. "The Arroyo Imbroglio in the Philippines". *Journal of Democracy* 19, no. 1: 141–55.

International Commission of Jurists (website). 2018. "Philippines: Supreme Court Decision Removing Its Chief Justice Contributes to Deterioration of the Rule of Law". 30 May 2018. https://www.icj.org/philippines-supreme-court-decision-removing-its-chief-justice-contributes-to-deterioration-of-the-rule-of-law/ (accessed 15 January 2021).

Kim, Young Hun. 2014. "Impeachment and Presidential Politics in New Democracies". *Democratization* 21, no. 3: 519–53.

La Viña, Tony. 2018. "It's Not Over for Sereno, the Rule of Law". *Manila Standard*, 12 May 2018. https://issuu.com/thestandardph/docs/mspdf20180512/ (accessed 17 December 2022).

Landé, Carl. 1965. *Leaders, Factions and Parties: The Structure of Philippine Politics*. New Haven: Southeast Asia Studies, Yale University.

Lorena, Nicole. 2018. "TIMELINE: The Many Times Duterte and Sereno Clashed". *Rappler*, 20 May 2018. https://www.rappler.com/newsbreak/iq/202763-timeline-maria-lourdes-sereno-rodrigo-duterte-clashes (accessed 17 December 2022).

Mendoza, Ronald U., Jan Frederick Cruz, and David Barua Yap II. 2014. "Political Party Switching: It's More Fun in the Philippines". *Asian Institute of Management (AIM) Working Paper* No. 14-019. https://dx.doi.org/10.2139/ssrn.2492913 (accessed 15 January 2021).

Mercado, Carolyn, and Steven Rood. 2012. "Philippine Judiciary: The Dawning of a New Era?" *VERA Files*, 8 June 2012. https://verafiles.org/articles/philippine-judiciary-the-dawning-of-a-new-era (accessed 17 December 2022).

Miller, Jonathan. 2018. *Duterte Harry: Fire and Fury in the Philippines*. Melbourne: Scribe Publications.

Neumann, Richard Jr. 2007. "The Revival of Impeachment as a Partisan Political Weapon". *Hastings Constitutional Law Quarterly* 34, no. 2: 161–327. https://scholarlycommons.law.hofstra.edu/faculty_scholarship/679/ (accessed 23 December 2022).

Official Gazette. n.d. "The 1987 Constitution of the Republic of the Philippines". http://www.officialgazette.gov.ph/constitutions/1987-constitution/ (accessed 11 December 2022).

Panganiban, Artemio V. 2017. "Impeachment Yesterday, Today and Tomorrow". *Philippine Daily Inquirer*, 3 September 2017. https://opinion.inquirer.net/106829/impeachment-yesterday-today-tomorrow (accessed 15 January 2021).

Patag, Kristine Joy. 2018. "Law Deans, Professors Join Call for Quo Warranto Dismissal". *Philstar.com*, 10 May 2018. https://www.philstar.com/headlines/2018/05/10/1813940/law-deans-professors-join-call-quo-warranto-dismissal/ (accessed 15 January 2021).

Quezon, Manuel L. III. 2017. "What Impeachment Is and Isn't". *The Explainer ANC*, 20 March 2017. https://www.quezon.ph/2017/03/20/the-explainer-what-impeachment-is-and-isnt/ (accessed 5 February 2022).

Ranada, Pia. 2018. "Duterte Tells Congress to Fast-Track Sereno Impeachment". *Rappler*, 9 April 2018. https://www.rappler.com/nation/199862-duterte-congress-fast-track-chief-justice-sereno-impeachment/ (accessed 15 January 2021).

Reuters. 2008. "Impeachment Case Filed Against Philippines' Arroyo". *Reuters*, 13 October 2008. https://www.reuters.com/article/idINIndia-35930720081013/ (accessed 15 January 2021).

Rose-Ackerman, Susan, Diane A. Desierto, and Natalia Volosin. 2011. "Hyper-Presidentialism: Separation of Powers without Checks and Balances in Argentina and the Philippines". *Berkeley Journal of International Law* 29, no. 1: 246–333. https://lawcat.berkeley.edu/record/1124427.

Santos, Eimor P. 2018. "House Panel Junks Impeachment Rap vs. De Castro, 6 Justices". *CNN Philippines*, 11 September 2018. https://www.cnnphilippines.com/news/2018/09/11/Impeachment-complaint-Chief-Justice-de-Castro-Supreme-Court.html (accessed 15 January 2021).

Shin, Gi-Wook, and Rennie Moon. 2017. "South Korea After Impeachment". *Journal of Democracy* 28, no. 4: 117–31.

Sy, Marvin. 2003. "Davide Hits 'Evil Plotters'". *The Philippine Star*, 27 October 2003. https://www.philstar.com/headlines/2003/10/27/225622/davide-hits-145evil-plotters146 (accessed 9 January 2023).

Teehankee, Julio. 2015. "Institutionalizing Political Party Reforms in the Philippines". In *Building Inclusive Democracies in ASEAN*, edited by Ronald U. Mendoza, Edsel L. Beja Jr., Julio C. Teehankee, Antonio G.M. La Viña and Maria Fe V. Villamejor-Mendoza, pp. 308–18. Mandaluyong City: Anvil Publishing.

Thompson, Mark R. 2016. "The Early Duterte Presidency in the Philippines". *Journal of Current Southeast Asian Affairs* 35, no. 3: 3–14. https://doi.org/10.1177/186810341603500301 (accessed 15 January 2021).

Tiojanco, Bryan Dennis Gabito. 2018. "The Worst Kind of Charter Change". *New Mandala*, 24 August 2018. https://www.newmandala.org/worst-kind-charter-change (accessed 15 January 2021).

Torres-Tupas, Tetch. 2018. "SC Rejects Sereno Ouster Appeal". *INQUIRER.net*, 19 June 2018. https://newsinfo.inquirer.net/1002048/sc-rejects-sereno-ouster-appeal/ (accessed 15 January 2021).

9

Tipping the Balance? Politics, Personalities and Institutions in the Philippine Supreme Court

Imelda Deinla and Maria Lulu Reyes

INTRODUCTION

The 2018 removal from office of Maria Lourdes Sereno, the first woman chief justice of the Philippine Supreme Court, provokes us to rethink our assumptions about the power of the judiciary within the democratic system of government. The judiciary is often regarded as the weakest branch of government, having no power of coercion and being dependent on the executive or the legislative branches of government for enforcement or compliance. The democratization movement that swept many parts of the world in the 1980s brought a new salience for courts in policing constitutional overreach and abuse of power that had been the hallmark of authoritarian regimes (Ginsburg 2003). Constitutional developments that granted courts review powers and autonomy have created opportunities for the judiciaries to test the efficacy of their authority and reshape their relations with political actors. Courts' performances in consolidating democracy and forging the rule of law in democratizing countries have been uneven; their authority has also been constantly challenged or under threat.

The seeming rise of illiberal democracies in contemporary times has put the judiciary under greater stress. How courts relate to political actors and respond to political pressures or demands has become even more critical for countries where liberal democracy is constantly challenged. In the Philippines, the 2016 ascendance to power of Rodrigo Duterte ushered in a march towards illiberal democracy. The judiciary and judicial actors have become focal points for political contestation. In a country that had previously overthrown an authoritarian regime (that of Ferdinand Marcos in 1986), the Supreme Court was known to have resisted attempts at illiberal revival, despite the highs and lows of its democratic consolidation process (Deinla and Dressel 2019). The court and the judiciary have been regarded as "beacons of democracy" since the promulgation of the democratic 1987 Philippine Constitution.

When members of the Philippine Supreme Court removed their own chief justice in May 2018 through a *quo warranto* procedure that aligned with presidential intentions, did this mean that the court has become acquiescent to the power of the executive? In practical terms, why would a court that has gained so much power become so readily compliant with presidential wishes? Is the loss of judicial independence simply a function of executive pressure or dominance?

We argue in this chapter that judicial power—and independence—is conditioned by the internal dynamics of the courts as much as by external factors. The manner by which the judiciary has used its power has helped shape the success or failure of constitutional democracy in many democratizing countries (Ginsburg 2003; Dressel 2010; Moustafa 2007). Three factors have been identified as necessary in allowing courts to fulfil their functions in conducting their constitutional mandate and exercising independent judgment: political support (Rosenberg 1992; Finkel 2008; Domingo 2000), public support (Nardi 2018; Deinla 2014) and institutional support (Helmke and Rosenbluth 2009; Clark 2010). These three conditions are interlinked, but as argued in this chapter, leadership and institutional cohesion are necessary for building the support network required for the Supreme Court to resist political pressures and assist in forging judicial independence. Moreover, the ability of a chief justice to provide capable and strategic judicial leadership is critical in navigating complex and difficult conditions in building strong judicial institutions and gaining broad support (Widner 2001). This leadership is crucial in situations where the court has been historically weak, such as when a court had been marginalized or undermined by autocratic regimes in the past (Hendrianto 2016).

THE PHILIPPINE SUPREME COURT: FROM "KANGAROO COURT" TO THE RISE OF THE "GODS OF PADRE FAURA"[1]

The Philippine Supreme Court has undergone institutional evolution after the 1986 People Power EDSA Revolution that has made it a "powerful" court capable of leveraging its influence with the other branches of government. During the authoritarian regime of former president Ferdinand Marcos, the court was widely perceived to be a "kangaroo court", a pejorative term for a rubber-stamp court that sustains government actions and those of its agents and allies (Moustafa 2014; Bello 1984). The court was "empowered" after it was restored as a coequal branch and an essential component of the institution of checks and balances of a democratic government. An independent and empowered court was a key consideration in drafting the 1987 Constitution, a product of broad public consultation to pave the way for reinstalling liberal democracy.

The democratic 1987 Constitution provided broad powers by the court, such as the power to determine constitutional boundaries, review and strike down government acts and legislation, and exercise exclusive jurisdiction over special legal remedies (art. V). Like other judiciaries in democratizing countries, these powers have empowered the court vis-à-vis other branches of government, the executive and the legislative, through its ability to bridge or balance competing political interests or provide judicial solutions to political conflicts (Roux 2013). In doing so, the judiciary has itself become an object of political disputes.

That the Philippine Supreme Court has been "empowered" is seen in the way trust in the court has been re-established after the institution of liberal democracy. Relative to other key government institutions such as the Senate, the House of Representatives and the Executive, the Supreme Court made progressive strides towards becoming one of the most trusted institutions over twenty years, 1990–2011 (see Figure 9.1). It overtook the Senate as the most trusted between 1993 and 2003, a period we can call the court's judicial renaissance. The highest points recorded in this period by the Supreme Court were between 1993 and 1998, coinciding with liberal reformism under President Fidel Ramos (1992–98), and in 2001, coinciding with the impeachment on the grounds of massive corruption and ouster (through the second People Power Revolution in 2001) of President Joseph Estrada (1998–2001).

FIGURE 9.1.
Public Satisfaction with the Supreme Court (1990–2018)

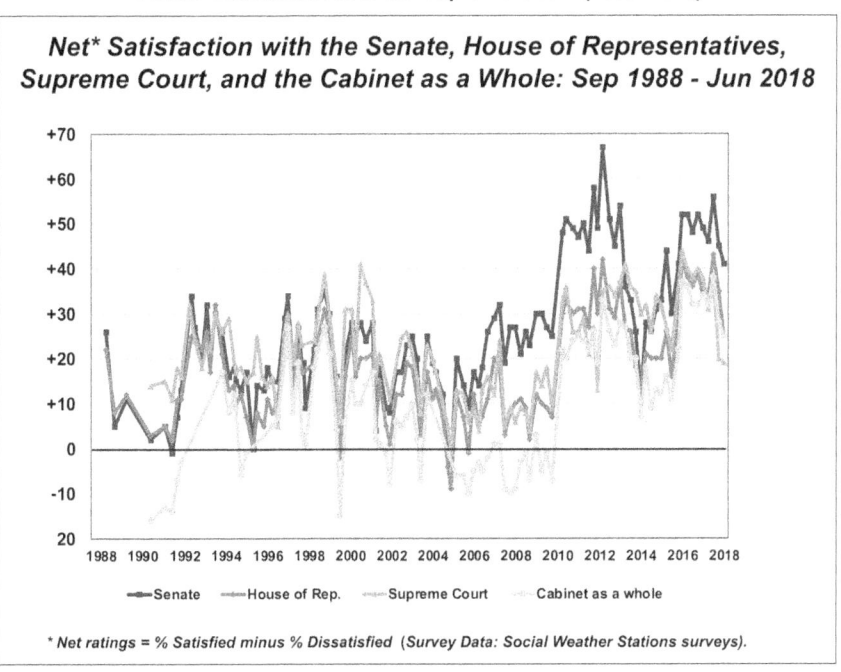

Source: Social Weather Stations Public Satisfaction Surveys.

Periods of judicial crisis can be observed during impeachments: one, during the impeachment of Chief Justice Renato Corona in 2012 during President Benigno Aquino III's term in office (2010–16) and two, during Chief Justice Sereno's impeachment in 2017 under President Rodrigo Duterte's government (2016–22). Public satisfaction with the court recorded the lowest satisfaction in Corona's removal. However, the dip in court satisfaction during Sereno's ouster lasted longer than Corona's, which could be attributed to the more prolonged proceeding to remove Sereno through the *quo warranto* proceeding that ended on 11 May 2018. It must be noted that the impeachment proceeding against Chief Justice Hilario Davide in 2003 did not affect the court's satisfaction standing relative to other state institutions. This could be a subject for deeper exploration of how the public perceived the legitimacy or illegitimacy of these impeachment proceedings.

Individually, the court members have also become powerful actors in their own right and are highly sought-after for their alliances and loyalties. The Supreme Court, vested with the power to determine with finality what the law is and how it applies to particular situations, has become the "gods of Padre Faura" (Abogado 2017). They are so-called "gods" because the cases become the ultimate law, and justices are beyond reproach for their decisions. Politicians increasingly see the court as a critical ally—or enemy—of government policies or political interests. Hence, court appointments have become more strategic, calculated and very contentious since the reinstatement of liberal democracy after the People Power Revolution (Vitug 2018). In the last fifteen years, we have seen that the Office of the Chief Justice has become the object of political machinations. Sereno's removal from office is the third episode since an ouster initiative was unsuccessfully launched in 2003 against Chief Justice Davide during the presidency of Gloria Macapagal-Arroyo (2001–10). In 2012, the first successful impeachment was of Chief Justice Renato Corona during the Aquino administration.

An examination of Sereno's ouster through the unconventional means of *quo warranto* is important as this incident points to the weakness of all the three support pillars—political, institutional and public—during the critical times of the justice's removal. The confluence of these conditions allowed the use of this unprecedented measure without consequent detrimental political and legal backlash. Sereno's removal is exceptional compared to the other two previous impeachment proceedings. The use of a *quo warranto* proceeding against a high state official has no legal precedent in Philippine jurisprudence. Voting 8–6 (for and against the removal), the "gods" have turned against their own (Abogado 2018).

Why the justices themselves exercised that power of removal—although most Philippine legal scholars believed that it could only be done through impeachment—could best be explained by the institutional dynamics and personalities within the court. As we explain below, the justices' action in removing a colleague is not a unique phenomenon; this has happened in other jurisdictions where political and institutional support is weak for the courts and judges. The Sereno removal saga also raises questions about the salience of a "standard" institutional design that had been thought to safeguard or enhance judicial independence, such as the provisions of lifetime (or long) tenure, financial independence and constitutional standards on removing justices from office.

LACK OF POLITICAL AND INSTITUTIONAL SUPPORT

Political support, particularly from key political actors and the elites, is critical in resisting the impeachment of a chief justice. Support of political actors for an independent bench has been explained in terms of "insurance"; the court would rule fairly towards the incumbent when they are out of office (Ginsburg 2003). Sectors of the elites and the general public can also be supportive of the judiciary as a feature of liberal democracy or as part of the political settlement embodied in a democratic constitution after social upheaval, as happened in the Philippines. Support, however, could mean that the public is merely satisfied with the work of the judiciary, as in the public satisfaction survey (see Figure 9.1). In the Philippines, it has been observed that higher public satisfaction with the court is linked to periods where there is democratic stability that, in turn, allows for the proper functioning of democratic institutions and empowers the court to perform an "activist" role (Deinla 2017).

The Sereno removal saga underscores the emergence of a powerful and highly popular presidency that could command obedience or acquiescence from other political actors within and outside the state system. Currently, the Philippines has a capricious executive bent on going after members of the opposition and critical media by filing criminal cases against them, such as former senators Leila de Lima and Antonio Trillanes IV and Maria Ressa of the online news site *Rappler*. The saga also demonstrates that institutional division in the court—seen in the lack of collegiality, perception of lack of "leadership" by the chief justice, personal conflicts and administrative issues besetting the office—facilitated the convergence of interests between the executive, the lower house of Congress and justices who opposed Sereno's continued tenure. Hence, former presidential spokesperson Harry Roque had to quip,

> In other words, she doesn't need to be bullied by the president; she has done a magnificent job at alienating her own colleagues. Even her own colleagues are saying that she doesn't deserve to be in that position. The president has been spared from doing that by her own colleagues (PCOO–NIB 2018).

Sereno's appointment as chief justice by former president Aquino on 24 August 2012 went against the "norm" of appointing senior justices to the top post in the judiciary. It was a surprising appointment that was considered a break from tradition. Sereno was the first woman chief justice and the youngest chief justice in the court's more than a hundred-year history. When she rose to the highest court in 2010 as associate justice, seemingly plucked from obscurity, she was only the thirteenth woman compared to 169 men who had sat on that bench before her. While trailblazing for Filipino women, Aquino's selection of Sereno as chief justice was unwelcome within a judiciary steeped in the unwritten tradition of seniority: that the incumbent justice serving longest in the court gets the plum prize of the chief justice post. She bypassed eleven of the more senior associate justices of the Supreme Court. Sereno would have served as chief justice for eighteen years until she retired at age seventy. None of her older colleagues would have had a hope of ever getting a taste of the position. Moreover, her alleged insular leadership style and inexperience in the workings of the judiciary did not help maintain the collegiality that is an intrinsic part of the court's institutional design. In fact, restoring the collegiality of the court is what the succeeding chief justice, Teresita de Castro, expressed as her legacy to the judiciary (Buan 2018b).

The Supreme Court was a deeply divided court during Sereno's tenure. The cracks within the court were an open secret and blamed on the high magistrate's management style, lack of political savvy in bridging divides and failure to create trust. This was evident from allegations of lack of consultation in decision-making and personal rifts with some judges. Her colleagues asked her to take a leave of absence while the removal proceedings were pending, while five judges went so far as to testify against her during 2017 impeachment proceedings in the lower house of Congress. Fissures and cleavages, even among lower court judges and personnel, were apparent in the line-up of those who supported her ouster or resignation and those who advocated for maintaining judicial independence (Buan 2017). Lawyer Antonio La Viña, a political analyst and friend of Sereno, remarked, "The chief must honestly look at her way of managing, whether she has to change her tone and practices. They need to go into the process of rebuilding trust" (ibid.).

The timing for initiating Sereno's ouster could not have been more opportune. When President Duterte picked a very public and rancorous fight with the Philippine chief justice over the latter's objections to the war on drugs in 2016, many were only too willing to assist him, including her colleagues in the judiciary. However, weak articles of impeachment, even with the approval of the House of Representatives, where Duterte had a supermajority, would not have passed the upper chamber of the legislature, the Senate, which has the power to conduct a trial and vote on Sereno's impeachment. The filing of the *quo warranto* in the Supreme Court itself sidestepped this nearly insurmountable barrier.

IMPEACHMENT: FROM A MECHANISM OF ACCOUNTABILITY TO A POLITICAL WEAPON

The impeachment process has been in place since the 1935 Constitution, but only in recent memory under the 1987 Constitution did Philippine democracy see it used. Whether the increasing propensity of its use over past and present administrations is a testament to the thriving democracy in the country or an undeniable indicator of the abuse of the process itself is a question that has haunted Philippine constitutional jurisprudence.

The first impeachment proceeding was in pursuit of accountability over a massive corruption scandal involving a sitting president of the republic, Joseph Ejercito Estrada, in 2000. Before Estrada's impeachment, only three impeachment complaints were filed in the Philippine Congress, none of which passed beyond the committee level (Diaz 2000). The first impeachment proceeding under the 1987 Constitution generated the widest publicity. With the emergence of news about receiving money from *jueteng* sources (a local form of illegal lottery), the president was peppered with allegations of corruption and bribery. In an allusion to the "Watergate" scandal, President Estrada's name and reputation became saddled with his very own *"Juetengate* Scandal" (Tatad 2017a).

Not long after this, an impeachment complaint was filed and initiated in the House of Representatives on 12 October 2000. The complaint against Estrada was grounded on bribery, graft and corrupt practices, betrayal of public trust and culpable violation of the Constitution (Chan Robles Virtual Law Library n.d.). The House of Representatives, dominated by Estrada allies, was cold to the move. But after the complaint garnered the signatures of the minimum one-third of all the members of the House, then-Speaker (and later presidential aspirant) Manuel Villar bypassed the House Committee on Justice process and immediately sent the Articles of Impeachment to the Senate for commencement of trial.

For several months, Estrada's impeachment trial was covered live on television, closely watched and widely followed by a public upset by corruption scandals at the highest echelons of government. It abruptly halted after discussing whether to open key evidence for the prosecution allegedly obtained from questionable sources, the so-called "envelope" containing details of Estrada's other secret bank accounts. When most of the Senators, sitting as impeachment judges and identified with Estrada, voted to deny opening the said evidence, the prosecutors walked out with the presiding officer, Supreme Court Chief Justice Hilario Davide Jr. The walkout sparked thousands of protestors to gather at EDSA demanding Estrada's resignation; the gathering became known as *"EDSA Dos"* (EDSA 2). Not long after that, Chief Justice Davide swore in Gloria Macapagal-Arroyo as the new president of the Philippines, prompting an embarrassed Estrada to leave the presidential palace.

While the first-ever impeachment proceeding in the country never came to its full conclusion, it precipitated widespread protest that ended the Estrada presidency. Later, former president Estrada would question Arroyo's presidency, saying he remained president because he was never convicted and was merely a president on leave. In *Estrada v. Desierto*,[2] the Supreme Court ruled that the totality of Estrada's actions taken together, despite an impeachment conviction not pushing through, indicated that he had resigned from office.

The next impeachment complaint was directed at the Supreme Court chief justice. On 2 June 2003, Estrada himself filed an impeachment complaint against Davide for corruption and misuse of the Judiciary Development Fund. The impeachment complaint was subsequently referred to the House Committee on Justice, which dismissed the complaint on 22 October 2003 (Tatad 2017b). A second complaint was filed the next day by Estrada-loyal members of the House of Representatives itself, supported by the required endorsement of at least one-third of all its members. Before the House of Representatives could transmit the Articles of Impeachment to the Senate, the second complaint was challenged before the Supreme Court, whose chief was under fire. The main argument in the Supreme Court was that filing the second complaint violated Section 5 Article XI of the 1987 Constitution, providing that no impeachment proceedings shall be initiated against the same official more than once within one year.[3]

The Supreme Court, in voiding the second impeachment complaint, played a critical role that was perceived as protecting its own. Unlike the later Sereno proceeding, Davide enjoyed wide public and judiciary support (Deinla 2017). The court, however, made a ruling that would also be utilized to defeat the very tenets of accountability that the process of impeachment seeks to approximate and objectify. This legal interpretation would be exploited to the hilt by Arroyo and her supporters over her nine-year corruption-marred and scandal-ridden presidential tenure, creatively skirting multiple attempts to impeach her. Former president Aquino and President Duterte were also beneficiaries of the decision in *Francisco v. House of Representatives*.

To stop the impeachment of Davide, the Supreme Court ruled in *Francisco v. House of Representatives* that "initiate" should be construed as the physical act of filing the impeachment complaint coupled with an action by the House of Representatives taking cognizance of it.

Using the constitutionally mandated legislative process, the Supreme Court said that it is the referral of the impeachment complaint to, or resolution by, the proper House Committee (the House Committee on Justice) that "initiates" an impeachment complaint. Putting the ruling in context, the court stated that the first complaint by Estrada himself, eventually dismissed by the House Committee on Justice, is considered a properly initiated impeachment complaint. This fact would trigger the one-year constitutional ban against another impeachment complaint, rendering the second complaint filed against Davide, even if endorsed by one-third of the total members of the House of Representatives, unconstitutional. Thus ended the threat of Davide's ouster, and he retired as chief justice at the mandatory age of seventy. He would later occupy the position of Permanent Representative to the United Nations, a job he would have been prevented from assuming had he been impeached.

The Davide impeachment attempt marked the first episode in turning impeachment into a tool for political vendetta. But it was during President Arroyo's term that impeachment was progressively thwarted or stripped of its accountability model. Starting in 2005, we can see the efficient and effective utilization of the *Francisco v. House of Representatives* ruling tactically to avoid legitimate impeachment complaints against President Arroyo. With the public outcry resulting from the "Hello Garci" scandal that referred to the alleged cheating in the 2004 presidential elections, impeachment threats against President Arroyo were inevitable. Thus, the public would see the filing of successive complaints against Arroyo in 2005, 2006, 2007 and 2008 (GMA News 2007). Her allies would file impeachment complaints deliberately fraught with gaffes, sure to be dismissed by the House Committee on Justice. The one-year prohibition was therefore triggered, sparing Arroyo. The administration continuously utilized this process until the end of Arroyo's term so that no actual threat of impeachment during her tenure existed. Her term expired as one of the most corruption-ridden and hated administrations. Thus, the Supreme Court ruling that had favoured its own Chief Justice Davide would be abused and exploited to defeat the constitutional mechanism of impeachment in the years that followed, further marring a process that had originally been envisioned to exact accountability for wrongdoing in office.

The subsequent administration of President Aquino sought to bring back the accountability function of impeachment. It was intended to carry out his popular anti-corruption crusade *"Daang Matuwid"* (straight path) against officials in the past Arroyo government. But these proceedings were also highly political and capitalized on the weight of executive power. Division within the judiciary also surfaced between the Arroyo and Aquino appointees in the High Court. This is seen in the clear division in voting patterns when dealing with corruption cases that arose under the past Arroyo government (Malasig 2018).

The first impeachment under Aquino was initiated against Ombudsman Merceditas Gutierrez, an Arroyo appointee whose fixed seven-year term would coincide with Aquino's term as president. Gutierrez was considered an obstacle to the prosecution of corruption charges against Arroyo officials. Two impeachment complaints were filed against her in July and August 2010, both of which were found sufficient in substance and referred to the House Committee on Justice (Dalangin-Fernandez 2010). Gutierrez challenged the two complaints by filing a petition for certiorari and prohibition to the Supreme Court on the ground that the one-year ban under Section 5 Article XI of the 1987 Constitution had been violated when the House Committee on Justice took on two impeachment complaints at the same time.[4] The Supreme Court issued a status *quo ante* order suspending impeachment proceedings. However, the court ultimately ruled that the one-year ban under the Constitution was not violated when the House Committee entertained two complaints. It reasoned that the two complaints were received at the same time. As long as there is only one proceeding, regardless of the number of complaints, the impeachment proceeding can go on, and the one-year ban is not violated. However, the impeachment process against Ombudsman Gutierrez came to a halt on its first step. Before the Aquino administration could commence a public display of political will, Ombudsman Gutierrez tendered her resignation personally to President Aquino on 29 April 2011. Aquino accepted it on the same day with a press statement (Official Gazette 2011a).

The second impeachment under the Aquino administration was filed against Chief Justice Corona on 12 December 2011, barely a year after the initiation of the Gutierrez impeachment. Corona was a so-called "midnight appointee" by Arroyo as he was appointed chief magistrate in the waning days of her presidency, thus depriving then newly elected president Aquino his chance of naming his choice for the vacancy. When Aquino took his oath as president, Corona was shunned. The chief justice traditionally administers the swearing-in ceremony, but Aquino asked Associate Justice Conchita Carpio-Morales to preside instead. Allegations of corruption and accumulation of ill-gotten wealth propelled the complaint against Corona. In the complaint for impeachment filed in the House of Representatives, he was being impeached initially on eight articles (Official Gazette 2011b). The eight articles were later reduced to three, and the House of Representatives focused on only one of the charges. One hundred eighty-eight representatives signed the document purportedly without reading the complaint first (Tatad 2017a). The complaint was transmitted to the Senate the next day.

The trial within the Senate chambers revealed the workings of an impeachment process in its political and legal aspects. Evidence dubiously obtained was presented during the trial (Suarez 2012). This prompted Corona to file a petition for certiorari with the Supreme Court, asking the court to issue a temporary restraining order claiming that the Senate had acted with grave abuse of discretion in the trial. At the same time, he asked that the court prohibit the implementation of subpoenas to bank managers in releasing documents for the trial (Aning 2012). However, before the court could act on the part regarding the bank records, the chief justice surrendered the information to the trial by his execution of a bank waiver.[5]

In May 2012, twenty senators voted to convict Corona, well beyond the two-thirds vote required under the 1987 Constitution. Corona's removal as chief justice thus became the first impeachment process to be taken to its conclusion in the Philippine jurisdiction. However, the following year, a Senate privilege speech revealed that the executive branch released PHP 50 million or more to each of the senators who voted to convict the chief justice in the form of a "bribery" through the Disbursement Acceleration Program (DAP) (Tatad 2017a). The DAP was designed to finance high-impact and priority programmes and projects using savings and unprogrammed funds. It was supposed to be a budget reform intervention to speed up public spending and boost economic growth (DBM 2018). Aquino's use of the DAP was invalidated by the Arroyo appointees dominating the Supreme Court on 4 February 2015, more than two years after Corona was removed.[6]

After the end of the term of the Aquino administration in 2016, a new and more sinister era of deploying impeachment and other legal rules came with the Duterte government. The first impeachment was filed against Commission on Elections (COMELEC) Chair Andres Bautista. The impeachment complaint was filed for betrayal of public trust and culpable violation of the Constitution over allegations of ill-gotten wealth (Cayabyab 2017). The impeachment complaint was dismissed by the House Committee on Justice. The plenary of the House of Representatives overturned this. Seeing the turn of events, Bautista eventually publicly declared his resignation, effective only on December 2017 (Cupin 2017). This pronouncement did not stop the House of Representatives from proceeding with the impeachment. On the same day, he was impeached in the lower house. The Articles of Impeachment were sent to the Senate for trial. But before the trial began, Bautista resigned immediately, avoiding the trial.

The second and third impeachment complaints were filed against Chief Justice Sereno on 2 August 2017 and Ombudsman Conchita Carpio-Morales on 13 December 2017. Both complaints were submitted by the Volunteers Against Crime and Corruption (VACC), a private organization seen as unflaggingly supportive of President Duterte, especially of his war on drugs. In the case of Sereno, another complaint was filed on 30 August 2017 by lawyer Larry Gadon, who represented former president Arroyo before the United Nations Working Group on Arbitrary Detention. In Morales's case, the complaint was not endorsed by any member of the House of Representatives (Buan 2017). As a result, the said impeachment complaint was not formally acted upon by the House of Representatives and died at birth. Carpio-Morales is the sister of the father-in-law of presidential daughter Sara Duterte-Carpio. Impeaching her a few months before her departure from office would have been a futile exercise. Carpio-Morales finished her term as the country's top graft buster in July 2018.

Prior to these complaints, two impeachment complaints were also lodged against President Duterte due to his alleged roles as mayor with the Davao Death Squad and president with the mass killings occurring in the country in pursuit of his drug war. However, both impeachment complaints were summarily thrown out by the House Committee on Justice without even conducting a full hearing (Tatad 2017a). An attempt to impeach Vice President Leni Robredo by then-Speaker Pantaleon Alvarez fell through, even as a draft complaint by Marcos's lawyer, Oliver Lozano, circulated in the media, could not find support within the House of Representatives (Cepeda 2017).

THE SUPREME COURT REMOVES ITS OWN CHIEF JUSTICE

Observers believe that the filing of the *quo warranto* against Chief Justice Sereno was brought about by the uncertainty of a Senate trial under duly transmitted articles of impeachment. The House of Representatives declared the impeachment complaint sufficient in both form and substance during its final hearing on 8 March 2018. At that point, transmittal of the Articles of Impeachment to the Senate was expected to be a mere formality. However, the intended outcome could not be predicted because sixteen senators out of twenty-four were needed to convict and remove the Chief Justice from office. It was believed that many senators were not sympathetic to having Sereno removed.

The wheels of the meta-constitutional remedy of *quo warranto* began to grind with a petition before the Supreme Court on 1 March 2018 by lawyer Oliver Lozano, the same person who submitted the failed bid for Vice President Robredo's impeachment. Five days later, the Philippine government's chief attorney, Solicitor General Jose Calida, submitted on behalf of the Republic of the Philippines another *quo warranto* petition (Buan 2018a).

Quo warranto comes from a Latin phrase, "By what right or warrant do you act?" (California Attorney General's Office 1990). *Quo warranto* proceedings are challenges or claims involving the right to hold a public office. It is a legal remedy for usurpation or intrusion into a public office. It is an action by which the right to an office or franchise is examined and results in the ouster of the holder from enjoying and exercising that office. In *Lota v. Court of Appeals*,[7] the court made a distinction between *mandamus* and *quo warranto* proceedings. In the Philippines, *quo warranto* may be brought in three instances: (1) against any person who usurps, unlawfully holds or exercises a public office, position or franchise; (2) against any public officer who does or suffers an act which, by provision of law, constitutes a ground for forfeiture of office; and (3) any association which acts as a corporation within the Philippines without being legally incorporated or without lawful authority so to act.[8] Thus, a *quo warranto* proceeding is the only way the right to an office can be contested. The right to public office cannot be questioned collaterally by any other means, not through *mandamus*, nor by a motion to set aside or annul an order.[9]

Sereno's *quo warranto* proceeding was anchored in her non-fulfilment of specific ethical requirements. Her fitness and moral integrity to be appointed as chief magistrate was the basis of the action against her, that is, her persistent failure in the past—as required by law, and until she applied for the position of chief justice—to file her annual Statement of Assets, Liabilities and Net Worth. The *quo warranto* provides a lower bar for removing a justice than the constitutional provision on impeachment, which needs to be grounded in culpable violation of the Constitution, treason, bribery, graft and corruption, other high crimes or betrayal of public trust (Const., (1987), art. XI (Phil.)).

In many ways, the Supreme Court staged a legal-political coup by firing its own chief justice in the controversial decision on 11 May 2018.[10] Her ouster by her own colleagues brought a deeply divided court to the fore, with eight of the fourteen justices voting against her, including fellow Aquino appointee Justice Francis Jardeleza, with whom Sereno had a very public squabble that signalled the *quo warranto* outcome. All the associate justices who testified against her in the House Committee on Justice during the impeachment proceedings voted to remove her. All Duterte appointees were in favour of her ouster. In the end, with her last-ditch attempt to reverse the vote by way of a motion for reconsideration denied, Sereno was declared by her colleagues in the Supreme Court as ineligible to sit among them.

Sereno's removal was blowback from President Aquino's disregard of the seniority rule in the court by appointing a newcomer as chief justice. The *quo warranto* decision declared Aquino's appointment of Sereno as chief justice void. Aquino's failure to appreciate the dynamics and nuances of the relations and personalities involved, in addition to Sereno's treacly effort to generate public support for her against the members of the court, finally doomed her.

Sereno's chief critic in the chamber, Teresita Leonardo-De Castro, would be selected by President Duterte to replace Sereno for a two-month stint as chief justice until De Castro retired at age seventy. De Castro vowed to heal the rifts in the judiciary during her short tenure. Subsequent Chief Justice Lucas Bersamin was not an unexpected choice by Duterte for the post, but the selection bypassed the most senior associate justice, Antonio Carpio, who has taken a very vocal stand against the Philippines' pivot to China in light of the West Philippine Sea issue. Sereno's leaving may have narrowed the cracks within the Supreme Court. Many keen observers, however, are wary. The court decided in 2019, with little debate, to extend martial law in Mindanao indefinitely. The court eventually upheld Duterte's unilateral denunciation of the Rome Statute, dismissed the recount of the 2016 vice-presidential election and declared various infrastructure loan agreements between the Philippines and China as valid and constitutional.

CONCLUSION

A popular executive with power and resources and little respect for the rule of law can tip the scales towards constitutional imbalance. Under the scheme of constitutional democracy, the framework and institutional arrangements are precisely designed to thwart or arrest such creeping expansion of powers. Judicial power—and judicial independence—are attributes that are built into the constitutional design so that this "least powerful" branch of government, the judiciary, should be able to resist external pressures when determining the law or interpreting constitutional boundaries. It has been often observed that power and independence go hand in hand, meaning the capacity for the court's decision to be obeyed (power) is dependent on its capacity to render decisions in an impartial manner (independence). This chapter has argued that judicial power and judicial independence are not mutually dependent, nor do they work together automatically to sustain judicial integrity. Only when that power is exercised judiciously is the court's integrity advanced.

The removal from office of former chief justice Sereno manifests the role that the judiciary plays in undermining its own power—or independence. While the Philippine Supreme Court gained much judicial power under the 1987 Constitution, its independence has never been under more severe doubt than during the Duterte administration. The court's decision to take on the power of removal, which had not been stated explicitly in the Constitution, signified its motivation to be part of political initiatives to strip Sereno of her position. Considering that the lower house voted to approve the Articles of Impeachment, the court could have chosen to "defer" to the Senate to proceed with the impeachment trial by ordering the transmittal of the Articles. Instead, the court willingly drew itself into the political process, with some members even testifying against Sereno and preempting the Senate's opportunity to exercise its prerogatives. While the *quo warranto* decision tries hard to contextualize the Sereno case to prevent its indiscriminate—or vindictive—use in the future, the court's decision opens Pandora's box for using this and other legal devices to unseat other high officials who may have displeased the president or the party in power.

This does not augur well for the stability and functioning of a constitutional government where independent bodies play a crucial role in ensuring accountability and preventing abuse of power. Thus, using legal rules as political weapons, with a judiciary that is not prepared to exercise judicial restraint in using those tools, can only serve to embolden political leaders intent upon undermining the constitutional balance of power and the rule of law.

A key lesson from this episode is that institutional cohesion and leadership are even more critical than mere possession of constitutional guarantees to enable the Supreme Court to be independent. Security of tenure, financial autonomy and a high bar for removal of justices are not *ipso facto* guarantees from political intrusions—or the politicization of the judiciary, as shown in the Philippines. As other jurisdictions have experienced, institutional cohesion and skilful leadership are essential in navigating the ups and downs of democratic transition. Under a climate of strongman rule, the judiciary is highly vulnerable to political machinations and pressure to alter the balance of power in a constitutional democracy. Institutional support from within the Supreme Court for the accused chief justice could have provided a barrier against malicious or arbitrary ouster initiatives.

Notes

1. The Supreme Court is located on Padre Faura Street.
2. Estrada v. Desierto, G.R. No. 146710-15 (2 March 2001) (Phil.), https://elibrary.judiciary.gov.ph/thebookshelf/showdocs/1/50524 (accessed 30 April 2023).
3. Francisco Jr. v. House of Representatives, G.R. No. 160261 (10 November 2003) (Phil.), https://elibrary.judiciary.gov.ph/thebookshelf/showdocs/1/47018 (accessed 30 April 2023).
4. Gutierrez v. House of Representatives, G.R. No. 193459 (15 February 2011) (Phil.), https://elibrary.judiciary.gov.ph/thebookshelf/showdocs/1/54669 (accessed 30 April 2023).
5. Philippine Savings Bank v. Senate Impeachment Court et al., G.R. No. 200238 (20 November 2012) (Phil.), https://elibrary.judiciary.gov.ph/thebookshelf/showdocs/1/55379 (accessed 30 April 2023).
6. Araullo et. al v. Benigno Aquino III, GR No. 209287 (3 February 2015) (Phil.), https://elibrary.judiciary.gov.ph/thebookshelf/showdocs/1/58859 (accessed 30 April 2023).
7. Lota v. Court of Appeals, G.R. No. L-14803 (30 June 1961) (Phil.), https://lawphil.net/judjuris/juri1961/jun1961/gr_l-14803_1961.html (accessed 30 April 2023).
8. Rule 66, § 1, Rules of Court in the Philippines (1 January 1964), https://elibrary.judiciary.gov.ph/thebookshelf/showdocs/11/373 (accessed 30 April 2023).
9. Topacio v. Ong, G.R. No. 179895 (18 December 2008) (Phil.), https://elibrary.judiciary.gov.ph/thebookshelf/showdocs/1/48116 (accessed 30 April 2023).
10. Republic of the Philippines v. Sereno, G.R. No. 237428 (11 May 2018) (Phil.), https://elibrary.judiciary.gov.ph/thebookshelf/showdocs/1/64003 (accessed 30 April 2023).

References

Abogado. 2017. "A Look at the New 'Olympus' for the 'Gods of Padre Faura'". 29 April 2017. https://abogado.com.ph/a-look-at-the-new-olympus-for-the-gods-of-padre-faura/ (accessed 11 April 2019).

———. 2018. "Pity Sereno! First Time 'Gods of Padre Faura' Have Turned Against One of Their Own". 16 January 2018. http://abogado.com.ph/pity-sereno-first-time-gods-padre-faura-turned-one/ (accessed 27 March 2023).

Aning, Jerome. 2012. "Corona Asks SC to Stop Impeachment Trial, Bank Subpoenas". *Philippine Daily Inquirer*, 8 February 2012. http://newsinfo.inquirer.net/142077/corona-asks-sc-to-stop-impeachment-trial-bank-subpoenas (accessed 20 April 2018).

Bello, Walden. 1984. "Benigno Aquino: Between Dictatorship and Revolution in the Philippines". *Third World Quarterly* 6, no. 2: 283–309.

Buan, Lian. 2017. "Sereno Impeachment: Cracks in the Supreme Court". *Rappler*, 12 December 2017. https://www.rappler.com/newsbreak/in-depth/191150-sereno-impeachment-cracks-supreme-court (accessed 20 April 2018).

———. 2018a. "Calida Petitions Supreme Court to Remove Sereno". *Rappler*, 5 March 2018. https://www.rappler.com/nation/197435-calida-sereno-quo-warranto-supreme-court (accessed 19 April 2018).

———. 2018b. "CJ De Castro: Collegiality Is Back at the Supreme Court". *Rappler*, 28 August 2018. https://www.rappler.com/nation/210560-collegiality-restored-supreme-court-de-castro-chief-justice (accessed 11 April 2019).

California Attorney General's Office. 1990. *Quo Warranto: Resolution of Disputes – Right to Public Office*. https://oag.ca.gov/sites/all/files/agweb/pdfs/ag_opinions/quo-warranto-guidelines.pdf (accessed 22 April 2018).

Cayabyab, Marc Jayson. 2017. "Impeachment Complaint vs Bautista Filed After Endorsement of 3 Solons". *INQUIRER.net*, 23 August 2017. http://newsinfo.inquirer.net/924928/impeachment-complaint-impeach-andres-bautista-comelec-ill-gotten-wealth-house-of-representative (accessed 20 April 2018).

Cepeda, Mara. 2017. "Still No Endorsers for Robredo Impeachment Complaint". *Rappler*, 3 May 2017. https://www.rappler.com/nation/168726-impeach-leni-movement-still-no-endorsers-robredo-impeachment-complaint (accessed 19 April 2018).

Chan Robles Virtual Law Library. n.d. "Complaint for Impeachment Against President Joseph Ejercito Estrada (2000)". http://www.chanrobles.com/legal11impeachmentcomplaint.htm#.WtiABC5ubIU (accessed 19 April 2018).

Clark, Tom S. 2010. *The Limits of Judicial Independence*. New York: Cambridge University Press.

Cupin, Bea. 2017. "From Resignation to Impeachment: Chairman Bautista's Longest Day". *Rappler*, 12 October 2017. https://www.rappler.com/newsbreak/inside-track/184990-andres-bautista-resignation-impeachment (accessed 20 April 2018).

Dalangin-Fernandez, Lira. 2010. "2 Impeach Raps vs Ombudsman Sufficient in Form – House Panel". *INQUIRER.net*, 1 September 2010. https://web.archive.org/web/20100907033857/http://newsinfo.inquirer.net/breakingnews/world/view/20100901-289928/2-impeach-raps-vs-Ombudsman-sufficient-in-formHouse-panel (accessed 19 April 2018).

DBM (Department of Budget and Management). 2018. "Disbursement Acceleration Program (Main)". 9 February 2018. https://www.dbm.gov.ph/index.php/budget-documents/previous-years/35-budget-documents/309-disbursement-acceleration-program-main (accessed 30 April 2023).

Deinla, Imelda. 2014. "Public Support and Judicial Empowerment of the Philippine Supreme Court". *Contemporary Southeast Asia: A Journal of International and Strategic Affairs* 36, no. 1: 128–58.

―――. 2017. *The Development of the Rule of Law in ASEAN: The State and Regional Integration*. New York: Cambridge University Press.

Deinla, Imelda, and Björn Dressel. 2019. "Introduction: From Aquino II to Duterte: Change, Continuity—and Rupture". In *From Aquino II to Duterte (2010–2018): Change, Continuity—and Rupture*, edited by Imelda Deinla and Björn Dressel, pp. 1–36. Singapore: ISEAS – Yusof Ishak Institute.

Diaz, Jess. 2000. "Estrada Impeached". *The Philippine Star*, 14 November 2000. https://www.philstar.com/headlines/2000/11/14/88756/estrada-impeached (accessed 19 April 2018).

Domingo, Pilar. 2000. "Judicial Independence: The Politics of the Supreme Court in Mexico". *Journal of Latin American Studies* 32, no. 3: 705–35.

Dressel, Björn. 2010. "Judicialisation of Politics or Politicisation of the Judiciary? Considerations from Recent Events in Thailand". *The Pacific Review* 23, no. 5: 671–91. https://doi.org/10.1080/09512748.2010.521253 (accessed 19 April 2018).

Finkel, Jodi S. 2008. *Judicial Reform as Political Insurance*. Indiana: The University of Notre Dame Press.

Ginsburg, Tom. 2003. *Judicial Review in New Democracies: Constitutional Courts in Asian Cases*. Cambridge: Cambridge University Press.

GMA News. 2007. "Impeachment Complaints Filed Against President Arroyo in 2005". 6 November 2007. https://www.gmanetwork.com/news/topstories/content/67288/impeachment-complaints-filed-against-president-arroyo-in-2005/story/ (accessed 19 April 2018).

Helmke, Gretchen, and Frances Rosenbluth. 2009. "Regimes and the Rule of Law: Judicial Independence in Comparative Perspective". *Annual Review of Political Science* 12: 345–66.

Hendrianto, Stefanus. 2016. "The Rise and Fall of Historic Chief Justices: Constitutional Politics and Judicial Leadership in Indonesia". *Washington International Law Journal* 25, no. 3: 489–564.

Malasig, Jeline. 2018. "How Supreme Court Justices Voted in Major Cases under Duterte Administration". *Interaksyon*, 15 May 2018. https://interaksyon.philstar.com/breaking-news/2018/05/15/126749/supreme-court-voting-patterns-duterte-administration/ (accessed 8 April 2023).

Moustafa, Tamir. 2007. *The Struggle for Constitutional Power: Law, Politics, and Economic Development in Egypt*. Cambridge: Cambridge University Press.

―――. 2014. "Law and Courts in Authoritarian Regimes". *Annual Review of Law and Social Science* 10, no. 1: 281–99.

Nardi, Dominic. 2018. "Can NGOs Change the Constitution? Civil Society and the Indonesian Constitutional Court". *Contemporary Southeast Asia* 40, no. 2: 247–78.

Official Gazette. 2011a. "Statement of President Aquino on the Resignation of Ombudsman Gutierrez, 29 April 2011". 29 April 2011. https://www.officialgazette.gov.ph/2011/04/29/statement-of-president-aquino-on-the-resignation-of-ombudsman-gutierrez-april-29-2011/ (accessed 30 April 2023).

———. 2011b. "Articles of Impeachment against Chief Justice Renato C. Corona". 12 December 2011. http://www.officialgazette.gov.ph/2011/12/12/articles-of-impeachment-against-chief-justice-renato-c-corona-december-12-20ff (accessed 20 April 2018).

PCOO–NIB (News and Information Bureau). 2018. "Interview with Presidential Spokesperson Harry Roque by Binibining Maharlika / FB Live". *Presidential Communications Office*, 9 March 2018. https://pco.gov.ph/media-interview/interview-presidential-spokesperson-harry-roque-binibining-maharlika-fb-live/ (accessed 24 April 2023).

Rosenberg, Gerald N. 1992. "Judicial Independence and the Reality of Political Power". *The Review of Politics* 54, no. 3: 369–98.

Roux, Theunis. 2013. *The Politics of Principle: The First South African Constitutional Court, 1995–2005*. Cambridge: Cambridge University Press.

Suarez, KD. 2012. "#CoronaTrial: Day 12". *Rappler*, 6 February 2012. https://www.rappler.com/nation/special-coverage/1334-coronatrial-day-12 (accessed 20 April 2018).

Tatad, Francisco S. 2017a. "A Unique Republic of Impeachments?" *The Manila Times*, 6 September 2017. http://www.manilatimes.net/unique-republic-impeachments/348909/ (accessed 19 April 2018).

———. 2017b. "The Ravages of Impeachment". *The Manila Times*, 11 October 2017. http://www.manilatimes.net/the-ravages-of-impeachment/355789/ (accessed 19 April 2018).

Vitug, Marites Dañguilan. 2018. "[OPINION] Aftershocks in the Supreme Court". *Rappler*, 20 March 2018. https://www.rappler.com/thought-leaders/198489-supreme-court-philippines-appointments-aftershocks (accessed 11 April 2019).

Widner, Jennifer A. 2001. *Building the Rule of Law: Francis Nyalali and the Road to Judicial Independence in Africa*. New York: W.W. Norton & Company.

10

Contesting Duterte's Drug War: Truth, Politics, Ethics[1]

Nicole Curato and Bianca Ysabelle Franco

Former president Rodrigo Duterte often spoke in hyperbole. "Shoot me", he dared soldiers during a speech in an army base if he overstays his six-year term. To ride a jet ski and plant the Philippine flag was his response when asked about his strategy for disputed territories with China. "I will eat them alive", he said in a speech in Vientiane, threatening Islamic State fighters that captured the city of Marawi. He just needs salt and vinegar, he added.

Over the years, observers have become familiar with Duterte's rhetorical style. The former Philippine president is a melodramatic performer, the quintessential celebrity politician befitting from the televisual age (Pertierra 2017). His vocabulary is meant to shock and amuse. His words are not meant to be taken literally.

But it is different when it comes to his war on drugs. In the first month after Duterte was elected president in May 2016, there were 581 documented cases of summary executions. This figure covers those killed in police operations and shot by unidentified gunmen (*ABS-

CBN News 2018). The death toll increased as the Philippine National Police (PNP) officially rolled out its anti-narcotics campaign, resulting in over 7,000 deaths in its first seven months (*Rappler* 2016). Duterte's claim that the war on drugs would be bloody differs from his other pronouncements. This statement was not an exaggeration.

Duterte's drug war proved popular, with polling data revealing 77 per cent of Filipinos finding it "satisfactory" (SWS 2017d).[2] Duterte himself enjoyed a "very good" net satisfaction rating of +66 a year into his term and stayed at that level throughout his presidency (SWS 2017c, 2022). The Philippines has embraced a strongman, so the story goes. By electing Duterte, Filipinos have forged a new social contract where they are willing to give up some of their liberties for the sake of the common good.

But there is danger in perpetuating a single story. Such a narrative about the drug war is not inaccurate but incomplete (Adichie 2016). Behind the coherent narrative of popular support for the president and the drug war are multilayered narratives of contestation, which challenge (1) the truths perpetuated by the state, (2) the politics that legitimize the drug war, and (3) the ethics of justifying the bloodbath. This chapter focuses on these angles of contestation. We aim to expose the different meanings associated with the drug war and prompt reflections for democratic practice.

IT WILL BE BLOODY

The story of the Philippines' drug war began much earlier than Duterte's presidency. One can trace it to Davao City, where Duterte served as mayor for two decades.

As Davao City mayor, Duterte earned the reputation of being the "butcher" (*SunStar* 2017). Human Rights Watch (2009) found evidence of death squad operations which accounted for the steady rise of targeted killings in the city from two in 1998 to 124 in 2008. The killings started with small-time drug pushers—men known in their neighbourhoods for petty theft and drug use (Human Rights Watch 2009; Canuday 2017; Miller 2018). Local media gave the label "Davao Death Squads" (DDS) to these vigilantes, a term lifted from American human rights lawyer Ramsey Clark's report about "death squads" during Corazon Aquino's administration (Canuday 2017, p. 128).

The killings follow a pattern. DDS get their cues from handlers (*"amo"* or boss) whose list of targets is compiled by the police or *barangay* officials. Handlers give killers the target's name, address and photograph and ensure that the police are slow to respond upon receiving reports.

> The assailants usually arrive in twos or threes on a motorcycle without a license plate. They wear baseball caps and buttoned shirts or jackets, apparently to conceal their weapons underneath. They shoot, or increasingly, stab their victim without warning, often in broad daylight and in the presence of multiple eyewitnesses, for whom they show little regard. And as quickly as they arrive, they ride off—but almost always before the police appear (Human Rights Watch 2009, p. 3).

The history of the DDS is essential to make sense of the Duterte administration's nationwide anti-narcotics campaign. In both arenas, the public's complicity, if not vocal support, is hinged on the view that vigilante killings are not worse than experiences of violence in the past. Jowel Canuday (2017, p. 132), a founder of Davao-based news service MindaNews, explains this in the context of Davao.

> It stems from the idea that the city, the region had seen worse times: the Marcos era, the rise of communists, urban insurrection units—there were plenty of violence before. The streets were militarized. It was difficult to go out at night. And you had this sense that, at any moment, society—even the country—would collapse.

Duterte won the backing of the Davao populace for improved peace and order that allowed the city to become a thriving commercial and tourist hub (Coronel 2016). Supporters drew a comparison between Davao and Singapore to demonstrate what can be achieved when a benevolent strongman governs a nation. Scaling up the Davao model has been the legitimizing discourse of Duterte's tough-handed approach to crime in the country.

The anti-drug campaign was anchored on Operation Plan (Oplan) Double Barrel. The "lower barrel" refers to the implementation of *"tokhang"* (knock and plead) operations in drug-affected *barangay*s in coordination with local government units. In contrast, the "upper barrel" focuses on "high-value targets" (National Police Commission 2016). Central to Oplan Double Barrel is the simulation of a strong state to secure public acquiescence. For Peter Kreuzer (2016, p. 3), this signals the return of national boss rule, where the PNP is established as the president's power base while democratic checks and balances are hollowed out (Sidel 1999).

Using the police as the primary institution to execute Duterte's nationwide drug war spells its significant difference from the Davao model. For Nathan Quimpo (2017, p. 156), DDS better fits the description of a "murderous private army" that rivals the infamous Ampatuan clan of Maguindanao. The direct link between Duterte and the DDS has yet to be proven in legal avenues. Still, it is fair to say that contract killers in Davao, and by extension Manila, after Duterte assumed power, enjoy "the comfort of state-protected impunity" (Human Rights Watch 2009, p. 4). Oplan Double Barrel, on the other hand, has a different character. As Canuday (2017, p. 133) observes,

> The police hardly figured in the Davao killings. But here in Manila, the deaths are usually the result of police raids, supposedly buy-bust operations. They didn't do as much buy-bust operations in Davao. Maybe there were a few, but that wasn't a common method... In fact, the suspicion there was that the gunmen were probably former NPA [New People's Army] Sparrow members because their methods were similar.

Duterte, to be sure, was not the first president to use the police with impunity. "[The] template for police killings already existed", as argued by investigative journalist Sheila Coronel (2017, p. 169). Alfred McCoy (2002) narrates and Kreuzer (2018) presents a detailed subregional mapping of deadly police violence even before Duterte was elected president. Duterte's drug war reveals not new patterns of police behaviour but further renders the institution vulnerable to criminal activities such as corruption and human rights abuses "in which the police are both enforcers of the law and its worst offenders" (Coronel 2017, p. 168).

The excesses of the drug war have not escaped the international community's attention. A United Nations committee urged the Philippines to end extrajudicial killings. In 2016, then-US President Barack Obama advised Duterte to follow the rule of law (Placido 2016). Colombia's former president, César Gaviria (2017), wrote an opinion piece in the *New York Times* urging Duterte to learn from the mistakes of Latin America's failed drug wars. Meanwhile, the Duterte administration dismissed these contestations as nothing more than foreign intervention over a sovereign state with its own history and cultural sensitivities (McKenzie and Liptak 2016). The administration concedes that the drug war will be bloody, but it will be worth it. This has been the storyline of both Duterte's Davao and the Philippines.

This narrative, however, has not gone unquestioned within the country. Contestations take place on three fronts—truth, politics and ethics. We argue that it is essential to place the contested character of the drug war in the foreground to illustrate the spaces for democratic debate and deliberation in what appears to be an increasingly repressive regime (Bello 2017). While not denying the democratic erosion in the Philippines under Duterte's rule (Freedom House 2018), we also find these levels of contestation as evidence not only of the vibrancy of political discourse in the Philippines but also the emergence of demands to hold the state accountable for its excesses.

CONTESTING THE TRUTH

Numbers are one of the main topics of contestation. The rationale of the drug war is itself based on questionable figures. During the presidential campaign, Duterte declared that there were three million addicts in the Philippines, while in 2017, this figure shifted to four million, as mentioned in another speech (Ranada 2017). Official statistics from the Dangerous Drugs Board (DDB) (2015) belie this. The number of drug users was pegged at 1.8 million in 2015, while the prevalence rate of drug use was 2.3 per cent—a figure below the global rate of 5.3 per cent (United Nations Office on Drugs and Crime 2017). In May 2017, Duterte fired DDB Chairperson Benjamin Reyes for "contradict[ing] the] government" (Gavilan 2017).

Citizens have called out these inconsistencies. Online news platform *Rappler* investigated how Duterte's questionable estimate of four million addicts became the official government figure (Ranada 2017). Students from the University of the Philippines (2016) provided data visualization of credible statistics to advocate for policy reforms based on sound evidence.[3] German media website Deutsche Welle also published an inquiry into the Philippine war on drugs, presenting the various discrepancies in the publicly available information about Oplan *Tokhang* (Santos and Ebbighausen 2018).

Why does this battle over numbers matter? It is because numbers justified the administration's brutal drug war. Duterte's political capital was drawn from his constant performance of a crisis. During the campaign, he warned that the country could become a narco-state if the proliferation of illegal drugs continues. Two years into his presidency, he claimed that the "rampant crime" in the country was cause for a national emergency (Regalado 2018). These declarations lend legitimacy to an administration that captured the seat of power because of its portrayal of a nation on "the brink of fragmentation" (Curato 2019, p. 129).

Numbers become even more contentious when it comes to the death toll. Police figures published in its database #RealNumbersPH place the death toll at 3,451 in the first year of the Duterte administration. This figure excludes 8,200 "homicides under investigation". The title of the database, "#RealNumbersPH", one can surmise, is a jab at human rights groups and journalists who, according to Duterte's spokespersons, are presenting inflated figures that portray the Philippines in a negative light.

At the start of Duterte's term, media organizations monitored the number of drug-related killings. The *Philippine Daily Inquirer*'s "The Kill List", *ABS-CBN*'s "Death Toll" and *Rappler*'s "Impunity Series" all consolidated numbers and narratives of casualties of both police and vigilante killings.[4] Human Rights groups like Amnesty International (2017) and Human Rights Watch (2017), meanwhile, reached the count of 7,000 deaths as of January 2017 based on media reports. The academic community has also published an archive of killings from 10 May 2016 to 29 September 2017 on the website drugarchive. ph. This website is based on a collaboration between the Ateneo de Manila University, De La Salle University, University of the Philippines Diliman and the Stabile Center for Investigative Journalism at Columbia University. The goal of this archive is to maintain a comprehensive database that provides evidence of the scale of casualties in Duterte's anti-narcotics campaign (*The Drug Archive* 2018). More recently, in November 2021, the Armed Conflict Location & Event Data Project (ACLED) released a review on the drug war killings with their data indicating that "at least 7,742 Philippine civilians have been killed in anti-drug operations since 2016" (Kishi and Buenaventura 2021). Another academe-led effort to track violence in the drug war is DahasPH (@dahasph on Twitter). The website dahas.upd.edu.ph provides timely updates on drug-related executions, detailed timelines and profiles of the casualties. In contrast, as of 28 February 2022, the Philippine Drug Enforcement Agency (PDEA) reports that 6,235 have died during anti-drug operations, which is more than 21 per cent lower than the 2021 ACLED data.

If the number of addicts justifies the war, the number of deaths is important in establishing accountability. The high number of drug-related killings has been used as the basis to file a case against Duterte before the International Criminal Court. A complaint lodged by human rights groups and families of fatalities in the drug war considered "the extrajudicial killings of thousands of Filipinos" as causing "great suffering to the victims and their families" (*ABS-CBN News* 2018). Therefore, contesting the state's casualty count is crucial for citizens that seek to assign responsibility and determine appropriate responses from the state and the international community.

CONTESTING POLITICS

There has been little dispute over the importance of addressing the problem of illegal drugs. Even some of Duterte's critics preface their statements with an acknowledgement that the problem of illegal drugs demands attention. The disagreement lies in the violent methods of the drug war.

There are various ways in which this disagreement is expressed. Some local government units promote alternative approaches to community policing instead of a tough-handed approach to crime. In the municipality of Pateros, for example, the mayor has publicly spoken against the killings and instead organized night patrols composed of mothers and police officers to keep the streets safe (Cabalza 2017). In the House of Representatives, opposition members launched investigations on using death squads to kill drug suspects. The Senate Committees on Justice and on Public Order and Dangerous Drugs have respectively conducted investigations into pay-per-kill allegations versus police officers and the use of hospitals to cover up the killings (Romero 2017; Baldwin et al. 2017). Despite the Duterte administration's supermajority in the legislature, the politics of the drug war has not gone unchallenged in the formal political arena.

Outside the state, contestations are most visible in the form of regular protests. Organized by human rights networks, faith-based groups and victims' families, protests have served various functions in challenging the narrative of the drug war. We conducted a cursory inventory of protests in the first two years of the Duterte administration. We find that protest action serves three main functions.

To express solidarity

Rituals of grieving have served as spaces for public displays of mourning. Wakes, funerals, and the 40th day of bereavement have been incorporated into the repertoires of protests to draw attention to the sorrow the drug war has brought to victims' families. Most prominent of these events is the funeral march for Kian Delos Santos, a seventeen-year-old student shot at close range in a police operation. Hundreds of protesters accompanied Kian's motorcade to the cemetery, such that a part of Metro Manila's busiest avenue was temporarily closed to traffic to give way to the procession. In this protest, mourners wore white t-shirts printed with a black ribbon to express grief and indignation.

The protest repertoire of mourning challenges the view that some lives are not worth grieving (Butler 2004). It asserts the victims' presence in the public sphere at a time when the public appears to become desensitized or feigning ignorance about the killings (Curato 2019). The website paalam.org serves a similar function by honouring the lives of the drug war's victims by providing digital eulogies. The private act of grieving is rendered a public issue when acts of mourning are incorporated into the protest repertoire.

To disrupt everyday spaces

During Duterte's second State of the Nation Address in 2017, the group #BlockDuterte laid down pairs of shoes and slippers along a highway leading to Congress, where Duterte delivered his speech. Reminiscent of the empty shoes taking the place of marchers at the Paris Climate Rally, the footwear along Commonwealth Avenue symbolizes those murdered in the drug war—victims who could no longer speak for themselves. This example of public installation illustrates how protest art disrupts everyday spaces to draw attention to the drug war's brutality. Not too far from the highway where empty shoes were scattered are communities that have witnessed a spate of drug-related killings. This visual disruption of a main thoroughfare, albeit temporarily, draws attention to what is often seen on the news but hidden from the view of everyday life in an urban metropolis.

Disruption also takes place in "elite spaces" such as the annual Art Fair in Manila's central business district, where a chilling installation on "everyday impunity" was featured alongside contemporary art for sale. Universities are also elite spaces where sculptors and painters create artwork about political repression and human rights. The use of art in disrupting everyday spaces offers a vocabulary of resistance based on the affective power of culture and imagery.

To draw connections to tyranny

Protests have also established the link between the drug war and broader practices of tyranny. Multisectoral organizations launched Movement Against Tyranny, which links Duterte's authoritarian tendencies and disregard for the rule of law to the country's history of repression. Protests during the anniversary of the 1972 declaration of Martial Law make this connection explicit. In 2017, protesters burned a ten-foot effigy of Rody's Cube—a version of Rubik's cube that shows four faces of Duterte that matches his image with Ferdinand Marcos Sr., Adolf Hitler and a puppet. The following year, protesters brought various protest art that placed Duterte's caricature alongside former president Gloria Macapagal-Arroyo and the dictator's son Ferdinand Marcos Jr. These visual forms of protest assert the continuity of repressive practices from the 1970s to current times.

This list of protest functions is by no means exhaustive but demonstrates the different angles of contestation on the politics of the drug war. Like contesting truth, contesting politics reflects the breadth of resistance against the narratives the Duterte administration offers about the drug war.

CONTESTING ETHICS

While the nation has witnessed numerous protest actions against the drug war, one could not help but ask why the popularity of both Duterte and the drug war persisted. Has the Philippines become a nation that has a questionable moral compass—a kind that applauds Duterte's call for genocide? A closer look is warranted. Empirical research puts forward another layer to this story.

Polling data is an excellent place to start. While headlines tend to highlight public satisfaction with the drug war, the finer detail of survey data presents a complex picture. Consider the following polling data from Social Weather Stations (SWS) taken in June 2017.

- Most Filipinos (90 per cent) think it is important to keep drug trade suspects alive. This can be read as an indication of the rejection of killings as a state-sponsored policy (SWS 2017b).
- A majority think that only the poor are killed in the drug war (60 per cent) and that those who have already surrendered to the police are nevertheless still killed (63 per cent) (SWS 2017a).
- Most worry that someone they know will be a victim of extrajudicial killings (73 per cent) (SWS 2017b).
- Half of the survey respondents disagree with the president's view that those engaged in illegal drug trade do not have the capacity to change anymore (51 per cent) (SWS 2017e).

These survey data provide a mixed picture of the specifics of the drug war. They reveal a certain level of anxiety about the policy and register differences in opinion about the appropriate treatment of drug addicts.

Our research among communities that have witnessed a spate of killings finds similar observations. From July 2017 to February 2018, we conducted over 20 interviews with family members affected by drug-related murders, 12 community leaders of religious and faith-based groups, 27 inmates detained due to drug-related charges and several local officials. We heard different stories in our interviews, leading us to observe that support for the drug war is beyond the binary choice for or against. Rather, most of our interviews demonstrate shades of grey regarding ethical judgment. Within this community, evaluating the drug war reveals layers of contestation. We categorize our analysis into three levels of contesting ethical calculations: (1) unqualified support, (2) ambivalence and (3) dissent. These different levels of support demonstrate the contested character of Duterte's popularity instead of one that polling numbers can simply summarize.

For this chapter, we use code names for all our respondents to protect their anonymity. We are also not disclosing our field site to honour our promise to our respondents.

Unqualified support

It is hardly surprising that *barangay* workers expressed unqualified support for the drug war. What we find insightful are their justifications for the policy. We spoke to Josie, a *purok* (zone) leader who testified to the audacity of the drug trade in her neighbourhood. "It's much better that the people are afraid today", she told us. "Drug dealers used to be shameless", she added, narrating how exchanging cash for crystal meth used to be brazenly done on street corners. She expressed concern that these conditions put her children's futures at risk. We also spoke to a *barangay* chairperson who shared the same apprehensions as Josie. *Kapitana* Edith articulated her worries for the youth victimized by illegal drugs. She said this when we asked about her views on the drug war: "I'm impressed with Duterte's platform against drugs because it benefits the youth. Their lives are exposed to the perils of the drug trade." Alex, a *barangay* employee studying to be a police officer, defends the killings, especially for those who refuse to change. As part of his work in a Quezon City Anti-Drug Advisory Council *barangay* office, Alex has witnessed how some addicts can be reformed when committed to rehabilitation and "graduate" from the *barangay*'s rehab programme, while there are those who are beyond redemption. He defends Duterte's line, "kill all addicts", by saying that there are those who "really refuse to change, those who fight back, and go astray from the law". We observed how both *barangay* workers are committed to their jobs and recognize how illegal drugs have broken their communities. While articulated in rather confident terms, their justifications are not easy to make, considering they also engage with community members seeking their help when turning over family members who have been addicted to drugs.

Aside from *barangay* officials, we also met religious officials who justified the anti-drug campaign based on their theological interpretation (Cornelio and Marañon 2019). One religious leader compared drug users to "swine", invoking Jesus's injunction to cast not "your pearls before swine, lest they trample them under their feet, and turn against and rend you". For some religious leaders, God has anointed Duterte to compel people to recognize the need for spiritual renewal. This view welcomes a higher purpose in Duterte's drug war by making users realize their moral depravity. This point became clear when we interviewed a pastor who leads an Evangelical congregation who said, "God needed to appoint Duterte to get Filipinos to repent." To approach Duterte's rule in this manner is to spiritualize drug abuse and frame it as a renewal of values and the soul's salvation (Cornelio and Medina 2018).

These religious reasons resonate with some of our respondents. Socorro, an eighty-four-year-old mother of four whose son was shot execution-style in his own home, considers Duterte "an instrument of God", someone who can "set straight the lives of addicts because there are many addicts who kill other people". In these justifications, we find that while the Catholic Church and faith-based groups have been at the forefront in organizing protests against the drug war, various layers of reasoning are present in everyday life that justify violence. Religion is not homogenous but a malleable source of rationalities that sometimes justify a brutal policy.

Ambivalence

To express support for the campaign against illegal drugs but disagree with killings is a frequent justification we hear from our interviews. We heard these narratives, particularly from relatives of men who died from drug-related murders. We met Bea, a mother in her twenties whose husband was killed in a police operation. "He [Duterte] probably has good reasons, but the process is wrong", she told us when we asked her about her thoughts on the anti-drug campaign and Duterte's leadership style. We also talked to Aya, the aunt of a boy killed by unidentified assailants inside their home. Aya works as a saleslady at a local hardware store. "The policy is okay; there is nothing [wrong] I could say", she said. "The part that we did not like was when *tokhang* started." Aya narrated the circumstances of her nephew's death. After his shift as a garbage collector, he was relaxing on the couch when a stranger went into their house and shot him dead. These stories, among others, reflect the polling data we cited above, where support for the anti-narcotics campaign is present, but the killings are rejected.

We also met respondents who shifted the blame to the police. "I am impressed with the president", said Libby, the mother-in-law of a drug runner shot by unidentified men weeks after being tailed by cops. "Oplan *Tokhang* is good", she added, "but the police are too rough; they became too arrogant." Mike, a drug offender, thinks the police are to blame too. "They are blindly following orders", he observes, "and you don't stand a chance when you fight the cops."

The distinction made between Duterte and the police is hardly surprising. For many residents of urban poor communities we have interviewed, the police have always been an agent of violence, whether in evictions or extortion rackets. The drug war opens doors to further excesses, but the direct link between the drug war and Duterte was not made. From their perspective, police brutality is an everyday reality (Jensen and Hapal 2018).

Dissent

Just as it is hardly surprising to find *barangay* employees supporting the drug war, hearing inmates and left-behind families contesting the administration's justifications is also expected. We found two main arguments when we unpacked their reasons for contesting the drug war.

The first argument relates to due process. Bob, a middle-aged construction worker in jail for drug-related charges, told us that the police have become too brutal. "It's not right that people are dying that way. They should just be imprisoned." Orly, a young vendor in his early twenties from Manila, takes a similar position, explaining that rehabilitation is a better alternative. "Everybody can change", he said in a somewhat frustrated manner. "If only people are given a chance to change, they will change." Meanwhile, Cindy, a twenty-three-year-old widow, expressed her frustration. "They should stop killing innocent people, or even those that peddle drugs", she said as she raised her voice. "They have to give people a better life, a chance to change. It's not good that they just kill anyone they fancy." In these narratives, we find evidence that the language of human rights and due process are present in everyday politics of justification among communities affected by the drug war. While we did hear references to the importance of keeping communities safe, we also listened to arguments that assert the importance of giving people a proper hearing and a second chance.

The second argument relates to the inequalities of the drug war. Clarita, a sixty-two-year-old mother of three, lost her son in 2016 after police officers ransacked his house, insisting he was a drug peddler. Witnesses said he was tortured before getting shot in the head. She was visibly upset when we talked to her. She asked, "Why don't they go after the big-time drug dealers?" She added that there wouldn't be small-time pushers if it were not for the big fish. Similarly, Cathy, a mother of three in her late thirties whose ex-husband was killed by a masked man on a motorcycle, expressed her frustration about Duterte's desire to protect police officers but not ordinary citizens. "He doesn't want cops getting hurt but turns a blind eye when average Filipinos get killed", she asserted. "That's not right." Simon's main sentiment is regret. "I regret voting for that man", he said in our interview when we discussed his views about the Duterte administration's policies.

In these narratives, we find that the support for the war on drugs is not as straightforward as it seems. Although a majority of Filipinos may consider the anti-drug campaign to be this administration's greatest achievement (Pulse Asia 2018), there are conflicting ethical calculations underpinning public opinion.

UNSETTLED CONFLICTS

In this book chapter, we put forward three aspects of contestations in Duterte's drug war. We started by situating the administration's narrative of the drug war in historical developments in Davao City and how the Davao imaginary feeds into the administration's vision for the nation. We challenged the implicit assertion that Filipinos have entered a new social contract where individual rights are given up for the sake of the collective good. Instead, we find different forms of resistance and ethical calculations that define today's political condition.

It remains an open question as to how these contestations will evolve. Will conflicting numbers be resolved? Will alternative policies surface? Will there be a national consensus against killings? More than the question of "will" is the question of "how". How will numbers be resolved, how will alternative policies be articulated and how will a national conversation about the killings ensue?

Contestations fuel public deliberation in democratic societies. Diverse and conflicting options prompt democratic citizens to consider a range of views before making collective decisions and reaching for common ground. This, in turn, allow democracies to generate epistemically robust decisions (Landemore 2020). The question is what these contestations do to the quality of political life and what lessons the nation learned from the Philippines' dark times.

Notes

1. This project is funded by the Australian National University's Philippines Project Small Research Grant "Who will bury the dead? Community responses in Duterte's bloody war on drugs" (Application 4). This grant is a collaborative project with Jayeel Cornelio and Erron Medina (Ateneo de Manila University) and Filomin (Ging) Candaliza-Gutierrez (University of the Philippines).
2. Survey question: "Please tell me how satisfied or dissatisfied you are with the performance of the administration in its campaign against illegal drugs. Are you… (SHOWCARD)?"
3. https://dahas.upd.edu.ph/drug-wars-visual-regime/.
4. Noticeable, however, is the decision of these news outlets to stop the count. Inquirer's last count was capped at 30 June 2016, while *Rappler*'s "In Numbers" counter was last updated on 23 April 2017.

References

ABS-CBN News. 2016. "MAP, CHARTS: The Death Toll of the War on Drugs". 13 July 2016. https://news.abs-cbn.com/specials/map-charts-the-death-toll-of-the-war-on-drugs (accessed 18 September 2018).

———. 2018. "Duterte Faces Fresh Case at ICC over Drug War". 28 August 2018. https://news.abs-cbn.com/news/08/28/18/duterte-faces-fresh-case-at-icc-over-drug-war (accessed 28 September 2018).

Adichie, Chimamanda. 2016. "The Danger of a Single Story". *National Geographic Learning*, 2016. https://ngl.cengage.com/21centuryreading/resources/sites/default/files/B3_TG_AT7_0.pdf (accessed 13 September 2018)

Amnesty International. 2017. *"If You Are Poor, You Are Killed": Extrajudicial Executions in the Philippines' 'War on Drugs'*. https://www.amnesty.org.uk/files/2017-04/ASA3555172017ENGLISH.PDF?9_73DdFTpveG_iJgeK0U13KUVFHKSL_X (accessed 21 September 2018).

Baldwin, Clare, Manuel Mogato, and Andrew R.C. Marshall. 2017. "Philippine Senate Committee to Investigate Actions of Anti-Drug Police". *Reuters*, 3 July 2017. https://www.reuters.com/article/us-philippines-duterte-doa-senate/philippine-senate-committee-to-investigate-actions-of-anti-drug-police-idUSKBN19O1KZ (accessed 28 September 2018).

Bello, Walden. 2017. "Rodrigo Duterte: A Fascist Original". In *The Duterte Reader: Critical Essays on Rodrigo Duterte's Early Presidency*, edited by Nicole Curato, pp. 77–91. Quezon City: Ateneo de Manila University Press.

Butler, Judith. 2004. *Precarious Life: The Powers of Mourning and Violence*. London: Verso.

Cabalza, Dexter. 2017. "Moms, Grandmas, Aunts, 'Lose Sleep' for Safer Pateros". *Philippine Daily Inquirer*, 22 October 2017. http://newsinfo.inquirer.net/939717/women-volunteer-patrollers-war-on-drugs-extrajudicial-killings-rodrigo-duterte-sitio-pagkakaisa-women-volunteers (accessed 28 September 2018).

Canuday, Jose Jowel. 2017. "Locating Duterte in Davao: An Interview with Jose Jowel Canuday". *Social Transformations Journal of the Global South* 5, no. 1: 121–36.

Cornelio, Jayeel, and Ia Marañon. 2019. "A 'Righteous Intervention': Megachurch Christianity and Duterte's War on Drugs in the Philippines". *International Journal of Asian Christianity* 2, no. 2: 211–30.

Cornelio, Jayeel, and Erron Medina. 2018. "Duterte's Enduring Popularity Is Not Just a Political Choice—It Is Also Religious". *New Mandala*, 3 September 2018. http://www.newmandala.org/dutertes-enduring-popularity-not-just-political-choice-also-religious/ (accessed 27 September 2018).

Coronel, Sheila. 2016. "'I Will Kill All the Drug Lords': The Making of Rodrigo Duterte". *The Atlantic*, 20 September 2016. https://www.theatlantic.com/international/archive/2016/09/rodrigo-duterte-philippines-manila-drugs-davao/500756/ (accessed 13 September 2018).

———. 2017. "Murder as Enterprise: Police Profiteering in Duterte's War on Drugs". In *The Duterte Reader: Critical Essays on Rodrigo Duterte's Early Presidency*, edited by Nicole Curato, pp. 167–98. Quezon City: Ateneo de Manila University Press.

Curato, Nicole. 2019. *Democracy in a Time of Misery: From Spectacular Tragedy to Deliberative Action*. Oxford: Oxford University Press.

DDB (Dangerous Drugs Board). 2015. *Nationwide Survey on the Nature and Extent of Drug Abuse in the Philippines*. https://pcij.org/uploads/5be017bdced4d-

DDB-2015-Nationwide-Survey-Final-Reportc.pdf (accessed 21 September 2018).
Drug Archive, The. 2018. https://drugarchive.ph/ (accessed 28 September 2018).
Freedom House. 2018. *Freedom in the World*. https://freedomhouse.org/sites/default/files/FH_FITW_Report_2018_Final_SinglePage.pdf (accessed 28 September 2018).
Gavilan, Jodesz. 2017. "Duterte 'Fires' DDB Chair: You Do Not Contradict Your Own Gov't". *Rappler,* 24 May 2017. https://www.rappler.com/nation/170839-duterte-fires-ddb-benjamin-reyes-contradict-government/ (accessed 4 January 2023).
Gaviria, Cesar. 2017. "President Duterte Is Repeating My Mistakes". *The New York Times,* 7 February 2017. https://www.nytimes.com/2017/02/07/opinion/president-duterte-is-repeating-my-mistakes.html (accessed 28 September 2018).
Human Rights Watch. 2009. "'You Can Die Any Time': Death Squad Killings in Mindanao". https://www.hrw.org/sites/default/files/reports/philippines0409web_0.pdf (accessed 13 September 2018).
———. 2017. "'License to Kill': Philippine Police Killings in Duterte's 'War on Drugs'". https://www.hrw.org/report/2017/03/02/license-kill/philippine-police-killings-dutertes-war-drugs (accessed 21 September 2018).
Jensen, Steffen, and Karl Hapal. 2018. "Police Violence and Corruption in the Philippines: Violent Exchange and the War on Drugs". *Journal of Current Southeast Asian Affairs* 37, no. 2: 39–62.
Kishi, Roudabeh, and Tomas Buenaventura. 2021. "The Drug War Rages On in the Philippines: New Data on the Civilian Toll, State Responsibility, and Shifting Geographies of Violence". https://acleddata.com/2021/11/18/the-drug-war-rages-on-in-the-philippines-new-acled-data-on-the-civilian-toll-state-responsibility-and-shifting-geographies-of-violence/ (accessed 20 January 2023).
Kreuzer, Peter. 2016. *"If They Resist, Kill Them All": Police Vigilantism in the Philippines.* Germany: Peace Research Institute Frankfurt. http://www.hsfk.de/fileadmin/HSFK/hsfk_publikationen/prif142.pdf (accessed 13 September 2018).
———. 2018. "Excessive Use of Deadly Force by Police in the Philippines before Duterte". *Journal of Contemporary Asia* 48, no. 4: 671–84.
Landemore, Helene. 2020. *Open Democracy: Reinventing Popular Rule for the Twenty-First Century.* New Jersey: Princeton University Press.
McCoy, Alfred. 2002. *Policing America's Empire: The United States, the Philippines, and the Rise of the Surveillance State.* Madison: University of Wisconsin Press.
McKenzie, Sheena, and Kevin Liptak. 2016. "After Cursing Obama, Duterte Expresses Regret". *CNN,* 6 September 2016. https://edition.cnn.

com/2016/09/05/politics/philippines-president-rodrigo-duterte-barack-obama/index.html (accessed 4 January 2023).

Miller, Jonathan. 2018. *Duterte Harry: Fire and Fury in the Philippines*. Melbourne: Scribe Publications.

National Police Commission. 2016. *PNP Anti-Illegal Drugs Campaign Plan – Project 'Double Barrel'*. https://didm.pnp.gov.ph/images/Command%20Memorandum%20Circulars/CMC%202016-16%20PNP%20ANTI-ILLEGAL%20DRUGS%20CAMPAIGN%20PLAN%20%20PROJECT%20DOUBLE%20BARREL.pdf (accessed 20 September 2018).

PDEA (Philippine Drug Enforcement Agency). 2016. *#RealNumbersPH*. Updated as of 28 February 2022. https://pdea.gov.ph/2-uncategorised/279-realnumbersph (accessed 4 January 2023).

Pertierra, Anna C. 2017. "Celebrity Politics and Televisual Melodrama in the Age of Duterte". In *The Duterte Reader: Critical Essays on Rodrigo Duterte's Early Presidency*, edited by Nicole Curato, pp. 219–29. Quezon City: Ateneo de Manila University Press.

Placido, Dharel. 2016. "Obama to Duterte: Do War on Drugs 'the Right Way'". *ABS-CBN News*, 8 September 2016. https://news.abs-cbn.com/news/09/08/16/obama-to-duterte-do-war-on-drugs-the-right-way (accessed 21 September 2018).

Pulse Asia. 2018. *June 2018 Nationwide Survey on the State of the Nation Address (SONA)*. http://www.pulseasia.ph/june-2018-nationwide-survey-on-the-state-of-the-nation-address-sona/ (accessed 20 September 2018).

Quimpo, Nathan. 2017. "Duterte's 'War on Drugs': The Securitization of Illegal Drugs and the Return of National Boss Rule". In *The Duterte Reader: Critical Essays on Rodrigo Duterte's Early Presidency*, edited by Nicole Curato, pp. 145–66. Quezon City: Ateneo de Manila University Press.

Ranada, Pia. 2017. "Is Duterte's '4 Million Drug Addicts' a 'Real Number'?" *Rappler*, 6 May 2017. https://www.rappler.com/rappler-blogs/169009-duterte-drug-addicts-real-number (accessed 21 September 2018).

Rappler. 2016. "IN NUMBERS: The Philippines' 'War on Drugs'". 13 September 2016. https://www.rappler.com/newsbreak/iq/145814-numbers-statistics-philippines-war-drugs (accessed 18 September 2018).

Regalado, Edith. 2018. "National Emergency? Duterte to Act vs Rampant Crime". *The Philippine Star*, 7 June 2018. https://www.philstar.com/headlines/2018/06/07/1822378/national-emergency-duterte-act-vs-rampant-crime (accessed 21 September 2018).

Romero, Paolo. 2017. "Senate to Probe Pay-per-Kill Report vs Police". *The Philippine Star*, 8 February 2017. https://www.philstar.com/headlines/2017/02/08/1670180/senate-probe-pay-kill-report-vs-police (accessed 28 September 2018).

Santos, Ana, and Rodion Ebbighausen. 2018. "Duterte's Drug War – Facts and Fiction". *Deutsche Welle*, 5 September 2018. https://www.dw.com/en/investigating-dutertes-drug-war-in-philippines-facts-and-fiction/a-43695383 (accessed 28 September 2018).

Sidel, John. 1999. *Capital, Coercion, and Crime: Bossism in the Philippines*. Stanford: Stanford University Press.

Students from the University of the Philippines. 2016. "EXPLAINER: How Serious is the PH Drug Problem? Here's the Data". *Rappler*, 27 August 2016. https://www.rappler.com/newsbreak/iq/144331-data-drug-problem-philippines (accessed 28 September 2018).

SunStar. 2017. "Duterte on Drug War: 'I Might Go Down in History as the Butcher". 9 January 2017. https://www.sunstar.com.ph/article/119529/duterte-on-drug-war-i-might-go-down-in-history-as-the-butcher- (accessed 4 January 2023).

SWS (Social Weather Stations). 2017a. *June 23–26, 2017 Social Weather Survey: 3 out of 5 Filipinos Agree That Only Poor Drug Pushers Are Killed*. https://www.sws.org.ph/swsmain/artcldisppage/?artcsyscode=ART-20171002135108 (accessed 28 September 2018).

———. 2017b. *June 23–26, 2017 Social Weather Survey: 90% Say It Is Important That Drug Suspects Be Captured Alive*. https://www.sws.org.ph/swsmain/artcldisppage/?artcsyscode=ART-20171005100742 (accessed 28 September 2018).

———. 2017c. *Second Quarter 2017 Social Weather Survey: Pres. Duterte's Net Satisfaction Rating a New Personal Record-High of "Very Good" +66*. https://www.sws.org.ph/swsmain/artcldisppage/?artcsyscode=ART-20170706173742 (accessed 28 September 2018).

———. 2017d. *September 23–27, 2017 Social Weather Survey: Satisfaction with National Admin's Campaign against Illegal Drugs at Net +63*. https://www.sws.org.ph/swsmain/artcldisppage/?artcsyscode=ART-20171016170928 (accessed 28 September 2018).

———. 2017e. *Third Quarter 2017 Social Weather Survey: 65% Disagree with Giving Cash Rewards to Cops for Every Drug Suspect They Kill*. https://www.sws.org.ph/swsmain/artcldisppage/?artcsyscode=ART-20171031204402 (accessed 28 September 2018).

———. 2022. *Second Quarter 2022 Social Weather Survey: Pres. Rodrigo Duterte's Final Net Satisfaction Rating at +81*. https://www.sws.org.ph/swsmain/artcldisppage/?artcsyscode=ART-20220923101814 (accessed 4 January 2023).

United Nations Office on Drugs and Crime. 2017. *World Drug Report*. https://www.unodc.org/wdr2017/field/WDR_2017_presentation_lauch_version.pdf (accessed 21 September 2018).

11

Prioritizing Prison Reform: The Real Challenges behind Managing Violent Extremist Prisoners in the Philippines

Clarke Jones and Raymund Narag

The large number of violent extremist offenders (VEOs) in the Philippines correctional system has generated intense interest from overseas governments, non-government organizations, academic institutions and think tanks, all trying to offer capacity-building solutions for managing this "special needs offender" cohort (Gideon 2013). Correctional authorities in the Philippines—the Bureau of Jail Management and Penology (BJMP) and the Bureau of Corrections (BuCor)—have welcomed these offers of support but have often also questioned the type of assistance because it tends to conflict with other correctional priorities. No one denies the difficulties in managing VEOs in any prison system. Yet, efforts to reduce their associated risk would have a greater likelihood of success if the more pressing correctional issues in the Philippines, such as overcrowding, corruption and general prison reform, were addressed in the first instance (Jones and Narag 2018).

In many cases, the capacity-building assistance offered by other countries lacks local context and an understanding of the Philippines' correctional management. As most of the proffered Western-centric strategies or programmes have been developed overseas, they have tended to lack cultural relevance in the Philippines. Cultural relevance here refers to the critical elements contained in the assistance offered, which should be "relevant to the targeted culture, make use of the language of the population and reflect the values and beliefs of the members of the culture" (Nastasi 1998, p. 169). Inherent in this understanding is the assumption that one cannot separate the type of assistance from the target culture and that understanding the culture is essential to creating organizational change and overall programme success and sustainability (ibid.). Furthermore, the various types of assistance offered by overseas governments lack coordination, are often conflicting and tend not to distinguish between remand and convicted offenders. In the end, much of the assistance offered results in unsustainable programmes, wasted resources and counterproductive outcomes. This potentially jeopardizes the security, rehabilitation and safekeeping of VEOs in the Philippines' correctional system.

One major issue impeding the success of international capacity-building efforts in promoting better management of VEOs is overcrowding. The Philippines has one of the most congested correctional systems in the world. Without effective strategies to manage and reduce the bulging inmate population, the correctional system could potentially tip into chaos, jeopardizing the safekeeping of VEOs. If a system cannot cope, there is potential for escapes, tension and violence can escalate, and the safety of inmates and guards can be jeopardized. In these chaotic conditions, inmates can control outside criminal or terrorist activity from within the jail or prison walls.

Overcrowding has partly emanated from "tough on crime" policies, which have resulted in many arrests, prosecutions and larger jail and prison populations. The increase in prison numbers has placed incredible pressure on correctional resources, compromising security and inmate safety. It has also translated into inmates' inability to access healthcare, rehabilitation or livelihood programmes. This results in higher recidivism rates and an overall failure of the correctional system (Knaus 2017; Chamberlen 2016).

With overcrowding now at critical levels, this chapter argues that any foreign aid to the Philippines correctional system must address this issue before any impact can be made on the safekeeping and rehabilitation of VEOs. In doing so, this chapter will also discuss the unique challenges around the current practices of managing, assessing, classifying and programming offenders in Philippine jails and prisons. The authors' discussions here are based on over ten years of ethnographic and longitudinal studies examining inmate shared governance, prison gangs, overcrowding and corruption in the correctional system. These interrelated problems hinder the potential to reform the prison and jail systems and generate additional problems when managing special needs offenders such as VEOs. From participant observation studies and interviews with prison administrators, staff (uniformed and non-uniformed), gang leaders and inmates, the authors have seen the correctional system operate through a precarious system of gang control and shared governance where the balance between order and disorder is continually threatened.

CONGESTION AND THE CORRECTIONAL SYSTEM

Throughout the participant observation period of this study, the authors have witnessed the number of inmates in the Philippines correctional system rise by more than 120 per cent from approximately 96,000 adult offenders in 2007 to over 215,000 in 2019. In New Bilibid Prison (NBP), a maximum-security compound that is one of the largest facilities of its kind in the world, the population rose from 12,450 in 2007 to over 19,000 in 2019. With over 19,000 inmates kept in a facility measuring only nine square hectares, overcrowding not only is about lack of bed space and accommodation, but also results in significant stress to the system and the safekeeping of high-risk offenders like VEOs. The number of VEOs in the Philippines' prisons and jails has risen just over 280 per cent, from 245 in 2007 to approximately 930 in 2019. This rise includes the addition of around 90 militants following their capture from the Islamic State-inspired conflict in Marawi in 2017 (Jones and Narag 2018).

It is an understatement to say that the correctional system is over capacity. The congestion rate has already exceeded 600 per cent in many prisons and jails. At the time of writing, the Philippines had the most overcrowded correctional system in the world, ahead of Haiti at around 450 per cent. In some jails in the Philippines, the rate is substantially higher than 600 per cent. The Quezon City Jail Male Dormitory, for example, has a bed capacity of 286 yet currently holds over 3,900 inmates—an overcrowding rate of almost 1,500 per cent, although this overcrowding rate has recently been addressed with the opening of a new jail in 2022. Other jails in Metro Manila have recorded over 3,000 per cent congestion levels, with one jail hovering around 3,600 per cent. Even specialized segregation and isolation units for high-risk offenders suffer from overcrowding. Before the onset of the COVID-19 pandemic, there was an isolation area called Building 14 in NBP, which was originally designed to house forty-eight high-risk offenders in twenty-four cells. As a result of the drug war, Building 14 came to house 128 offenders, including VEOs and drug lords—a potentially toxic mix. With a high arrest rate of drug offenders (Curato and Franco, this volume), the population growth continued to rise, stressing all areas of the correctional system (Jones and Narag 2018).

The judicial system is notoriously slow for those awaiting trial or appeal from their conviction, further impacting high congestion levels. Inmates now spend longer in remand jails, forming a bottleneck of offenders. The surge in drug cases from former president Duterte's drug war increased the overall congestion rate even further. At the time of writing, there were around 700,000 outstanding cases, with only 1,665 state prosecutors to clear these cases. Each state prosecutor, therefore, has an average of 426 cases, resulting in a limited capacity to reduce numbers in the overcrowded jail system. Even before the drug war, the judicial system was struggling to clear cases. Two VEOs affiliated with the Abu Sayyaf Group have been on remand for nineteen years. Around 20 per cent of the detainees have stayed in jail for at least two years. Some inmates remain in jail for more than twenty years, only to be acquitted. Ironically, it takes longer to be acquitted than to be convicted, which suggests that time on remand has become a *de facto* mechanism to punish detainees, even though some may be innocent.

The Philippines' correctional system consists of approximately 1,344 prisons and jails, including national prisons, provincial jails, sub-provincial jails, district jails, city jails, municipal jails and regional rehabilitation centres. It is essential to highlight the distinction between a "jail" and a "prison" in the Philippines. The BJMP runs jails, defined as places of confinement for inmates under investigation, undergoing trial or serving short-term sentences of up to three years. "Jail" is differentiated from "prison", which refers to the national prisons or penitentiaries managed and supervised by the BuCor. Prisons hold inmates who are convicted and sentenced to three years or more. The longest sentence is "life", usually forty-five years or more.

The BuCor operates seven national prisons dispersed around the country's different regions. BJMP run 478 jails nationwide; however, there are also 87 provincial and sub-provincial jails supervised by provincial governments. There are also numerous "lock-up jails" and detention centres maintained by the Philippine National Police (PNP), the National Bureau of Investigation, the Philippine Drug Enforcement Agency and the Bureau of Immigration. The latter facilities are generally utilized as temporary detention cells for those under investigation and those awaiting transfer to jails under court orders. All offenders are initially managed through the various lock-up jails awaiting investigation and trial. VEOs, however, are treated differently. Once their main investigations have been completed and they are charged, those on remand are usually quickly transferred to the high-security facilities in the Bicutan jail complex in Metro Manila (Jones and Narag 2018).

Due to overcrowding, most facilities within the Philippines' correctional system struggle to meet the United Nations Standard Minimum Rules for the Treatment of Prisoners (UNODC 2012). This is primarily due to archaic facilities and outdated equipment, inadequate supervision of staff and inmates and excessive corruption. Overcrowding is detrimental to an inmate's physical and mental health. In PNP lock-ups, most cells are single detention ones where fifty to one hundred detainees are cramped in an area designed for only four to six people. There is usually only one toilet, washing facilities are inadequate and food is scarce. The PNP does not have a budget for food and medicine for detainees. This is different from BJMP and BuCor, which both have a budget of PHP 60 per day per inmate for food. However, even this amount is inadequate as the food budget in BJMP of PHP 2.32 billion is based on an inmate population of 106,280. Yet, they now must cope with over 170,000 offenders (as of October 2019). This budget shortage has forced jail wardens to find other means to feed their inmates from third sources such as private concessionaires, loans from local governments and personal initiatives until the Philippine Congress initiates the next budget round. In the meantime, with congestion levels soaring, inmates must either face the possibility of malnourishment or rely on outside food sources from families and other visitors.

The over-reliance on resources from the outside can have significant security complications. For example, it can increase the chances of contraband (e.g., weapons, cell phones, drugs) entering the jail and prison system. Often this contraband enters the system through food items brought in by visitors or is concealed inside visitors' body cavities. Another outcome is creating a black market, with corrupt guards and inmates selling additional food or contraband items at overinflated prices. Selling such contraband also creates competition between inmate groups and gangs, leading to increased violent and often deadly institutional security incidents. These violent events often translate into further disruptions to the prison routine, resulting in many lockdowns, searches, time spent in cells and staff refusals to work on occupational health or safety grounds.

Overcrowding also places considerable pressure on inmates' correct placement, access to prison facilities and participation in education and rehabilitation programmes. Overcrowding can also lead to violence among inmates, often resulting in serious injuries or fatalities. It also increases stress and tension between inmates and therefore creates problems for staff and prisoner health and safety. When large groups of inmates are forced to live together in minimal space, they fight over things like washrooms, televisions, phones, food, recreational areas, equipment and space in general. Crowding can translate into higher rates of aggression, violence and injury. Self-harm may also rise due to increased anxiety and demands on already stressed individuals (Haney 2006). Inmates generally deal with this type of anxiety as they deal with feelings of depression or aggression by withdrawing from programmes and vocational and recreational activities, which greatly diminishes their chance of succeeding with any correctional plan.

THE IMPACT ON CORRECTIONAL MANAGEMENT

As congestion increases, prison control decreases. Inmates can no longer rely solely on the security and safety provided by correctional authorities. Over time, gangs (*pangkats*) have formed to provide protection from unscrupulous guards or hostile inmates. These gangs begin to undermine the custodial administrator's authority over the prisons and jails, resulting in a system of shared or even self-governance (Narag and Jones 2016). In these situations, Sykes (1958, p. 123) argues that prison officials obtain inmate cooperation through a system of illicit rewards. For example, guards allow contraband to circulate and disregard petty infractions by inmates. Inmates accept these minor illicit benefits and, in return, maintain prison order. Inmate leaders help the administration preserve order by restraining the more violent inmates and keeping violence to a minimum (Jones, Narag and Morales 2015).

But keeping this form of shared governance in check can become even more problematic when there are insufficient operational resources to adequately prevent the facilities from becoming totally run by prisoners. An inmate-to-guard ratio of one guard to eighty inmates means that there is an insufficient number of personnel to run facilities. Often, those recruited are poorly trained and underqualified to work in such difficult correctional settings. The ideal ratio is 1:7, as mandated in BuCor and BJMP operational policies. Most facilities have become dilapidated from years of neglect, making staff working conditions extremely poor. Though there are variations between the jails and prisons in terms of severity of conditions (i.e., some jails and prisons are more crowded, understaffed and dilapidated than others), all currently fail to meet the minimum standards set by the United Nations on the treatment of prisoners (the Nelson Mandela Rules) (UN General Assembly 2016).

Structural limitations arising from archaic facilities have necessitated the creation of informal organizational practices that have been tacitly allowed; however, BuCor and BJMP officially deny that they are allowed. Due to the lack of personnel, for example, selected inmates are allowed to render custodial, rehabilitation and administrative functions such as conducting inmate head counts, controlling cell keys, looking after prison or jail paperwork and accounting or acting as quasi-custodial officers—often referred to as "God Marshals". Due to a lack of facilities and services, inmates are allowed to bring in their own resources, such as materials to construct their beds (*tarima*) or bring in amenities like electric fans to overcome poor ventilation. As there are limited resources, inmates can bring their food, clothing, medicine or toiletries to meet their basic needs. Due to a lack of inmate programming, inmates develop and implement their rehabilitation programmes, including art, spiritual, educational, livelihood and sporting activities. Because of the lack of guard numbers, inmate leaders mediate conflicts, discipline inmates who violate informal cell rules and collect funds from their constituents to support cell maintenance. All these practices are informal coping mechanisms that are tacitly allowed and recognized by jail and prison officers. These informal practices are observed in all correctional facilities around the country, with some variations depending on location. For example, the central location of NBP in Manila makes it more accessible to visitors, thus allowing inmates to bring more resources to the prison. Prisons in rural areas, like the Sablayan penal farm on the island of Mindoro, are less accessible to visitors, thus limiting the resources generated through inmate contributions.

These informal coping mechanisms help keep the BuCor and BJMP facilities operational despite the decades of neglect. The structural deficits (lack of facilities, personnel, equipment and resources), coupled with the formation of informal coping practices, have translated into the evolution of a unique jail and prison culture. In Western prison systems, for example, administrators provide inmates with basic human rights such as safe accommodation, programmes for rehabilitation, a regular diet, and health and mental health support to maintain their well-being. Inmates are rarely given opportunities to take on leadership roles or undertake custodial duties. Prison gangs and other dominant inmate groups are usually associated with rule violations and overall inmate hostilities, and there are distinct operational policies and strategies to prevent such an occurrence. Usually, in high-security facilities where VEOs and other high-risk inmates are held, there are strict procedures to separate influential or violent inmates from others. There are usually no opportunities for inmates to do their own thing or be creative.

These coping mechanisms found in Philippines prisons and jails are facilitated by outside values imported into the jails and prisons. The coping mechanisms are rooted in the Filipino cultural values of helping one another (*damayan*) and community spirit (*bayanihan*), which are imported into the jail facilities. They are anchored in Filipino resilience and are vital in overcoming extreme adversities. While this setup has several benefits for correctional officers in the short term, it has also compromised the overall mandates of the BJMP and the BuCor. Informal practices, which are recognized by correctional officers and inmates alike, have become ingrained in the jail and prison culture. It has also provided the foundation for both developmental and predatory relationships among inmates, inmate leaders and correctional officers.

The coping mechanisms that result from the wide discretion given to correctional officers result in unique opportunities for inmate rehabilitation. The closeness of inmates and officers, however, can also often result in corrupt or careless practices. In relation to rehabilitation, since inmates are used for co-managing the cells and brigades, they are given opportunities to develop leadership and social skills that are helpful for their eventual release. Inmates are also actively involved in self-reformation activities like mentoring other inmates and providing them with mechanisms to maintain a positive self-identity while in prison. The presence of markets (*talipapa*) and other money-making opportunities also train inmates to be entrepreneurial, and anecdotal reports are rife with stories of inmates successfully starting businesses upon release from prison. For example, one former inmate well-known to the authors ran a café in NBP Maximum Security Compound, where inmates were trained to bake bread and make pastries and cakes. The inmate also ran several bakeries in Muntinlupa (the suburb surrounding NBP), employing the families of inmates and ex-offenders. With the power to generate income from their fellow inmates, inmate leaders contribute to jail and prison operational expenses like paying the BuCor's electricity bills or providing gasoline for correctional officers' visits to other offices.

Nevertheless, coping practices can also come at a considerable cost and are subject to abuse and corruption. For example, correctional officers can utilize their arbitrary discretion to obtain favours from selected inmates. Favoured inmates are given access to alternative coping mechanisms such as using extra accommodation space if they hand over the right amount of money. In this scenario, the correctional officers justify decisions based on the informal rules of the game, usually using a humanitarian narrative to explain their actions. However, inmates who are not favoured by the jail or prison officers or are unwilling to provide bribe money are denied access to legitimate services. For example, correctional officers can utilize the formal rules of the jail or prison manual as a basis for denying privileges. The ability to "code switch" from formal to informal policies and rules gives the jail and prison officers a level of influence and power over the inmates. Inconsistencies in the application of the rules lower the morale of well-intentioned correctional officers and heighten their cynicism about the system (Narag and Jones 2016).

In the process, a patron (*padrino*)–client relationship between correctional officers and inmates develops. Inmates are forced to cultivate a personal relationship with correctional officers to receive favours. A correctional officer also develops relationships with inmates to be assured of continued financial kickbacks. Inmates and correctional officers without a support group continually feel threatened by other inmates and other correctional officers. As such, inmates form gangs to protect themselves against other inmates but once in a gang, their own gang leader preys on them. Correctional officers can also serve as a *padrino* to gangs or become gang members themselves. They can also develop cliques based on family, school and religious ties with other correctional officers to strengthen their local positions. Creating a support base is necessary for protection from the whims and caprices of people above them in the hierarchy and from the unnecessary demands of people below them. While a semblance of peace and order is maintained amidst the overcrowding and noise, deep-seated violence can erupt anytime. Inmates can be killed if they do not follow the informal rules and are continually cautioned by their gang leader about when to invoke the formal and informal rules to survive. Furthermore, correctional officers are insecure in their positions as any step out of place can have them transferred, suspended or removed from the job.

The interplay of formal and informal rules is reinforced in every transaction. Newly recruited correctional officers, idealistic as they may be, are quickly socialized to the ways of the jail and prison. Those who lack comprehension of the mechanics or do not adhere to unstated rules are ostracised. Prison officers admit that they are in a bind. While they do not morally agree with the corrupt practices inside the prisons or jails, they are forced to adapt to them to survive. They concur with the Filipino adage, "dance to the tune of music (*kung ano ang tugtog, 'yun ang sayaw*)". As such, an ethically upright prison guard may be forced to accept bribes to keep their position. Newly arrived inmates are socialized to the setup and learn the acceptable and unacceptable behaviours in due time. Inmates who know how to negotiate around the setup can become inmate leaders and access privileges not given to other inmates. The inmate leaders can also have favourites and utilize formal and informal rules depending on the context.

The interplay of formal and informal rules has also generated many positive features that make the management of prisons and jails in the Philippines unique. For example, these mechanisms normalize the conditions of inmates by creating a sense of family and community. Inmates are managed like cells (*barangay*s) and towns (*brigade*s) where inmates can choose their leaders through established selection or election procedures. In the process, inmates are given roles deemed important by outside community members, such as being respected as a leader for serving as a cell leader (*mayor*). Since inmates are also allowed to develop and initiate their own rehabilitation programmes, their identities and sense of self-respect are maintained. Inmates are also allowed to continue to practise their pre-prison profession. For example, if an inmate was a doctor, they could practise in the jail or hospital. They could help construct new accommodations or maintain the existing jail or prison facilities if they were a builder. Inmates are, therefore, motivated to maintain the informal setup, making it easier for prison and jail management to control inmates. These informal mechanisms also mediate the pains of imprisonment for inmates, thus reducing the incidence of violence, disturbances and escapes. Finally, it improves the chances for successful reintegration into the community upon release as they maintain their sense of identity and self-respect. Thus, despite the extreme levels of overcrowding, the lack of personnel and the lack of operational resources, BuCor prisons and BJMP jails do not collapse into chaos.

Despite these positive features, these informal and unofficial policies are inherently subject to abuse. Without a clear policy on the informal mechanisms, prison and jail officers utilize unbridled discretion in granting and suspending privileges which inmate leaders replicate in managing their cells and brigades. Though the community setup varies from prison to prison and jail to jail, the inherent tensions generated by the reliance of BuCor and BJMP on inmate resources have a uniform deleterious effect on the correctional system. Due to the reliance on inmate leaders and the privileges and status attached to these positions, power struggles among inmates arise. Inmates strive to become cell and brigade leaders to acquire resources and maximize their cell space.

A market economy thrives with the informal entry of resources and cash into the prison and jail communities from visitors and families. In the past, before President Duterte's election, this economy sustained a lucrative drug economy where the inmate leaders captured profits. In some prisons, such as the Maximum Security Compound of the NBP, a number of gang leaders served as protectors for the drug dealers. More recently, Abu Sayyaf Group members have acted as bodyguards for an inmate leader who participated in the prison drug business. With large amounts of money generated from drug sales inside and outside the prison, inmates could replicate their pre-incarceration luxurious lifestyles. This setup reproduced the inequalities inherent in Philippine society, where the more resource-endowed inmates enjoyed unlimited benefits such as flat-screen televisions, air-conditioned cells, queen-sized bed, spa baths, saunas and ornately tiled bathrooms. Inmates with limited or no resources were used as pawns in power struggles between inmate leaders, drug lords, and participating guards and prison staff. However, not all inmates engage in power struggles and politicking; most simply want to serve their time peacefully by actively participating in prison activities and rehabilitation programmes.

The BJMP and the BuCor facilities and their operational practices require urgent modernization. Problems arise from outdated policies, inadequate personnel and physical security practices, operations and management issues, and organizational disparities. Very little, if any, information or intelligence is passed from the BJMP to the BuCor when inmates are convicted and transferred from remand jails to prison. The organizational disparities between the BJMP and the BuCor primarily result from the two organizations coming under different parts of government. The BJMP is overseen by the Department of Interior and Local Government, whereas the Department of Justice oversees the BuCor. There is very little formal cooperation between the two organizations; each has different correctional policies, procedures and standards.

There are also significant differences in the levels of professionalism between the BJMP and the BuCor, with the BJMP appearing to operate at a more skilled level than the BuCor. The BJMP has a national training facility for its uniformed personnel called the National Jail Management and Penology Training Institute. The BuCor personnel, on the other hand, have no such facility and only undergo basic correctional training with little possibility of supplementary or additional education. There have also been major challenges for the BuCor's progress with reform as there has been no stable leadership. Since 2010, there have been sixteen BuCor directors, each promoting their own vision for the prison system. None of these directors have come from the prison ranks, nor have they had previous correctional experience. Most have come from either police or military backgrounds with little experience in correctional management. By the time a new director upskills himself or herself in correctional management, particularly in the Filipino context, they retire, resign or are fired due to corruption or other prison scandals. BJMP, on the other hand, has had relatively stable leadership, all coming up from the jail ranks and all staying their full terms of around four years without controversy. The net result is that each organization runs differently, although informal practices continue to undermine the principles of effective correctional management in both organizations. This is making the management of high-risk offenders even more problematic.

Modern correctional management identifies four key domains in running an effective correctional institution: inmate classification, security housing, inmate programming, and documentation and assessment. In the Philippines, inmates are not classified according to risk or needs but to the length of sentences. The overcrowding naturally compromises any secure housing based on risk. Rehabilitation programmes usually are stand-alone and implemented without consideration for an inmate's security classification or whether the inmate needs the programme. An inmate's performance is also not documented or evaluated. There is limited utilization of methods such as psychological tools and assessments to determine an inmate's needs or whether they can be reformed or rehabilitated.

CONCLUSION

Before any real progress can be made to improve the management of special needs offender cohorts like VEOs in the Philippines, any assistance or solutions offered by overseas governments should first concentrate on overcrowding and prison reform more generally. From the brief, yet complex, description of prison and jail conditions provided above, overseas government assistance will require a significant cultural shift which will not happen quickly. To reduce violence and corruption in prisons and jails, for example, the entire culture will need to change. Like in the Scandinavian prison systems, Filipino guards and inmates work side-by-side, "sharing the same space instead of fighting for it". There is an emphasis on cooperation, sharing resources and rehabilitation rather than punishment and confinement (Pishko 2016).

Nonetheless, most other Western correctional systems are very different from the Philippines' and solutions developed in a Western context often have very little cultural relevance to the Philippines. To ensure sustainability and effectiveness, introducing correctional practices found effective in the developed world must be made in full awareness of the context to which they will be exported. Past experiences adopting foreign correctional practices without considering local conditions, resources and culture have been counterproductive and unsustainable. A failure to account for contextual differences between correctional systems has translated into cultural barriers raised by correctional personnel and inmates alike.

As with many other countries in the developing world, the Philippine government aims to professionalize its correctional system. Over the past ten years, it has been common for the heads of both BuCor and BJMP to look for guidance on correctional reform from experiences of the West. In doing so, they have tended to adopt whatever has been deemed best practice in other jurisdictions to ensure the safe custody, rehabilitation and reintegration of inmates into the community. However, the vast contextual differences mean correctional knowledge is not easily transferable. Correctional priorities are different and conflicting, and best practice in one jurisdiction or between countries is not the same in the next.

Before overseas assistance can be made more relevant, it is essential to understand the numerous organizational and political challenges facing BJMP and the BuCor that jeopardize the safe supervision of inmates, particularly the high-risk offender cohort. Traditional constraints faced by these agencies—such as lack of qualified personnel and resources, shortage of bed spaces and prolonged court trials—were made even more pronounced by the rising inmate population stemming from President Duterte's "war on drugs". In addition, the 2017 conflict in Marawi City and the resulting arrests of militants have led to the rapid growth of the VEO population. The combination of these organizational and political factors has led to the precarious state of correctional management in the Philippines.

Given these conditions, the principles of effective correctional management in BuCor prisons and BJMP jails continue to be undermined as most correctional staff in both BJMP and BuCor, and the inmates in jails and prisons, grow resigned to the fact that correctional reform cannot be sustained. However, it is essential to recall that the structural deficiencies we have observed and outlined here indirectly produced the formation of informal and important coping strategies. As such, the authors do not advocate for their complete elimination. The coping strategies are rooted in the Filipino cultural values of *damayan* and community spirit, *bayanihan*, which are imported into the jail facilities. They are anchored in Filipino resilience and are vital in overcoming extreme adversities.

In looking for the right balance between modern correctional reform and the Filipino way of correctional management, the authors suggest that informal coping strategies should be formalized and rationalized through the shared governance model. With appropriate and judicious implementation, the shared governance model can mitigate the structural deficits currently faced by the Philippines' correctional system (Narag and Jones 2016). With all its faults, the authors have seen that the current shared governance model has given inmates, including VEOs, opportunities for rehabilitation and new pathways to reduce recidivism. Further research is underway to examine recidivism rates in the Philippines to see whether shared governance has a measurable positive effect on reducing future offending and an inmate's successful reintegration into the outside community.

References

Chamberlen, Anastasia. 2016. "The Real Prison Crisis is the Damage the System Does to Its Prisoners". *The Conversation*, 24 November 2016. https://theconversation.com/the-real-prison-crisis-is-the-damage-the-system-does-to-its-prisoners-68609 (accessed 5 February 2023).

Gideon, Lior, ed. 2013. *Special Needs Offenders in Correctional Institutions*. Los Angeles: Sage Publications.

Haney, Craig. 2006. "The Wages of Prison Overcrowding: Harmful Psychological Consequences and Dysfunctional Correctional Reactions". *Journal of Law & Policy* 22, no. 1: 265–93.

Jones, Clarke R., and Raymund E. Narag. 2018. *Inmate Radicalization and Recruitment in Prisons*. London: Routledge.

Jones, Clarke R., Raymund E. Narag, and Resurrecion S. Morales. 2015. "Philippine Prison Gangs: Control or Chaos?" *RegNet Working Paper*, no. 71. Canberra: Regulatory Institutions Network.

Knaus, Christopher. 2017. "Prisons at Breaking Point but Australia Is Still Addicted to Incarceration". *The Guardian*, 28 December 2017. https://www.theguardian.com/australia-news/2017/dec/29/prisons-at-breaking-point-but-australia-is-still-addicted-to-incarceration (accessed (accessed 5 February 2023).

Narag, Raymund E., and Clarke R. Jones. 2016. "Understanding Prison Management in the Philippines: A Case for Shared Governance". *The Prison Journal* 97, no. 1: 3–26.

Nastasi, Bonnie K. 1998. "A Model for Mental Health Programming in Schools and Communities". *School Psychology Review* 27, no. 2: 165–74.

Pishko, Jessica. 2016. "When Prison Guards Are Violent Blame Culture – Not Bad Apples". *The Guardian*, 20 January 2016. https://www.theguardian.com/commentisfree/2016/jan/20/prison-guards-violence-culture (accessed 5 February 2023).

Sykes, Gresham M. 1958. *The Society of Captives: A Study of a Maximum Security Prison*. New Jersey: Princeton University Press.

UN General Assembly. 2016. *Resolution 70/175, United Nations Standard Minimum Rules for the Treatment of Prisoners (the Nelson Mandela Rules)*, adopted by the General Assembly on 17 December 2015. https://www.ohchr.org/Documents/ProfessionalInterest/NelsonMandelaRules.pdf (accessed 5 February 2023).

UNODC (United Nations Office on Drugs and Crime). 2012. *United Nations Prison-related Standards and Norms*. http://www.unodc.org/newsletter/pt/perspectives/no02/page004a.html (accessed 5 February 2023).

PART III

Reshaping the State under Duterte

12

Local Civil-Military Relations during Emergency: Lessons and Norming from Marawi[1]

Rosalie Arcala Hall

INTRODUCTION

On 23 October 2017, the Philippine government officially announced the end of the five-month battle in Marawi against Islamic State militants under Isnilon Hapilon and the Maute group. The Maute group centred on a family with ties to extremists in the Middle East and Indonesia, and the assault in Marawi was led by two brothers (Fonbuena 2017b).

The campaign by the Armed Forces of the Philippines (AFP), which featured aerial bombardment and urban warfare, resulted in over a hundred civilian deaths, hundreds of thousands displaced and the destruction of the city's infrastructure and neighbourhoods at "ground zero". The humanitarian response drew from a diverse set of government and civil society actors, working in multilayered coordination platforms which knitted together civilians and the military in crucial tasks such as rescue, retrieval and relief provisioning to displaced populations (Fonbuena 2020; Yabes 2020).

This chapter describes the armed and humanitarian responses to the Marawi crisis by highlighting in-theatre engagements between local civilian elites, civil society actors and military leaders in combat, rescue and retrieval operations and humanitarian provisioning. It describes the various coordination platforms and how they structure such engagements. It identifies the norming, gains and gaps in local civil-military relations. We see that civil-military relations during the Marawi war were spatial and task-based: the military focused on combat, while local government authorities and humanitarian responders focused on relief provisioning. The multilevel (national and provincial) government and cluster-based coordination platforms that pre-date the Marawi conflict were in place. Still, they functioned separately from platforms established by the military for civil-military coordination to support their combat mission. Military control over space and civilian cognisance of the martial law conditions during the Marawi conflict adversely affected humanitarian deliveries. A significant finding of this chapter is that there was no institutional norming of previous peacetime civil-military frameworks. In the face of an unexpected and intense military campaign, these frameworks fell away. Divergent views about who held informal power and how this would be exercised led to contestation over the conduct of rescue missions, aerial bombardment and accounting for the dead and missing. The military exhibited rule-based and culture-sensitive behaviour in the security measures they undertook but had little interface with local humanitarian actors. These responses occurred against the backdrop of the 23 May 2017 declaration by President Duterte of martial law in Mindanao (Proclamation 216, series of 2017), which legally privileged the military and the police to carry out stricter security measures.

An essential prologue to civil-military relations during the Marawi conflict was the evolution of more democratic civil-military relations in the Philippines following defence reforms instituted after 1986. While the Philippines military remained focused on internal security in its missions, its human rights norming in the conduct of armed operations and more people-oriented counterinsurgency strategies yielded positive gains in the military's relationships with local civilian authorities (Hall 2018). Democratic oversight of the military has also been strengthened by robust civil society and empowered political elites (Sombatpoonsiri 2018, p. 390). In Mindanao, in what is termed the "Bangsamoro theatre", institutional platforms such as local monitoring teams and area-based inter-agency task forces (e.g., in Zamboanga City, Basilan) have emerged, allowing these two sets of actors to interface and build personal ties (Russell 2013; Ilagan 2014; Adam, Verbrugge and Boer 2014). Under the army's new rules, co-located military units are required to engage stakeholders, especially mayors, governors and the Peace and Order Councils (POCs). Civil-military operations (CMO) officers are now standard in deployed units, tasked to bridge military objectives and civilian support. Institutional mechanisms, such as the Army Division-level Multi-Sector Advisory Board (MSAB) and local government-led Disaster Risk Reduction Management Councils, provide venues for working relationships during peacetime.

The presence and functionality of these civil-military platforms have been uneven. In North Cotabato towns bordering Maguindanao, municipal and barangay POCs are relatively functional in establishing, operating and monitoring government-linked militias (Hall 2017). By contrast, municipal POCs in Samar towns where big government construction projects were carried out have not been convened or are poorly performing, as per accounts of the Department of Interior and Local Government (Hall 2020). Where they are convened, military involvement is usually framed through a counterinsurgency lens (i.e., as tools to gather intelligence with bearing on military operations or a way to exert influence over project site selection that dovetails with their kinetic operations). Bohol's Provincial Peace and Order Council (2001–6) was the only documented case of a local government-led localized solution to the communist insurgency problem, which drew upon civil society participation with the military lending support (Arugay 2008).

Military-civil society engagement varies depending on the type of mission. In disaster response, where the military's role is confined to logistical support, engagements between military units and civil society actors have been scant, selective and based on personal ties (Kiba and Hall 2014; Hall and Espia 2015). In non-traditional missions such as support for development initiatives, local military units in Panay island have nominal outward linkages, resource and expertise sharing with preferred private foundations, but not with NGOs with broader project credentials (Hall 2016). Informal channels for dispute settlement anchor most engagements by the military and local leaders in North Cotabato and Maguindanao, where the military is mainly seen playing a symbolic role (Adam and Verbrugge 2014).

MARAWI AND THE MARANAOS: A PRE-CONFLICT MAPPING

Marawi City has a relatively homogenous ethnic Maranao population, where Muslims comprise the majority of residents. It is the commercial hub of the Lanao provinces, where the intersection between militancy, illicit activities and strong clan relations is most clearly illustrated. The city has a reputation as a hotbed of Islamic extremism, where recruits for the Abu Sayyaf Group (ASG) received instruction in ideological nodes such as the Dar Imam Shafii and Markazasos Shabab al-Muslim (Ramakrishna 2018, pp. 116, 120). It has been dubbed the "centre of [the] drug trade in Mindanao", with elected local government officials previously identified by law enforcement agencies as key persons in the operations (*SunStar* 2016, 2017; Cagoco-Guiam and Schoofs 2013, p. 95).

The province of Lanao del Sur hosts various non-state armed groups and is heavily militarized. Numerous military and paramilitary detachments under three battalions (103rd Infantry Brigade headquartered in Marawi City) are scattered through the province, with another mechanized battalion within earshot at nearby Iligan City. There are strong municipal mayors with their private armies, themselves part of rival political clans like the Alonto-Adiongs. Several mayors were included in President Rodrigo Duterte's narco-list and had been targets of police operations. Moro Islamic Liberation Front (MILF) units of the 102 Base Command of Commander Abdullah Makapaar (alias Bravo) control *barangay*s in Piagapo and Munai (Özerdem and Podder 2012, p. 525). MILF Commander Bravo, who had previously gained notoriety in 2008 from spearheading attacks on Lanao del Norte towns following the collapse of the Memorandum of Ancestral Domain (MOA-AD), ran a shadow government in MILF-controlled areas.

The Mautes, whose group earlier broke off from the MILF command and pledged support to ISIS, ran a training camp in Butig to which members of the Cotabato cell and presumably other ISIS recruits in central Mindanao were sent (Jones 2018, p. 7).

Before the Marawi siege, there had been numerous incidents in the province. The Mautes attacked a military outpost of the 51st Infantry Battalion in Butig in February 2016 (Ansis 2016). In August 2016, they brazenly broke into the provincial jail in Marawi to free their comrades who had been netted at checkpoints for possessing illegal firearms. In November 2016, they laid siege to the disused municipal hall of Butig for five days (Remitio 2016). In early 2017, there had also been encounters between the military and the Mautes in Masui, Pagayawan, and Pantar (including the 25 April 2017 encounter at Piagapo immediately preceding the Marawi crisis) (Jerusalem and Umel 2017).

Decades of fighting and displacement have had adverse effects on Maranao society. Studies covering Marawi have repeatedly pointed to the population's distrust of government and its representatives and trust towards insurgent groups, specifically the Moro National Liberation Front (MNLF), the MILF and the Bangsamoro Islamic Freedom Fighters (BIFF) (Deveans et al. 2013, p. 28). Özerdem and Podder (2012, p. 537) also found strong support for and participation in the MILF amongst respondents from towns in Lanao del Sur. This was in contrast to Lanao del Norte towns, which have seen more frequent displacements, given their proximity to MILF camps. Clan wars (*rido*) have become more frequent and intense in Lanao del Sur as local elected positions become key to accessing the state's coercive apparatus and financial resources (Adam and Boer 2015). These resources are leveraged to generate patronage and support from clans/ family members, and so winning elections becomes paramount—and so does armed mobilization.

The elements of this complicated environment are anchors for understanding the dynamics of engagement between civilian and military actors and the layers of authority responding to the Marawi crisis. It was a military operation which evolved from an army division using special forces to a full-blown Philippine armed forces-wide undertaking. Joint task groups were drawn from the infantry, police, navy, coast guard and air force and had communications and logistics support from the United States and Australia. The humanitarian platform during the conflict was supra-local in the early stages, partly because of the overwhelming number of displaced people. It drew in assistance from areas outside Lanao del Sur and needed coordination with the Autonomous Region of Muslim Mindanao (ARMM), Regions X, XII and then the National Emergency Operations Command (NEOC). It was an armed conflict in which government security forces enjoyed little trust from local Maranaos and had scant experience working with local humanitarian actors (Searle 2017).[2] While the fighting was contained in Marawi City, Lanao local chief executives with their private armed groups were also apprehensive about the possibility of the conflict spilling over and the implications of the presidential declaration of martial law for their ability to defend their communities against ISIS groups.

WHO'S IN CHARGE? MARAWI AND BEYOND AS A CONFLICT AREA

The Marawi crisis began with an army-police raid of a house at Barangay Basak Malutlut, where Isnilon Hapilon, Abu Sayyaf's leader, was said to be hiding (Fonbuena 2017c). The state security forces were met with gunfire and surprised by the high number of armed men in the area. Fighting between outgunned and outnumbered government troops and the militants followed for several days, with the militants waving black ISIS flags moving towards the city centre. They targeted government establishments—police stations, the fire station, prison and district hospital—established defence positions and a logistics base to gather guns/munitions, medicines, food and water. The militants killed many civilians during this period—mainly Christians who were summarily executed after having been identified as such (Amnesty International 2017, pp. 14–15). The Marawi police force on duty at the time was decimated, a new firetruck of the City Bureau of Fire was torched, and the prison opened with the prison warden killed on site. The militants tried to advance towards the 103rd Brigade headquarters but were repelled.

Two weeks of sustained fighting confined the ISIS fighters within what the military designated the "Main Battle Area" (MBA), bordered by the Agus River. A cordon was established around the MBA, with access points controlled by state security forces on the West bank of the Agus River at the Mapanggi and Banggolo bridges. These blocking forces prevented ISIS militants from escaping and receiving reinforcements from outside the MBA. The bridges and the river were also the only means for civilians trapped inside the MBA to exit. Many civilians, including 71 persons escorted by former deputy ARMM governor Norodin Alonto Lucman, escaped through this route, but many more died or were wounded in the process (Lagsa 2017).

The military divided Marawi into two zones—the MBA (combat zone) and Controlled Area (CA)—with separate deployments and command structures but under one umbrella—the Joint Task Force Marawi (JTF Marawi). Of the 76 *barangays* making up Marawi City, 24 were inside the MBA. In the MBA, task groups (Tiger, Vector and Musang) were assigned areas of operation by sector. The task groups were composite teams of Army Scout Rangers, Light Infantry, Special Forces, Marines, Philippine National Police (PNP) Special Action Forces (SAF) units and Philippine Coast Guard (PCG). Aerial bombing continued with increasing frequency well into September 2017. Ground combat operations were complemented by water operations in Lake Lanao under Task Group Lawa.

Combat task groups inside the MBA had a threefold mission: neutralize the ISIS militants, prevent them from escaping and receiving reinforcements from the outside and rescue civilian hostages (Rene Glenn Paje, pers. comm., 6 June 2018). While preoccupied with fighting, some of the commanders admitted to having rescued civilians (Danilo Pamonag, pers. comm., 3 May 2018). According to the TG Musang commander assigned to the lakefront by Dansalan College, they came across a sixty-plus group of women and children believed to be family members of the ISIS fighters in the final stages of the fighting. The procedure observed was for such rescued civilians to be turned over to the military medical unit for first aid, subjected to interrogation or questioning by the PNP Criminal Investigation and Detection Group and then turned over to the Provincial Capitol for social workers or Red Cross personnel to process. PNP personnel from Region XII confirm having interviewed rescued civilians from the MBA. In its report, Amnesty International (2017, pp. 18–20) cited civilians who escaped the MBA who had been physically abused by soldiers during interrogation or were held by them for multiple days before being released.

The CA included portions of Marawi city which had been "cleared" by the military of ISIS militant presence, and remains of those who perished were retrieved. These included Barangays Basak Malutlut, areas around Sarimanok, Amai Pakpak Medical Center and the City Hall and Datu Soboy, where many buildings still bear marks from artillery fire, and with gates spray painted "AFP/PNP cleared". By July 2017, civilians were allowed to return to their homes and businesses in "cleared" areas. Termed *kambalingan* (return) and *kambisita* (visits), the military controlled the timing of civilians' movements. Most of the Mindanao State University (MSU)-Marawi campus residents did not evacuate throughout the crisis, although three checkpoints were installed around its perimeter. MSU-Marawi, which halted classes at the onset of the fighting, resumed operations in August 2017, months before the formal combat ended.

Joint Task Group Ranao (JTG Ranao) had operational jurisdiction over the CA. JTG Ranao manned numerous checkpoints along the highways linking Marawi to Iligan City and around Lake Lanao. Numerous checkpoints were argued to be necessary to ensure the safety of the supply road for government troops operating inside the MBA. The blocking forces on the West bank of the Agus river were under the operational control of JTG Ranao.

In the CA, JTG Ranao's mandate was law enforcement. Because martial law was imposed early in the Marawi crisis, the military, in effect, took the lead position concerning law enforcement in the city. The local police force, which had suffered substantial casualties in the early weeks, was relieved and replaced by officers from the National Capital Region (NCR), including a new Police Chief who was a Maranao.[3] Additional police forces from the ARMM were also assigned to Marawi. The military and police in Marawi ran joint checkpoints and did evening *ronda* (drive-bys) in line with the curfew imposed throughout the city. Marawi Chief of Police Ebra M. Moxsir (pers. comm., 1 March 2018) said the procedure was to arrest people who violated the curfew and to turn them over to the police for processing. In villages already cleared by the military, Barangay Police Auxiliary Teams (BPATs) operated the checkpoints. A city joint security coordination command was put in place for checkpoint operations and curfew enforcement.

The checkpoints and clearing operations (including raids) restricted the mobility of residents and humanitarian workers. Safe conduct passes were required for residents, and gate passes for vehicles and passengers entering the CA. Only local government unit vehicles, emergency vehicles (e.g., ambulances), and vehicles carrying relief goods were issued passes for entry into Marawi. Entry to the MBA was restricted to combat troops, members of the PNP Scene of Crime Operations and Bureau of Fire Protection (BFP) personnel tasked with rescue and cadaver retrieval.

The security restrictions also adversely affected neighbouring towns. Marantao and Balindong, less than 20 kilometres south on the eastern side of Lake Lanao, had to position "local forces", fearing attacks on their town centre by ISIS militants or supporters.[4] In August 2017, a group of ISIS fighters tried to seize Marantao town but were repelled by a handful of soldiers and the mayor's private armed force. Similar concerns about attacks were raised by the incumbent Balindong mayor in light of prior military encounters with Maute fighters and MILF troops (under Commander Bravo) in the border *barangay*s with Piagapo.

Marawi is Lanao del Sur's commercial hub, with the main highway artery cutting through the city. Thus the flow of goods and humanitarian assistance was constrained by the checkpoints and entry pass requirements. By July 2017, displacements were also happening in the First District of Lanao del Sur, not because of actual fighting but because the residents feared hunger since no supplies were reaching them. Many of these displaced people found their way to Malabang.

LOCAL CRISIS MANAGEMENT PLATFORMS

Multiple coordination bodies were created at various levels throughout the five-month crisis. The military platform was set up first and coordinated activities for the first two weeks. The platforms led by local government units became more established and functional later, as the displacement intensified and humanitarian assistance began to flow from outside in heavier volumes. Consequently, there were two different coordination platforms—one for humanitarian efforts (province and national, civilian) and another for security and combat operations (JTF Marawi, military).

The Marawi City government, having suffered severe losses in its police and fire protection agencies, could not set up a humanitarian platform. Mayor Majul Gandamra was held up for a few days at the City Hall before being extracted by government troops. In the following weeks, satellite offices were set up in Iligan City and Baloi, Lanao del Norte. The Marawi City government transferred most of its services (social work, registry and justice) to where most evacuees were, including city government employees. Mayor Gandamra convened a Peace and Order Council meeting five times throughout the crisis, mainly in Iligan City.

The Lanao del Sur province created the Provincial Crisis Management Committee (PCMC), which was headquartered at the Provincial Capitol.[5] The PCMC was an inter-agency cluster for different government agencies doing response (e.g., retrieval of dead bodies, relief operations, rescue operations, media communications) (Ishii 2017). According to Vice Governor Mamintal Adiong (pers. comm., 19 September 2018), the PCMC made it possible for tasks to be divided among various agencies, for response teams to be accurately identified and for activities to be centrally coordinated, thus avoiding replication. Volunteer rescue groups and the Red Cross also coordinated with the PCMC (Arguillas 2017). It is important to note that while the PCMC coordinated humanitarian operations, security operations were outside its ambit. However, Adiong said that the military held closed-door meetings with the PCMC on sensitive matters and coordinated their activities with those of the PCMC.

As Marawi was part of the ARMM, the ARMM government also set up a Crisis Management Committee in Cotabato on day one. The ARMM Humanitarian Emergency and Action Response Team (HEART) deployed a search and rescue team which arrived in Marawi on day two, while dispatched relief goods arrived in Iligan on day four of the crisis. The ARMM rescue team was tasked with the retrieval of dead bodies at Barangay Basak Malutlut. ARMM HEART ran relief operations from satellite offices and warehouses in Iligan and in Malabang, Lanao del Sur, with goods transported from Cotabato to these sites. An untoward incident in Saguiaran (angry locals mobbed the truck) made ARMM HEART decide to stock goods inside the 6th Infantry Battalion headquarters in Malabang. A 24/7 hotline manned by ARMM employee volunteers was also set up in Cotabato City.

The hotline gathered SMS, phone calls and social media reports of civilians and kin stranded or trapped. Information about the identity of the civilian victims, their location and contact details were, in turn, relayed to ARMM HEART operating in Marawi.

A National Emergency Operations Center (NEOC) was also set up in Iligan City, evolving from a Region X Command and Control Center (Ric Jalad, pers. comm., 21 April 2018). The setting up of NEOC was unprecedented but was widely perceived as necessary to referee confusion and overlap in the relief responses of ARMM, Region X (which includes Lanao del Norte and Iligan City) and Region XII (where relief activities were considered supplementary) (Mark Torres, pers. comm., 31 January 2018). Undersecretary Ric Jalad called the Marawi response "national government-led, local government unit complemented", in recognition that most resources provided to those in evacuation camps were drawn from national government agencies such as the Department of Social Welfare and Development (family packs), Department of Health (medicine), Bureau of Fire (water) and Department of Public Works and Highways (toilet facilities). According to Adiong, the Lanao del Sur PCMC reported directly to the NEOC.

The UN cluster system was a separate coordination platform for non-government humanitarian providers. Groups focused on education, health, nutrition, water and sanitation, camp management, non-food item delivery, etc., met and coordinated their activities across various areas. In a report issued by UNOCHA (2017), activities were mainly concentrated in Iligan City, Baloi, Saguiaran, Pantar and Pantao Ragat, where the big evacuation centres were located. Apart from the World Food Programme and the International Organization for Migration, many other international non-government organizations were listed as having provided support. Many local NGOs with years of experience in terms of advocacy and development work in the Lanao area (e.g., Al-Mujadilah Development Foundation, Kapamagogopa Inc., Ecoweb) stepped up early. Faith-based organizations like the Catholic Diocese of Iligan and the Redemptorists likewise mobilized. According to Sohaila Macadato from United Youth of the Philippines (pers. comm., 16 September 2018), NGOs made a conscious effort to distribute activities to cover underserved home-based internally displaced persons (IDPs) and those in evacuation centres located far from the main highway. The NGO providers independently engaged local authorities (*barangay* captains, municipal mayors and traditional leaders) where their activities were located.

On the military side, there was also a CMO Coordinating Council (CMOCC) headed by Army Lieutenant Colonel Jo-ar Herrera under the Army First Infantry Division. According to Herrera (pers. comm., 20 February 2018), the CMOCC was a "one-stop-shop for information and humanitarian undertaking". They informed the PCMC once buildings were cleared and retrieval teams could be sent to collect remains. As a CMO unit, its task included news management, providing updates on military activities (Colonel Herrera was the CMOCC spokesperson) and counteracting fake news on social media. The ARMM rescue teams reported receiving instructions from the CMOCC. The CMOCC was a bridge between the PCMC and the military doing security and clearing operations. In one case, adjacent municipalities from Marawi complained to PCMC that it was difficult for them to enter Marawi because they had to travel the farthest route for humanitarian aid delivery. It was CMOCC that relayed information regarding road clearance for humanitarian convoys. With the reconstitution of the military response into JTF Marawi, JTG Ranao became the military's coordination platform to link with civilians.

Early in the crisis, a Joint GPH-Moro Islamic Liberation Front (MILF) Crisis Management Committee was convened that subsequently established a peace corridor from Malabang to Marawi in September 2017 (Sabilo 2017). The peace corridor was intended to facilitate the safe delivery of humanitarian aid by having MILF and AFP units maintain checkpoints and sometimes offer to escort delivery vehicles.

The Marawi and Provincial coordination platforms were not immediately set up at the onset. According to Naguib Sinarimbo (pers. comm., 16 September 2018), few government personnel were left at the Capitol to staff the emergency response centre until additional personnel and relief goods from the ARMM HEART arrived on the fourth day. The PCMC's function as a coordination body for humanitarian response became more visible only after several weeks, with media given space at the Capitol grounds to cover events. The military ran the armed response at Brigade headquarters (across from the Capitol). The provincial government representatives and also some mayors crossed over to the Brigade to meet with Generals Eduardo Bautista (6th Infantry Division commander), Carlito Galvez Jr. (Western

Mindanao commander) and Eduardo Año (AFP chief of staff) for assessments on 24 May 2017. An MILF official said the closed-door meetings, which included heated discussions about how to conduct rescue operations (whether soldiers would accompany civilian rescuers or not) and bombardment (whether mosques should be spared), were not negotiations but rather restrained military information sharing to local government officials, on account of low trust (pers. comm., 18 January 2019).

From the beginning, the Marawi crisis was seen primarily as a military operation, with a quick decision to proceed with shelling in the MBA. The various civilian crisis management platforms dealt only with humanitarian concerns such as rescue, retrieval and relief provisioning, but their ability to do these was secondary to military considerations. Local intermediaries came forward to negotiate with the ISIS fighters for a humanitarian ceasefire in early June 2017 to allow trapped civilians to escape, but the offer was rejected by the military (Agence France-Presse 2017). Ranao Rescue Team requested a ceasefire from military leaders so their volunteers could extricate civilians trapped, but their request was rejected. One of its leaders felt that the military leaders did not believe their group was not in contact with Maute group and that they were mistrusted for going in to help ISIS militants (pers. comm., 28 February 2018). In the end, civilian-volunteer rescuers were only allowed access to the fringes of the fire zone but not to enter the bombed city blocks. According to PCMC Spokesperson Zia Adiong, the military rebuffed offers to negotiate by local political leaders with clan/familial connections to the ISIS fighters who were more familiar with this type of terrorism (PIA 2017).

RESCUE AND RETRIEVAL OPERATIONS

Military operational imperatives strongly conditioned rescue and retrieval operations. People evacuated Marawi voluntarily, with many opting to remain with the false expectation that the crisis would be over quickly. Hence, many were trapped as fighting intensified between the militants and the government. Information about those holed up in their homes and businesses was often lacking. The ARMM 24/7 hotline kept a database of SMS, calls and social media reports of persons needing rescuing and their whereabouts (filtered by *barangay*), relayed to the ARMM HEART representative stationed at the Marawi Capitol and to the PCMC rescue and retrieval cluster. Three sets of rescue teams were on standby: Ranao Rescue Team, the ARMM/province rescue team and the volunteer "suicide squad" composed of Marawi locals (*GMA News Online* 2018). The "civilian" rescue teams waited for military advice for open or cleared areas and a time window (e.g., two hours) within which they could go and pick up stranded individuals or cadavers. They were provided details on the persons to be rescued, such as the location of the building or house. Control of the battle space being paramount, the military required civilian rescuers to wear IDs.

Rescue operations were political, given the military's concern that a ceasefire would give the militants more opportunity to reposition to their advantage. After the second week, the only rescuing done was of civilians in the MBA making their way to exit points (by Mapanggi and Banggolo bridges), where they were received by the civilian rescuers and processed. Loudspeaker operations were maintained in this corridor, providing instructions such as having a white cloth when approaching security personnel. The ARMM rescue team was stationed with soldiers at these exit points but strictly followed instructions by the soldiers on when to move forward. Civilians rescued inside the MBA were rescued by the military, including the seventeen females and children (wives and children of fighters) in Datu Naga (an area in the direction of the lake where militants retreated towards the end of fighting) and the Marawi Catholic priest, Father Teresito "Chito" Soganub.

Retrieval operations were less contested but lacked policy direction on cadaver management and ambulance access. At first, retrieved cadavers were taken to funeral homes in Iligan City, where members of the PNP Scene of Crime Operations processed the remains for identification. However, as the number of retrieved cadavers increased, it became necessary to do mass burials immediately. The Province and City Bureau of Fire personnel were given this sordid task, many admitting that they were not given protective equipment and had to recycle cadaver bags.

The ARMM 24/7 hotline tallied 1,333 rescued and evacuated and 3,717 stranded cases throughout their five-month operation (Abdulhamid Alawi Jr., pers. comm., 14 September 2018). A news outlet pegged a low 170 rescued out of the estimated 2,000 people trapped (Fonbuena 2017a). JTF Ranao lists forty-seven civilians killed by ISIS militants and 978 militants killed (Romeo Brawner, pers. comm., 21 September 2018).

SECURITIZATION OF HUMANITARIAN ASSISTANCE

The pattern of displacement following the Marawi crisis peaked two weeks after the Basak Malutlut shootout. Evacuees fled to the nearby Lanao del Sur towns of Pantar, Saguiaran, Pantingao, Pantao-Ragat and Munai, in Baloi (Lanao del Norte) and Iligan City as well as towards Malabang. Most IDPs were in Iligan City, of which roughly 90 per cent were home-based. The others were housed in four recognized evacuation centres (Iligan City School of Fisheries in Barangay Buruan and gymnasiums in Barangay Maria Cristina, Barangay Sta. Elena and Tibanga). As host, the Iligan City government felt pressure mount on its public services with the increasing number of evacuees and residual concern of ISIS fighters attacking their city. The Iligan City Police, tasked with operating the checkpoints in key highways and guarding vital installations (including the evacuation centres), received reinforcement from the National Capital Region. To document the home-based IDPs and ferret out ISIS fighters, the police conducted a census in each *barangay*, asking residents to present IDs and to profile those who fled from Marawi (*GMA News Online* 2017).

Humanitarian assistance poured into Iligan City and Lake Lanao towns. Among the organizations that mobilized and provided relief assistance early on was Philippine Red Cross (Iligan City chapter). Iligan City-based and other Mindanao-based NGOs like Balay Mindanaw and Kapamagogopa, with established credentials in responding to humanitarian crises in Lanao, also organized promptly.[6] Faith-based groups like the Diocese of Iligan and the Redemptorists also organized and delivered relief assistance to interior Lanao del Sur municipalities. The relief goods were mostly procured from Iligan City or Cagayan de Oro or bought and shipped on-site.

The army did not have a good reputation in Marawi and Lanao provinces, to begin with, and many locals viewed the Marawi operation in conspiratorial terms. In any case, the military also provided direct humanitarian assistance to civilians. During the first week of the crisis, soldiers were sent to evacuation sites in Saguiaran town. Under Task Group *Tabang* ("Help") (TG *Tabang*), the military acted as conduits of relief donations to evacuees. They channelled relief goods, undertook psycho-social interventions and embedded female soldiers and police officers (called "hijab troopers" because they wore headscarves with their camouflage uniforms) in the evacuation camps. The military's involvement in providing direct assistance to civilians was premised on the need to shore up legitimacy for the troops' combat activities in the MBA and prevent public sympathy for the Maute group (Jo-ar Herrera, pers. comm., 20 February 2018). Colonel Thomas Sedano, then commander for TG *Tabang*, admitted that the army does not traditionally deal with service delivery but that there was a deliberate effort to locate their non-combat activities in areas where known service-delivery gaps exist (pers. comm., 20 April 2018). As part of the army's counter-propaganda, TG *Tabang* distributed leaflets at the MBA, set up a Radio Ranao programme in Iligan City to provide updates on military activities, provided transistor radios to IDPs in evacuation centres and worked with camp managers to have residents listen during the programme time slot. As destruction and fatalities from the combat operations mounted, the troops at the evacuation centres were supposed to act as gauges of the extent of civilian support, checking and registering sentiment on soldiers and the Maute fighters.

The military was able to obtain material and logistical support from Manila-based NGOs, doctors and civil society groups they had previous relationships with and from the corporate social responsibility (CSR) arms of major companies, including San Miguel, Asia Brewery and Aboitiz. Many of these donations were directed to soldiers, but TG *Tabang* donated any surplus to ARMM HEART. Deputy Commander Jose Cuerpo of the 101 Brigade, who headed TG *Ayuda* ("help"), said they received significant donations of food, drinks and hygiene kits and medicine for the soldiers that were delivered directly to the HQ (pers. comm., 19 April 2018). A Maranao male enlistee from an Army Signals Unit who operated at the MBA opined that the Marawi crisis was the best operation he participated in because they had good food, unlimited phone calls and internet access during combat operations.

Marawi residents and humanitarian service providers did not openly contest the setting up of checkpoints and the requirements for passes.

There appears to have been an accepted understanding that checkpoints were necessary for security (preventing ISIS fighters from coming into other cities and municipalities or accessing support from outside of Marawi) and that long queues and questioning by military personnel would be routine (Nawal 2017). While the notion that checkpoints are "dragnets" for ISIS elements was not questioned, there was one occasion when the military prevented a leftist group with Satur Ocampo from entering Marawi, even though the group maintained that they were going there to deliver relief goods. The military officers were candid that they made distinctions between friendly and hostile groups and did not hesitate to use their control over checkpoints to prevent the latter from inciting agitation (pers. comm., 20 April 2018). The military considered the checkpoints at Saguiaran and Marawi critical, given the high risk presented by stray bullets from the MBA. There was a case where humanitarian assistance intended for the evacuees was sequestered at the checkpoint. Military officers observed, however, that there was no one orchestrating deliveries and no clear guidance about the level of local government (*barangay*, municipality, city or province) with which the military had to coordinate.

The checkpoints and the raids were spaces of dissent. Several NGO representatives interviewed cited cases of rude treatment by soldiers at a checkpoint, of soldiers imposing additional checks (e.g., needing additional calls for verification), which caused delays, or soldiers insisting on opening packages. The military, in turn, complained about stubborn people who did not have passes but nonetheless demanded entry. The response to complaints was to have checkpoint personnel wear a mounted camera on their helmet to record vehicles and passengers, lest they be accused of misbehaving.

Complaints were raised about alleged looting by soldiers. The command response was to issue a directive requiring military personnel to turn over items found inside the MBA. A shakedown and inspection of personnel and company properties, especially vehicles exiting the MBA, were implemented. Officers interviewed by the author argued that outright corrective action was made for every complaint. The officers confirmed one case of looting but did not publicize the disciplinary action taken against the personnel involved. Items found in the MBA (e.g., furniture, motorcycles) were placed in the JTG Ranao office for owners to retrieve (Romeo Brawner Jr., pers. comm., 27 February 2018).

ANALYSIS

The Marawi Siege illustrates the inherent tensions between local civilian authorities and military leaders, framed within a discordant understanding of informal power and clan relations. As in many places in the Bangsamoro territory, Marawi has long hosted multiple army units and has had an institutional framework for civil-military interface through the *Kasalimbago* (Maranao word for "reform") since 2012 and local monitoring team protocols (for elections, disaster and ceasefire). *Kasalimbago* is a coalition of civil society organizations (CSO) and government agencies, including the 103rd Infantry Brigade in Marawi. Under former commander Brigadier General Daniel Lucero, the brigade had fruitful engagements with Lanao del Sur-based CSO groups in *Brigada Eskwela* (preopening school clean up and repair) and in monitoring local elections (*SunStar* 2013). As proof of its continuity, *Kasalimbago* had worked with the military in monitoring elections at Butig town, which the Maute laid siege to in 2016 (Basman and Alfonso 2016). However, these institutional mechanisms and the social capital gained from years of engagements were not harnessed when critical decisions had to be made in the early stages of the conflict. Save for Western Mindanao Commander General Galvez, whose previous stint was head of the government's Committee on the Cessation of Hostilities, and Lieutenant Colonel Romeo Brawner Jr., none of the Maranao local government leaders found a receptive ear within the military. It appeared to the Maranao leaders that their motives were distrusted; their offers to reach out to the Mautes for a negotiated end to the conflict and civilian rescue inside the MBA were seen as selling out to help their kin. While communication lines were open between the military commanders and local officials, the primacy of military objectives over other considerations was strongly conveyed.

Could more civilian lives have been saved by prolonging volunteer rescue efforts at the MBA? Should mosques have been spared from assault? Can the asymmetry in capabilities for urban warfare be addressed only with shelling and aerial bombardment? One officer interviewed simply argued, "It was war." In war, normative and textbook assumptions on stakeholder engagement were held to not apply. Admittedly, the declaration of martial law also made the local power holders less assertive, as they feared being targets of firearms confiscation.

Perhaps this points to the limits of institutional frames for civil-military engagements. They work for low-intensity conflict situations and short-duration armed operations like many previously experienced by people from Lanao provinces. But there was little room for manoeuvre for a full-blown war, like the Marawi siege, where the military was sustaining heavy losses.

When the shelling and aerial bombardment commenced, the military put its civil-military operations in high gear because it needed public support for the troops and validation for the military objective. The deployment of *hijab* troopers in evacuation centres and the independent relief provisioning carried out by the CMO group was pathbreaking for the military institution. While there had been sporadic experiences of military units penetrating Muslim communities for development projects and *rido* settlement, these engagements had been typically rife with challenges. The military's role in humanitarian assistance following a disaster was usually limited to logistics and providing security. Thus, the Marawi war expanded the military's role in the conflict area into direct humanitarian provisioning, further skewing the balance of power in favour of the military.

Civil-military engagements during the Marawi crisis were spatially and functionally segregated. By separating the MBA and the CA, the military was able to carry on its armed operations against the militants while civilian actors addressed the humanitarian needs of the displaced. In both spaces, the military set the terms for civilian mobility by requiring vehicle passes and identification cards for humanitarian workers and Marawi residents. Relief logistics were inevitably militarized because the same road was used for the military's supply line for combat operations in the MBA. Humanitarian actors did not contest these prerogatives, mainly because there was acceptance of the need for security measures during a war and the military's legal remit to do so under martial law. Complaints about maltreatment at checkpoints were articulated and addressed but were generally of low salience.

The military also determined when and under what circumstances civilians would be able to return to their residences. The *kambalingan* (return) and *kambisita* (visits) occurred within the military's time frame and risk assessments, weighing in concerns about potential support for the ISIS militants. As firearms were seized at checkpoints and raids were unannounced, civilians who remained or travelled to and from Marawi also had to submit to searches and questioning, even when they already had a permit or pass. For Maranaos, who are culturally stereotyped as having a strong sense of *maratabat* (honour) and being status-conscious (there are families descended from royal lineages), these are impositions which could only be tolerated because of the necessities of martial law.

The coordination platforms for humanitarian provisioning followed separate civilian and military streams. Government agencies worked within the PCMC and NEOC, while NGOs followed the UN cluster and sector-based platforms. From interviews, it appears that NGOs did not see any value in attending NEOC and PCMC meetings, nor did they influence their activities or take measures to inform these bodies about their deliveries. The only interaction with NEOC was to obtain the vehicle pass. Save for a few cases, local non-government humanitarian providers interviewed did not work with the military for logistics or security. While several Iligan-based NGOs had prior working relationships with units from the Mechanized Brigade, their representatives argued that they felt it unnecessary to burden the military for logistics support when they are busy fighting. The military labelled humanitarian organizations variously as "left", "yellow-linked" (connected with the opposition Liberal Party leaders) and "friendlies" (NGOs with whom the military had a good relationship) and dealt with them correspondingly. The military did their own relief provisioning, drawing from their pool of private donors. The CMOCC was akin to a "pier" upon which select, deep-pocket donors from Manila sending food and non-food items landed.

The Marawi war also points to institutional learning curves for the military and local civil society actors. The military personnel generally behaved well in dealing with civilians at checkpoints, clearing operations and rescue operations. The decision to have a separate platform to deliver information and updates about military operations and security protocols, paralleling humanitarian updates on the government side by PCMC, was a welcome innovation. Periodic consultations with local authorities and representatives of displaced Marawi communities allowed orderly return and visits to the MBA. Rather than dismissing allegations of looting by soldiers, the military responded by instituting screening measures into and out of the MBA for its personnel and putting up a lost-and-found corner for items found in the MBA. However, the military was less forthcoming when it came to the issue of civilian deaths and missing persons. No official tally has ever been provided for this, except for the number of civilians (forty-five) killed by ISIS militants. There are 329 graves in the Marawi cemetery from remains collected at the battle site, but the majority have not been identified (Arguillas 2022).

Local civil society actors have shown signs of maturity. Established NGOs with area-specific experience in advocacy and development work mobilized, as did faith-based organizations. Their activities penetrated interior communities and covered various services, including psychological interventions (Ilagan, this volume). Their work puts a premium on getting the approval and support of local authorities (*barangay* captains, municipal mayors and traditional leaders) where their activities were located. They worked within clusters and found merit in coordination to ensure services were distributed evenly across IDP communities.

CONCLUSION

Civil-military engagements during the Marawi crisis exhibited different tendencies from what has been previously observed in disaster response. Coordination platforms for humanitarian provisioning proceeded in two separate streams—military and civilian—with little interface between the two. The NEOC, PCMC and UN cluster system were functional, but the military did not subscribe to them. The military carried out independent and direct relief provisioning to generate public support for its combat mission. The armed operations at the MBA were paramount; thus, security measures in the CA were deemed necessary. Humanitarian activities throughout the CA and decisions on whether or not residents were allowed to return were securitized. Despite the culturally-sensitive and rule-based behaviour of military personnel in Marawi throughout the crisis, tensions with locals remain over the issues of looting and the missing or dead.

The end of formal fighting in October 2017 ushered in new arrangements and roles for the military in Marawi. With the extension of martial law in Mindanao until 31 December 2019, the military was deputized by the Department of Interior and Local Government to oversee the implementation of national government projects in Lanao del Sur province and keep an eye on the performance of mayors (Hall and Deinla 2021). The shift towards rehabilitation led by Task Force Bangon Marawi (TFBM) relegated the military to clearing debris and unexploded ordnance in the renamed main affected area. President Duterte's declaration establishing a ten-hectare second military camp in the cleared area did not sit well with locals, who argued that they would lose their land claims. There was strong local opposition to the national government's rehabilitation plan, which prioritized the reconstruction of public roads, utilities and buildings. Complaints over insufficient funds for temporary shelter construction and the slow pace of the clearing operations (less than half of the area had been cleared from unexploded ordnance) are resonant. In April 2022, Congress passed the Marawi Compensation Law and committed one billion pesos (US$18.33 million) to compensate war victims, including those who lost private properties. The Bangsamoro referendum in January 2019 and the 2022 national and local elections were carried out in the city with few violent incidents. The dominant Adiong clan retained control over local government seats. The fulcrum of post-Marawi war politics has shifted to a fight by local civil society groups like the Marawi Reconstruction Conflict Watch to keep rehabilitation and victim compensation on top of the national government's myriad priorities. The 103rd Brigade, which has gone on to capture remnants of the Daesh group and now has more muscle within the peace and order council, has shifted attention to getting civilian government agents into its campaign against youth radicalization. The long shadow of the Marawi Siege continues to inform local politics.

Notes

1. The author wishes to acknowledge funding from Philippine Project of the Australian National University for this research.
2. The 2008 MOA-AD crisis affected large numbers of Lanao del Norte towns and generated displacements toward coastal areas (Kolambugan, Kauswagan,

Maigo). Following retooling of the Army's counterinsurgency strategy in 2010, there had been more positive military-civil society engagements in these areas within the AOR of the 1st Mechanized Battalion (Hall 2017, pp. 66–67).
3. According to the Chief of Police Ebra Moxsir, the remaining Marawi policemen were rotated to serve in other areas of ARMM. He argued that this was done because the local Marawi police were ineffective given the prevalence of *rido* or clan fighting in the area.
4. Lanao del Sur is home to many private armed groups controlled by mayors. One critical point for discussion between the military and local leaders was whether the military would "strictly enforce" martial law and confiscate illegal firearms attached to these mayors. Attorney Naguib Sinarimbo (personal communication, 16 September 2018) who was present at these exchanges, and also the two mayors interviewed by the author, noted that the mayors needed means to protect themselves against ISIS militants; and that given the military's strained resources (from fighting in Marawi), that it was more pragmatic to allow the PAGs to take on this self-defence task.
5. The area around the Provincial Capitol and the 101st Brigade headquarters (at Signal Hill) was considered a safe zone.
6. Many of the NGOs who provided direct assistance to IDPs have been around since the flooding disaster that hit Iligan City in 2011 and the 2008 MOA-AD conflict.

References

Adam, Jeroen, and Boris Verbrugge. 2014. "Informal Conflict Management in Exclusivist Political Orders: Some Observations on Central Mindanao". *ASEAS – Austrian Journal of South-East Asian Studies* 7, no. 1: 61–74.

Adam, Jeroen, Boris Verbrugge, and Dorien Vanden Boer. 2014. "Peacemaking and State-Society Interactions in Conflict-torn Mindanao, Philippines". Justice and Security Research Programme (JSRP) Paper 18. London: London School of Economics.

Adam, Jeroen, and Dorien Vanden Boer. 2015. "Conflict Mediation and Traditional Authority in the Province of Lanao del Sur, Mindanao". Justice and Security Research Programme (JSRP) Paper 26. London: London School of Economics.

Agence France-Presse. 2017. "Broken Truce Ends Bid to Free Civilians in Marawi". *Straits Times*, 5 June 2017. http://www.straitstimes.com/asia/broken-truce-ends-bid-to-free-civilians-in-marawi (accessed 27 September 2017).

Amnesty International. 2017. *The Battle of Marawi: Death and Destructions of Marawi City.* https://www.amnesty.org/en/documents/asa35/7427/2017/en/ (accessed 10 November 2017).

Ansis, JC. 2016. "Butig Clashes: What We Know So Far". *CNN Philippines*, 2 March 2016. https://www.cnnphilippines.com/regional/2016/03/02/Butig-Lanao-del-Sur-clashes-Maute-group.html (accessed 14 February 2023).

Arguillas, Carolyn. 2017. "Preparing for the Worst in Marawi: From Rescue to Retrieval". *MindaNews*, 11 June 2017. http://www.mindanews.com/top-stories/2017/06/preparing-for-the-worst-in-marawi-from-rescue-to-retrieval/ (accessed 27 September 2017).

———. 2022. "The Graveyard of the Unidentified: 5 Years after Marawi's 'Liberation'". *MindaNews*, 23 October 2022. https://www.mindanews.com/top-stories/2022/10/the-graveyard-of-the-unidentified-5-years-after-marawis-liberation/ (accessed 16 January 2023).

Arugay, Aries. 2008. "Linking Security Sector Reform to Peacebuilding and Development in the Philippines: A Best Practice Case". *Journal of Peacebuilding & Development* 4, no. 2: 100–105.

Basman, Anna Tasmin, and Derkie Alfonso. 2016. "Amid Tensions, Lanao's Butig Municipality Holds Violence-Free Elections". *The Asia Foundation InAsia Insight and Analysis*, 11 May 2016. https://asiafoundation.org/2016/05/11/amid-tensions-lanaos-butig-municipality-holds-violence-free-election/ (accessed 16 January 2023).

Cagoco-Guiam, Rufa, and Steven Schoofs. 2013. "A Deadly Cocktail? Illicit Drugs, Politics and Violent Conflict in Lanao del Sur and Maguindanao". In *Out of the Shadows: Violent Conflict and the Real Economy of Mindanao*, edited by Francisco Lara and Steven Schoofs, pp. 85–117. London: International Alert.

Deveans, Thomas, Ronald Fricker, Jeffrey Appleget, Ben Cipperley, and Jonathan Alt. 2013. *Southern Philippines Public Perception Survey (SPPPS) Exploration and Analysis.* Monterey: TRADOC Analysis Center. https://apps.dtic.mil/sti/pdfs/ADA587718.pdf (accessed 2 February 2018)

Fonbuena, Carmela. 2017a. "Hundreds Still Trapped in Marawi as Crisis Enters 3rd Week". *Rappler*, 6 June 2017. https://www.rappler.com/nation/172084-marawi-tension-hostages-residents-impatient (accessed 14 February 2023).

———. 2017b. "Terror in Mindanao: The Mautes of Marawi". *Rappler*, 26 June 2017. https://www.rappler.com/newsbreak/in-depth/173697-terrorism-mindanao-maute-family-marawi-city/ (accessed 20 December 2022).

———. 2017c. "The War in Marawi: 153 Days and More". *Rappler*, 23 October 2017. https://www.rappler.com/newsbreak/in-depth/186075-marawi-series-rappler-timeline/ (accessed 14 February 2023).

———. 2020. *Marawi Siege: Stories from the Front Line.* Pasig City: Journalism for Nation Building Foundation.

GMA News Online. 2017. "AFP, PNP Do House to House Inspection in Iligan to Look For Possible Terrorists". 29 June 2017. http://www.gmanetwork.com/news/news/nation/616282/afp-pnp-do-house-to-house-inspection-in-iligan-to-look-for-possible-terrorists/story/ (accessed 2 February 2018).

―――. 2018. "'Suicide Squad' of Marawi Honored in US for Outstanding Rescue Work". 21 August 2018. https://www.gmanetwork.com/news/pinoyabroad/pinoyachievers/664937/suicide-squad-of-marawi-honored-in-us-for-outstanding-rescue-work/story// (accessed 18 February 2023).

Hall, Rosalie Arcala. 2016. "Guardians Reinvented: The Philippine Army's Non-Traditional Engagements in Panay Island, Philippines". *Philippine Political Science Journal* 37, no. 2: 135–58.

―――. 2017. "Maguindanao and Lanao del Norte: Civil-Military Engagements in a Contested Zone". In *Local Security in the Contested Bangsamoro Zone: Informality, Hybridity and Pragmatic Imperatives*, edited by Rosalie Arcala Hall, pp. 51–90. Manila: The Asia Foundation.

―――. 2018. "Civil-Military Relations: Norming and Departures". In *Routledge Handbook of Contemporary Philippines*, edited by Mark Thompson and Eric Vincent Batalla, pp. 144–58. New York: Routledge.

―――. 2020. "Recalibrating Counterinsurgency with Development Interventions: PAMANA Road Construction Projects and Their Effects on Civil-Military Dynamics in Samar Province". Philippine Political Science Association Visayas Regional Conference Proceedings, 26 August 2022, pp. 1–29.

Hall, Rosalie Arcala, and Imelda Deinla. 2021. "Shifts in the Humanitarian Space: Examining NGO-Military Engagements during the 2017 Crisis in Marawi, Philippines". *Asian Politics & Policy* 13, no. 3: 349–65.

Hall, Rosalie Arcala, and Juhn Chris Espia. 2015. "The Response to Typhoon Haiyan". In *Frameworks and Partnerships: Improving HA/DR in the Asia Pacific*, edited by Charles Aanenson and Jon Ehrenfeld, pp. 31–124. USA: Peace Winds America.

Ilagan, Gail Tan. 2014. "Multi-Stakeholder Security Strategies that De-escalate Armed Violence in Mindanao". *Open Journal of Social Science Research* 2, no. 3: 78–86.

Ishii, Mashako. 2017. "Interview with Assemblyman Zia Alonto Adiong". *Asia Peacebuilding Initiatives*, 14 September 2017. http://peacebuilding.asia/interview-with-assemblyman-zia-alonto-adiong/ (accessed 16 May 2018).

Jerusalem, Jigger J., and Richel V. Umel. 2017. "2 Maute Group Leaders Killed in Lanao del Sur Clashes – Army". *INQUIRER.net*, 25 April 2017. https://newsinfo.inquirer.net/891972/2-maute-group-leaders-killed-in-lanao-del-sur-clashes-army (accessed 25 September 2018).

Jones, Sidney. 2018. "Radicalisation in the Philippines: The Cotabato Cell of the 'East Asia Wilayah'". *Terrorism and Political Violence* 30, no. 6: 933–43. https://doi.org/10.1080/09546553.2018.1481190 (accessed 14 February 2023).

Kiba, Saya, and Rosalie Arcala Hall. 2014. "Regional Cooperation on Civil-Military Coordination in Disaster Response – Crisis or Opportunity?" In *Security Sector Reform: Modern Defense Force*, edited by Jennifer Santiago-Oreta, pp. 155–74. Quezon City: Ateneo de Manila University.

Lagsa, Bobby. 2017. "Trapped in Marawi, Muslims Shield Christians from Terrorists". *Rappler*, 4 June 2017. https://www.rappler.com/nation/171901-civilians-rescued-marawi-muslims-protecting-christians (accessed 29 September 2018).

Nawal, Allan. 2017. "Checkpoint Passes a Must to Guard vs Terror – AFP". *Philippine Daily Inquirer*, 26 October 2017. http://newsinfo.inquirer.net/940538/checkpoint-passes-a-must-to-guard-vs-terror-afp (accessed 26 October 2017).

Özerdem, Alpaslan, and Sukanya Podder. 2012. "Grassroots and Rebellion: A Study on the Future of the Moro Struggle in Mindanao, Philippines". *Civil Wars* 14, no. 4: 521–45.

PIA (Philippine Information Agency). 2017. "OPAPP Sec, Marawi Crisis Management Committee Work On Mechanism to Ensure Onetime Delivery of Relief to Civilians". 7 June 2017. https://reliefweb.int/report/philippines/opapp-sec-marawi-crisis-management-committee-work-mechanism-ensure-time-delivery (accessed 27 September 2017).

Ramakrishna, Kumar. 2018. "The Radicalization of Abu Hamdie: Wider Lessons for the Ongoing Struggle against Violent Extremism in Post-Marawi Mindanao". *Journal of Asian Security and International Affairs* 5, no. 2: 111–28.

Remitio, Rex. 2016. "Maute Group Holds Lanao Town under Siege". *CNN Philippines*, 27 November 2016. http://cnnphilippines.com/news/2016/11/28/Maute-Lanao-del-Sur-siege.html (accessed 25 September 2018).

Russell, Delilah Ruth. 2013. "Civil Military Operations (CMO) in the Philippines: Examining Battlespace Management in the Past and the Present". PhD dissertation, Graduate School of Asia-Pacific Studies, Japan.

Sabilo, Kristine Angeli. 2017. "Duterte Oks PH-MILF 'Peace Corridor' for Marawi". *INQUIRER.net*, 31 May 2017. http://newsinfo.inquirer.net/901245/duterte-oks-ph-milf-peace-corridor-for-marawi (accessed 27 September 2017).

Searle, Martin. 2017. "Martial Law and Trust: Humanitarian Challenges in Marawi". *RSIS Commentary*, 21 September 2017. https://www.rsis.edu.sg/rsis-publication/nts/co17173-martial-law-and-trust-humanitarian-challenges-in-marawi/#.Y9qsvHBBy3B (accessed 2 February 2023).

Sombatpoonsiri, Janjira. 2018. "Securing Peace? Regime Types and Security Sector Reform in the Patani (Thailand) and Bangsamoro (the Philippines) Peace Processes, 2011–2016". *Strategic Analysis* 42, no. 4: 377–401. https://doi.org/10.1080/09700161.2018.1482628 (accessed 14 February 2023).

SunStar. 2013. "Comelec Successful in Cleansing Voters List in Lanao del Sur". 28 January 2013. https://www.sunstar.com.ph/article/267260/comelec-successful-in-cleansing-voters-list-in-lanao-del-sur (accessed 16 January 2023).

_____. 2016. "Lanao del Sur Mayor, Ex-Mayor Linked to Drugs Surrender". 5 August 2016. https://www.sunstar.com.ph/article/90150 (accessed 26 September 2018).

_____. 2017. "Duterte: Narco Politicians 'Main Protagonists' in Marawi Crisis". 23 September 2017. https://www.sunstar.com.ph/article/165648 (accessed 26 September 2018).

UNOCHA (UN Office for the Coordination of Humanitarian Affairs). 2017. "Philippines: Marawi Armed Conflict 3W (as of 12 October 2017)". https://reliefweb.int/report/philippines/philippines-marawi-armed-conflict-3w-12-october-2017 (accessed 14 February 2023).

Yabes, Criselda. 2020. *The Battle of Marawi*. Davao City: Pawikan Press.

13

Emergency Mental Health and Psychosocial Support Provision for Marawi's Internally Displaced Persons

Gail Tan Ilagan

INTRODUCTION

When the Marawi crisis broke out on 23 May 2017, it set off a mass evacuation of Marawi residents to Iligan City and its immediate environs. By mid-June, the number of internally displaced persons (IDPs) was shaping into an alarming humanitarian crisis, with many residents from towns neighbouring Marawi evacuating. The displacement data as of 18 June 2017 placed the IDP figures at 338,536, with only 17,891 (5.28 per cent) housed in formal evacuation centres (NDRRMC 2017a). Caught flat-footed by the scale of the Marawi evacuees pouring into their jurisdiction, local governments were not ready to set up evacuation centres to host the displaced. While local government units have arrangements to address disaster- and emergency-related evacuations for their constituents, there are no protocols for hosting those coming in from adjoining municipalities. Thus, Marawi evacuees sought shelter among relatives if they could not find rentals. By April 2018, home-based IDPs tracked by the Department of Social Welfare and Development (DSWD) were dispersed in eight regions (DSWD-DROMIC 2018). One of the issues exposed by the Marawi crisis was the need to take a more coordinated, civil society-oriented approach to support the mental health needs of those affected by conflict and humanitarian crises.

Since 2010, the implementing rules and regulations (IRR) for Republic Act 10121 or the Philippine Disaster Risk Reduction and Management Act have required the Department of Health (DOH), the lead agency tasked to address post-disaster health, to address public mental health concerns (*Official Gazette* 2010). Since the law was promulgated, succeeding disasters forced the DOH to constantly adjust its policies and lines of coordination in an attempt to find the perfect fit. However, while the public mental health approach in humanitarian settings is advised (Szabo 2015), the DOH remains inadequately staffed for emergency mental health and psychosocial support (MHPSS) services. It relies mainly on the Department of Education (DepEd) and DSWD, United Nations (UN) agencies and international non-government organizations (INGOs) to deliver MHPSS in times of emergency and disaster situations. Local MHPSS clusters consistently fail to harness the resources of many home-grown organizations. It was not until after the 2013 Typhoon Haiyan tragedy in Eastern Visayas that the public health sector and its partner INGOs admitted to needing the help of other stakeholders, especially those that can employ more indigenous methods that may be more culturally appropriate (Asia-Europe Meeting 2014).

Early in the Marawi crisis, the DOH set up the Health Quad Cluster (for health, water, sanitation and hygiene [WASH], nutrition and MHPSS) and located its operation centre in Iligan City. By early June, the first three clusters were already operational. However, the DOH had yet to assemble the personnel for emergency MHPSS and disseminate information on the core MHPSS principles laid down by the National Disaster Risk Reduction and Management Council (NDRRMC) Memorandum No. 62, issued on 17 April 2017. Meanwhile, independent MHPSS responders were mobilizing resources and activating their networks to assist the IDPs. Among these were the Psychological Association of the Philippines and the Davao-based Center of Psychological Extension and Research Services (COPERS). COPERS, in particular, has a track record for researching the cultural context of disasters towards designing appropriate and peace-centred interventions for enhanced community resilience.

Weeks after the DOH Operations Centre was set up, it still could not deliver an MHPSS response. The inter-agency coordination, monitoring and evaluation system was grindingly slow in linking up with independent groups actively engaging the evacuees. But some among the twenty-five groups that signed the terms of reference for the MHPSS Cluster began needs assessments in the evacuation centres and reported results at the next meeting on 24 June 2017. They cited problems such as language barriers between MHPSS providers and IDPs and a lack of appropriate materials, space and venue for the conduct of MHPSS activities. They also reported that the IDPs were "already exhausted" and unwilling to participate. The DOH Operations Centre stated that independent MHPSS providers were not submitting the names of referred cases with mental health problems. The DOH lacked trained personnel for MHPSS work (DOH-HEMB 2017).

On the ground, the clamour for the delivery of psychosocial services was starting to get loud. By July, government officials took up the public mental health concern for the war-displaced in Marawi, Iligan and the Lanao provinces (Santos 2017; Doyo 2017; Tamayo 2017). They warned of dire psychiatric consequences should the trauma experience of the evacuees continue to be ignored.

But were mental health services really absent in the emergency humanitarian response to the Marawi crisis? I argue that they were not. Instead, they were not reflected in the official figures. Thus, I set out in this chapter to fill the glaring gap in the official reports and to explain why certain MHPSS activities were not captured in official reports. This review of MHPSS provision to Marawi IDPs examines data from the periodic bulletins issued by the Health Quad Cluster from June to October 2017 and data from the 5 August 2017 MHPSS

Best Practices forum among humanitarian response actors. It also draws from the field reports submitted by the MHPSS teams deployed by COPERS, supplemented by my experience directing the Task Force for the Psychological Association of the Philippines' Response to the Marawi Crisis, as well as from lessons learned in responding to previous disaster events.

THE MHPSS PROVIDERS

The official MHPSS Cluster on Marawi Emergency Response was activated on 11 June 2017 upon the arrival of the World Health Organization (WHO) personnel at the DOH Operations Centre. Discussions during its initial meeting on 24 June 2017, which I attended, harped on the "lack of clarity related to the number and categories of MHPSS workers, both government and non-government, who have been providing interventions *in evacuation camps*" (emphasis added). The needs of the home-based evacuees were not discussed. From the start, the concern of the MHPSS Cluster was focused on only the 5.6 per cent of Marawi IDPs housed in evacuation centres.

There were twenty-seven organizations listed in the MHPSS Cluster on Marawi Emergency Response, including six government agencies, three UN agencies, four INGOs, three local academic entities, three national NGOs, and eight local NGOs. Section V of the MHPSS Cluster Marawi Emergency Response Terms of Reference (TOR) specified that the cluster would be chaired by two government lead agencies. The Iligan City Health Office (CHO) was to be the cluster head for interventions within Iligan City. At the same time, the Integrated Provincial Health Office (IPHO) of Lanao del Sur was the cluster head for interventions outside Iligan City. Both clusters were to be co-led by the WHO, suggesting that the lead agencies needed a nursemaid on the matter of MHPSS response.

Moreover, the TOR also stated that the MHPSS Cluster articulated with both the Protection and Education Clusters. In particular, the MHPSS Cluster was to link up with the Child Protection Working Group and Gender-Based Violence Sub Cluster in areas of common interest. Thus, the chairs of the MHPSS Cluster were expected to participate in Protection Cluster meetings and provide feedback on main intercluster developments.

The setting up of two MHPSS Cluster lead agencies and the requirement of their participation in the meetings of both the Protection and Education Clusters, as well as participating in the activities of the Child Protection Working Group and the Gender-Based Violence Sub Cluster, left very little time for the MHPSS Cluster to see to MHPSS delivery among the IDPs.

Not many member organizations of the MHPSS Cluster have a regular MHPSS programme that refers to the first three layers (Tiers 1–3) of non-specialized support. Such support is crucial to reducing the risk for the population affected by trauma and acute stress to develop chronic mental illnesses.

Following the UN Inter-Agency Standing Committee MHPSS pyramid (IASC 2007, p. 12),

- Tier 1 refers to services that include advocacy for MHPSS delivery by responsible actors, documentation of the impact on mental health and psychosocial well-being, and guidance for delivery of participative interventions to promote mental health and psychosocial well-being.
- Tier 2 involves enhancing family and community support to those that need services such as family tracing and reunification, assisted mourning and communal healing ceremonies, mass communication on constructive coping methods, supportive parenting programmes, formal and non-formal educational activities, livelihood activities and the activation of social networks, such as through women's groups and youth organizations.
- Tier 3 involves non-specialized support for a smaller number of people that need focused individual, family or group interventions for psychological first aid or basic mental health care by trained and supervised workers.

Tiers 1 through 3 are non-pharmacological interventions that need to be delivered in the wake of a disaster.

Iligan CHO and Lanao del Sur PHO can provide Tier 4 services that refer to specialized mental health services and access to psychotropic drugs. Usually, such services are needed by less than 5 per cent of disaster-affected populations. Those that have the capability for Tiers 1–3 services are the INGOs and UN organizations. They, however, come from outside the affected area. They took time to get their bearings and set up shop before they could operate for MHPSS provision. They had to negotiate entry into affected communities for needs assessment before they could deploy the resources required to address these needs.

For over a month, the more mobile community-based groups carried the burden of emergency MHPSS provision to evacuees in the formal evacuation centres and outside these. But while these groups had the advantage of ready access to the affected populations, they had limited resources to sustain the work. Thus, they needed to raise funds. By July, their attendance at coordination meetings called by the DOH was dwindling. They opted instead to use their time for sourcing logistical support, checking up on the IDPs within their reach, and providing whatever stop-gap assistance they could. MHPSS service provision was indeed fragmented and piecemeal.

By late June 2017, the IDP figures breached the 380,000 mark, with less than 6 per cent housed in formal evacuation centres (NDRRMC 2017b). As the situation worsened in the following weeks, even government agencies tasked to coordinate with the MHPSS Cluster became notably absent from the weekly DOH Quad Cluster meetings. The dwindling attendance suggested that the MHPSS Cluster was not serving as "the reference body for coordination, guidelines development, technical advice, and oversight of MHPSS services in affected areas", as stipulated in the MHPSS Cluster Marawi Emergency Response TOR.

DISCUSSION

The invisibility of MHPSS services to public health humanitarian response authorities stemmed from the lag in activating the MHPSS Cluster, the lack of public health personnel to deliver Tiers 1–3 psychosocial support services and the failure of the DOH to sustain its link with the civilian stakeholders who carried on despite the lack of government support. I also take note of the limitations of the MHPSS Cluster's mandate to serve only those in the formal evacuation centres. The MHPSS Cluster did not have a protocol to support IDPs who were not in government-designated evacuation centres.

Through all the community disasters I have responded to since 2011, I have observed that the MHPSS Cluster is often the last cluster in the Incident Command System to be activated for disaster response. For Marawi, it took more than two weeks.

In 2014, the DOH trained its Mindanao personnel extensively in a bid to scale up public health services for mental, neurological and substance use disorders. However, the agency admits that it still lacks the personnel to deliver non-pharmacological interventions for general populations affected by man-made or natural hazard-induced disasters. During one of the discussions of the Technical Working Group for the crafting of the Davao City Mental Health ordinance in July 2017, DOH Region XI psychiatrist Reagan Villanueva explained how hard it is for the DOH to deliver stand-alone MHPSS services for disaster response. Trained for Tier 4 services (to assess and treat mental health disorders for individual clients), he admitted that he did not know what to do during a post-Typhoon Bopha medical mission in early 2012 because the IDPs that showed up needed Tiers 1–3 services. He mused that whoever set up the humanitarian health clusters lacked an understanding of what MHPSS is about.

Villanueva may indeed be right because the Notes for the Record sent out on the 3rd DOH Region X Quad Cluster Meeting for the Marawi crisis held on 27 June 2017 detailed that "Interventions which are mainly to address the basic needs of the IDPs (hygiene kits, dignity kits, etc.) will be considered as provision of Psychological First Aid." This glib definition of a core MHPSS activity, officially put out by the DOH, prompted psychologists to raise an incredulous howl. If the DOH did not know how to define interventions "to protect or promote psychosocial well-being and/or prevent or treat mental disorder" (IASC 2007, p. 11), how could it be a competent reference body for coordination, guidelines development, technical advice and oversight of MHPSS services in the affected areas?

In another meeting on the proposed Davao City Mental Health ordinance on 13 May 2017, Villanueva opined that it is improper for the MHPSS services to be designated as a stand-alone cluster. Instead, he said that MHPSS should be embedded in the service delivery of the other clusters that provide material support. This would indeed be reasonable, as it is during psychosocial support activities that the distressed communities air what they perceive to be their unmet needs. The persistence of these life stressors is a barrier to their return to normalcy (Budosan et al. 2016). Thus, it is not enough that the distressed populations are given the venue to vent their concerns, which is part of what psychosocial support services do for them. Concretely addressing these needs would alleviate their experience of felt difficulties (Ilagan et al. 2016). This could only be done when the emergency clusters responsible for providing these material needs promptly proceed from the information supplied by MHPSS service providers.

Stand-alone MHPSS services are indeed limited. Psychosocial responders may come to know what the evacuees need, but they cannot address these on their own. They need to coordinate with the designated Clusters for Health, WASH and Nutrition. Thus, in addition to reporting the what, where, when, who and how many MHPSS services to the DOH, there is also an urgent need to report the specific felt needs articulated by the affected population—and for this list to get to the mandated agencies in charge of meeting these needs. But even if responsible MHPSS providers were to report to the MHPSS Cluster what they discovered about their clients' needs, the information would not likely be acted upon by the agencies that control the distribution of relief goods.

In many instances, COPERS learned about the need for food distribution. While we reported this to the MHPSS Cluster, the information did not influence the distribution schedule set by the DSWD. This burden of information leaves many responsible psychosocial responders no practical and ethical recourse but to source the appropriate materials themselves to meet the needs articulated by the IDPs during MHPSS activities. As it is, however, it is also true that there are local NGOs and social formations that claim to deliver psychosocial support activities for the sake of reporting on the number of clients served. They may have no interest in documenting the impact of their one-shot intervention, much less reporting the results to the MHPSS Cluster.

As the delay in the distribution of humanitarian relief dragged on—especially for home-based evacuees—COPERS approached the Office of Civil Defense (OCD) on 26 June 2017 in the hopes of working out an arrangement where COPERS's local partners could help distribute government relief to the communities we were servicing. Earlier, COPERS had augmented its psychosocial services with meagre material support cadged from various donors, but the wellspring of goodwill was beginning to dry up by late June 2017. By then, we had an indication from the home-based IDPs we worked with that the continued denial of government provisions was a sore point for them. We thought it best to appeal to the OCD to firm up our partnership in this manner, in keeping with the intention of RA 10121 to "strengthen local capacities to manage disasters by institutionalising the involvement of civil society organisations (CSOs) and the private sector to complement government resources".

However, government regulations would not allow channelling government supplies through non-government entities. Government support could only be coursed through the designated evacuation centres. We were caught in a circle of futility, with the OCD advising us to coordinate with the place we started, the DOH Quad Cluster. We knew this arrangement would not speed up the delivery of material support and alleviate some distress felt by the IDPs we were serving.

We had learned early on from our response to Typhoon Washi in 2011 and Typhoon Bopha in 2012 that psychosocial support sessions ended on a lighter note, and follow-up sessions were more welcome, when we could somehow provide some token of the material requirements of the IDPs (Ilagan, Timonera and Benitez 2012). From Psychological First Aid sessions among home-based Marawi evacuees, our teams were able to draw up a list of essentials that evacuees had problems accessing. We sent this "wish list" to our donors with a prayer that they would not succumb to donor fatigue. However, the OCD would again cause us some operational problems when it issued its advisory in late June, just days after the agency turned down our offer to distribute relief on its behalf. Some potential donors who received the text blast from the OCD found it a reason to close their purse strings. The advisory read:

> ATTENTION: To all Donors for MARAWI CRISIS or for any other NATURAL DISASTER/HUMAN INDUCED DISASTER that would likely occur in the future. Kindly coordinate first with DSWD and DOH and other National Disaster Response Cluster Lead Member Agencies for your donations/assistance. The Government has enough relief goods from local and if exhausted, we level up to regional then to national. When DSWD, DOH and other Disaster Response Cluster Lead Agencies assess that their reserved relief items are already depleting, then that's the time they may accept donations from NGOs (OCD, text message forwarded to the author, 29 June 2017).

There was no question about the adequacy of government supplies for humanitarian relief. There were surplus food packs in the evacuation centres—so much so that there was no more floor space for people to sleep (Nawal 2017). This situation happened because relief supplies intended for 600,000 could only be received by the 25,000 people who were (ironically) lucky enough not to have relatives who would take them in. As in disasters past, it was not a question of lack; it remained a problem of distribution (Ilagan 2012). The many more directly affected by the Marawi crisis but not in the evacuation centres were technically disenfranchised from accessing government support.

Because of the delay in activating the MHPSS Cluster and the lack of trained government personnel to deliver emergency MHPSS services, many of the Tiers 1–3 services were by default provided by CSOs, especially those already working in the communities affected by the disaster. However, the MHPSS Cluster consistently failed to connect with these CSOs. The problem, I think, is that the public health system has not been in the habit of linking with local resources. From experience, I have found that lead government agencies do not welcome volunteer psychologists or the CSOs or institutions they represent. Government functionaries seem to labour under the notion that CSOs cannot sustain their services and, thus, do not need to be mainstreamed in the MHPSS service provision. Public health officials are more accommodating of INGOs and UN agencies because they are perceived to have the resources to sustain their work and the time to attend long inter-agency meetings. Public health officials seem not to mind if these foreigners seldom have a grasp of the local context and culture. This was a reprise of the situation following Typhoon Bopha in 2013 when the DOH Region XI sent its MHPSS Team to set up the Davao Oriental MHPSS Cluster. Rather than tap the local expert base to consolidate community resources for MHPSS, the DOH preferred to host retired nurses from Europe and visiting university instructors from Indonesia to train its staff in psychosocial first aid.

As the Marawi crisis further deteriorated, the Duterte administration pointedly refused to ask for humanitarian aid from international donors, thus depriving the DOH of their traditional partners in disaster response. By July 2017, the MHPSS Cluster desperately needed to engage the local service providers but did not know how.

When the MHPSS Cluster for Marawi Emergency Response was convened, more than two dozen groups signed up in the directory of MHPSS service providers. Perhaps to save on resources and foster closer coordination, the DOH adopted Quad Cluster meetings for WASH, Nutrition, MHPSS and Medical Services. The meetings were predictably long-winded, sometimes taking up all day. Discussions centred on WASH, Nutrition and Medical Services Clusters that had solid data to report by then. The MHPSS Cluster reporting was inevitably pushed back, requiring its members to sit through the reports before MHPSS matters were up for discussion. By July, only a handful of organizations were still sending representatives to the Quad Cluster meetings. Lyra Versoza, a volunteer MHPSS responder who attended most of the Quad Cluster meetings, shared they proceeded thus:

> There would be three hours devoted to discussing provisions of Health, WASH, and Nutrition, and about two minutes towards the end for MHPSS. Mostly it was just to complain that the local NGOs were not using the prescribed format when sending in their reports.

Understanding the nature of the CSOs that made up most of the community-based resources for MHPSS service delivery to Marawi IDPs is important. These were mostly faith-based groups, volunteers from the academe and professional groups that mounted operations when their schedule and resources permitted, local NGOs that had a stake in their adopted communities' peace and development agenda, and spontaneously emerging social formations seeking to respond to the crisis. Through the long, drawn-out period when these stakeholders were taking part in the MHPSS response for Marawi IDPs, they had no clear idea when the fighting would end. They were all scrambling to realign their budget, reassign their human resources and source extra funding to mount psychosocial missions. Many were based far from the DOH Operations Centre and could not spare the time and money to travel to the Cluster meetings. Aggravating the situation was the problem of travel within the affected areas due to the long lines at the checkpoints and the convoluted process of securing car passes. Thus, they could not prioritize attendance at the cluster meetings.

Then, too, there is the question of the appropriateness of MHPSS services delivered by non-specialists. Following Republic Act 10029 or the Philippine Psychology Act of 2009, only licensed psychologists and helping professionals can implement and supervise psychological interventions. Humanitarian emergencies happening on a grand scale would challenge emergency MHPSS service provision in this country of 105 million, with less than 1,200 registered psychologists.

At its peak, the Marawi crisis displaced over 600,000 people (Remitio 2017). The number of displaced people lent a sense of urgency to many volunteers, most of whom had not been trained to work with individuals in distress. During the conduct of Psychological First Aid, skilled responders can readily pick up on the felt needs of the distressed populations as they articulate the source of their current difficulties. By deploying various modalities, a clinician can assess acute stress symptoms from how the children play and what they draw or portray. These clinical considerations are, however, lost on the untrained. While well-meaning, non-professionals who deliver psychosocial support only have common sense notions about these opportunities for psychological assessment. In their desire to help, some ran programmes without the supervision of a licensed psychologist. Some appropriated psychological tools they were not qualified to use and delivered interventions they did not fully comprehend. Like the DOH, they, too, were motivated to deliver services so they could report on the number of activities and the number of IDPs served. Confronted with the urgency of numbers, the question of competence conveniently took a backseat. Alarming information on the supposed emergence of 2,500 cases of schizophrenia among the Marawi IDPs came from Lanao del Sur Crisis Committee spokesperson Zia Alonto Adiong who was not qualified to diagnose such conditions (Doyo 2017).

The Marawi crisis was unique in that it demanded that MHPSS providers negotiate the conservative cultural norms characteristic of the closed society of the Maranao. The Maranao environment was fraught with pitfalls for the unwary MHPSS service provider, with every decision representing the possibility of violating cultural norms and religious prohibitions or—as had often been warned against during security briefings—more than an acceptable risk to the responder's personal safety. The language barrier was a significant deterrent, but so were the traditional prohibitions on certain social interactions. For example, when working with adolescents and adults, there was a need to segregate participants and facilitators according to gender for interactive therapeutic activities. The lack of space to hold group processing was a perennial issue. Also, security concerns were raised by the IDPs and by some of my contacts in the military intelligence sector over the suspected presence of Maute sympathizers among the home-based evacuees we were working with.

Understanding the context of the local service providers, COPERS made an effort to consult religious leaders on the appropriateness of psychosocial activities and materials for use among home-based IDPs. We then set out to find community-based Maranao-speaking youth groups in order to enhance their understanding and skills for MHPSS service delivery to various populations. To sustain their work with the IDPs, COPERS also provided these local partners with culturally appropriate, peace-centred materials for running these activities and some transportation allowance. Every week, COPERS recalled these local groups for sessions on working through their difficulties in delivering MHPSS services. We also replenished their materials and operational funds at these sessions.

Apprehending the DOH's problem of linking up with the local service providers, COPERS organized a forum on best MHPSS practices for the Marawi crisis on 5 August 2017. Assembling the participants was not hard, as COPERS had already linked up with various organizations in response to Typhoon Washi in 2011–12. About 200 participants from seventy-nine organizations attended the forum, during which we could map the MHPSS service provision thus far and mediate for the participants to share resources. To standardize MHPSS service delivery, COPERS disseminated culturally appropriate and peace-centred MHPSS activity materials that it developed in collaboration with Maranao traditional leaders.

CONCLUSION

The delay in setting up the MHPSS Cluster and putting order to the ad hoc structure of mental health and psychosocial service delivery in Marawi masked the Incident Command System's poor fit as an emergency humanitarian response mechanism. Designed to be led by the local government unit (LGU), the Incident Command System could work best when the affected population converges in the evacuation centres. However, the Marawi IDPs reacted to the disaster by reverting to their cultural norms—they shunned the LGU-established evacuation centres that were set up perhaps too late, preferring to stay with relatives or take refuge in the *madaris* and Islamic boarding schools. Unsurprisingly, only a minuscule portion of the Marawi IDPs willingly located themselves in the formal evacuation centres because the Maranaos have always been clannish. The home-based IDPs expressed pity for their neighbours housed in evacuation centres because "they did not have relatives who would take them in".

Unhampered by bureaucratic operational strictures and geographical boundaries to their service delivery, the local NGOs could reach the home-based IDPs and those in the non-formal evacuation centres. Thus, it was not so much that there was a lack of MHPSS service provision to the home-based IDPs; it was a case of the official MHPSS Cluster not being mandated to extend humanitarian service provision outside the evacuation centres. Overwhelmed already with caring for the IDPs in the formal evacuation centres, the DOH did not prioritize tasks such as linking up, monitoring and regulating the MHPSS activities outside the formal evacuation centres. When this realization came to light during the 5 August forum, WHO Surveillance Point Person Julie Villadolid expressed relief at knowing how extensively local responders had provided psychosocial support to home-based IDPs. She entreated the local service providers to send in reports about their MHPSS activities in any form that was convenient for them, so these could be included in the official reports that the WHO was providing weekly (Versoza 2017).

The MHPSS provision during the Marawi crisis demonstrated glaring gaps in the appropriateness of the disaster response structure. These gaps ought to be addressed in the future to mitigate the impact of disasters on those who would be direly affected. Rather than relying on INGOs and UN agencies to save the day, as has been done in response to previous disaster events, the DOH must exert efforts to enhance working relations with community-based humanitarian groups with MHPSS capabilities.

There is a need to factor in the cultural responses and redesign the structure to be more capable of providing Tiers 1–3 MHPSS services, especially after a week or two when the absorptive capacity of the local psychosocial support network begins to fail. Host households could not sustain their relatives' needs for long without suffering unwarranted deprivation and inconvenience. Thus, humanitarian mechanisms should allow for the support of IDPs even when they are not in evacuation centres. In this way, host communities would not be burdened as much.

As disaster events that beset our communities become more intense and protracted, LGU leadership must push every disaster-prone community to the point of constant readiness to deploy MHPSS resources nearest to the occurrence of the disaster event. They must maintain an updated directory of local MHPSS providers and periodically update them on guidelines and standards of MHPSS provision even before a disaster event happens. LGUs must retool their respective disaster response structures so that during emergency response, the results of Tiers 1–3 interventions could be promptly addressed by the appropriate government agency, factoring in the cultural context of how their constituents would take to displacement. A swift and proper response does so much to help affected individuals recover their sense of normalcy and personal agency in the aftermath of a disaster.

References

Asia-Europe Meeting. 2014. "Post-Haiyan Tacloban Declaration". http://eeas.europa.eu/asem/docs/20140604_post-haiyan_tacloban_declaration_final_en.pdf (accessed 22 March 2018).

Budosan, Boris, Sabah Aziz, Marie Theres Benner, and Batoul Abras. 2016. "Perceived Needs and Daily Stressors in an Urban Refugee Setting: Humanitarian Emergency Settings Perceived Needs Scale Survey of Syrian Refugees in Kilis, Turkey". *Intervention: Journal of Mental Health and Psychosocial Support in Conflict Affected Areas* 14, no. 3: 293–304.

DOH-HEMB (Department of Health-Health Emergency Management Bureau). 2017. Health situation update no. 30 on armed conflict in Marawi. Iligan City: DOH-HEMB.

Doyo, Ceres P. 2017. "Schizophrenic in Marawi and Iligan". *Philippine Daily Inquirer*, 10 August 2017. http://opinion.inquirer.net/106227/schizophrenic-marawi-iligan (accessed 16 December 2017).

DSWD-DROMIC (Department of Social Welfare and Development-Disaster Response Operations Monitoring and Information Center). 2018. "DSWD DROMIC Report #103 on the Armed Conflict in Marawi City as of 03 April 2018, 6PM". https://dromic.dswd.gov.ph/armed-conflict-in-marawi-city-23-may-2017/ (accessed 12 February 2023).

IASC (Inter-Agency Standing Committee). 2007. *IASC Guidelines on Mental Health and Psychosocial Support in Emergency Settings*. Geneva: IASC.
Ilagan, Gail Tan. 2012. "WAYWARD AND FANCIFUL: Feed the Hungry Now". *MindaNews*, 10 December 2012. http://www.mindanews.com/mindaviews/2012/12/wayward-and-fanciful-feed-the-hungry-now/ (accessed 22 March 2018).
Ilagan, Gail Tan, Randolph R. Reserva, Rodge P. Lelis, and Lyra R. Verzosa. 2016. *Kadasig: The Leyte Community Resilience Enhancement Program*. Davao City: Terre des Hommes.
Ilagan, Gail Tan, Bob Timonera, and Isabelo Julio Benitez. 2012. *Recovery and Resistance in the Grassroots: The Mindanao Resilient Communities Report II*. Davao City: Center of Psychological Extension and Research Services.
Nawal, Allan. 2017. "Too Much Food Cramps Space for Marawi Evacuees". *Philippine Daily Inquirer*, 10 July 2017. http://newsinfo.inquirer.net/912405/too-much-food-cramps-space-for-marawi-evacuees (accessed 5 January 2018).
NDRRMC (National Disaster Risk Reduction Management Council). 2017a. *NDRRMC Response Clusters Situation Report #1 (as of 18 June 2017) - Marawi Siege*. https://reliefweb.int/report/philippines/ndrrmc-response-clusters-situation-report-1-18-june-2017-marawi-siege (accessed 6 February 2023).
_____. 2017b. *NDRRMC Response Clusters Situation Report #11 (as of 29 June 2017) - Marawi Siege*. https://reliefweb.int/report/philippines/ndrrmc-response-clusters-situation-report-11-29-june-2017-marawi-siege (accessed 6 February 2023).
Official Gazette. 2010. "Implementing Rules and Regulations of Republic Act No. 10121". https://mirror.officialgazette.gov.ph/2010/09/27/implementing-rules-and-regulations-of-republic-act-no-10121/ (accessed 29 January 2023).
Remitio, Rex. 2017. "Displaced Persons due to Marawi Crisis Reach 600,000". *CNN Philippines*, 14 August 2017. http://cnnphilippines.com/news/2017/08/14/displaced-persons-Marawi-crisis.html (accessed 8 May 2018).
Santos, Ana P. 2017. "Battle for Marawi Takes Huge Toll on Public Health". *Deutsche Welle*, 10 October 2017. http://www.dw.com/en/battle-for-marawi-takes-huge-toll-on-public-health-in-philippines/a-39626527 (accessed 8 May 2018).
Szabo, C.P. 2015. "A Public Mental Health Approach in Humanitarian Settings Is Worthy of Consideration, with Evidence". *Epidemiology and Psychiatric Sciences* 24, no. 6: 498–99. http://dx.doi.org/10.1017/S2045796015000839 (accessed 2 January 2018).

Tamayo, Bernadette E. 2017. "Displaced Families Need Mental Health Services". *Manila Times*, 4 July 2017. https://www.manilatimes.net/2017/07/04/news/top-stories/displaced-families-need-mental-health-services/336561 (accessed 10 December 2017).

Versoza, Lyra. 2017. "Report to PAP on Forum on Best Practices in Mental Health & Psychosocial Support in Response to the Marawi Crisis". Unpublished manuscript, last modified 5 August 2017. Portable Document Format.

14

A Tale of Two Towns: Patterns of Violent Conflict in Maguindanao since the Framework Agreement on the Bangsamoro

Georgi Engelbrecht

INTRODUCTION

The armed conflicts in the southern Philippines between the government and several separatist and insurgent groups for over forty years are some of the longest running in the world, as well as some of the most difficult to consequentially resolve (Majul 1973; Hashim 2001; Tan 2010). Whilst many peace treaties and agreements have been signed, a significant breakthrough occurred in 2012 with the Framework Agreement on the Bangsamoro (FAB), its follow-up Annexes, and ultimately, the groundbreaking Comprehensive Agreement on the Bangsamoro (CAB) in 2014. The Bangsamoro "homeland of the Moro" would be a new, autonomous region in Mindanao that would replace the previous Autonomous Region of Muslim Mindanao. The CAB was primarily based on the decade-long negotiation between the Moro Islamic Liberation Front (MILF) and the Government of the Philippines (GPH) and the compromise achieved by both sides after almost twenty years of negotiation that spanned numerous ups and downs. In their content and concept, the FAB and CAB finally marked milestones for many residents of Muslim Mindanao.[1]

However, a few years later, in 2017, arguably the most lethal armed conflict of the last decade in Mindanao occurred: the onset of the Marawi siege. Months of violence between a local militant group inspired by the Islamic State and government security forces (International Alert 2017) destroyed a chunk of the only Islamic city in the Philippines.[2] What the Marawi siege demonstrated was that the drafting of the FAB—and the subsequent birth of CAB—did not entirely prevent the emergence of an alternative to the negotiated idea of the Bangsamoro: a more violent and fierce manifestation of the Bangsamoro vanguard. What led to the 2017 Marawi conflict was an actual or perceived lack of confidence in the government on the ground, frustrations about local or regional grievances and the spread of Islamic State (IS)/Daesh allure over social media since 2014. These all contributed to increased mobilization and activity of Moro militant groups, some aligning themselves with the Marawi insurgency, even if only for rhetorical action.

Many feared that this violent counterforce, in the form of the Marawi siege, would stymie a negotiated settlement on the Bangsamoro. In 2018, however, President Duterte engineered the passage of the Bangsamoro Organic Law through Congress, which was ratified in a plebiscite in 2019. Months later, the Bangsamoro Autonomous Region in Muslim Mindanao (BARMM) was officially inaugurated in the spirit of the partial implementation of the CAB (Deinla, Rood and Taylor, this volume). However, understanding the enduring patterns of violence in Mindanao remains salient for fully understanding the Marawi conflict and assessing the likely success of a political settlement in Mindanao in the long term.

One of the origins of the Daesh-inspired outfits in the province of Maguindanao (a heartland of the Moro rebellion) lies in a remote *barangay* of Shariff Saydona Mustapha, an artificially created municipality close to the pulse of both MILF and other armed groups in Maguindanao. This patched-up town, which is essentially a combination of several *barangays* and not an organic location in itself, stands in historical contrast to another town just 15–20 minutes away, the once prosperous municipality of Datu Piang ("Dulawan"), the former seat of the Sultanate of Buayan which reached up to General Santos City in Mindanao's south. Since the FAB, Datu Piang has been affected by many violent encounters between the Bangsamoro Islamic Freedom Fighters (BIFF), a splinter of the MILF, and the Philippine Army. The same has been occurring in Shariff Saydona Mustapha. Interestingly though, both municipalities started to drift apart slightly in recent years in terms of their peace and order. Today, they can arguably stand for two types of Maguindanaon and Bangsamoro towns at the forefront of the various armed conflicts: the town of relative insecurity and the town of relative security. Whilst the former could be applied to Shariff Saydona Mustapha, which is likely to remain in a precarious state, despite some improvements unless many structural conditions change, the latter is a signifier of the marginally increasing success of Datu Piang.

This chapter argues that levels of contestation of power within certain municipalities contribute to the fragility or stability of those areas. In the following sections, I provide a brief overview of relevant literature on conflict in the Bangsamoro before turning attention towards the socio-political reality of Maguindanao, using these two towns as a case study. I conclude by showing that the realities of contested local zones complicate, while making more important, the success of the nascent Bangsamoro.

LITERATURE REVIEW

Most of the current literature on the different conflicts in the Bangsamoro is tied to day-to-day reporting, policy briefs and papers, and analytical and op-ed pieces in the media. Theoretically coherent or empirical scholarship on ongoing patterns of violence, Moro armed groups (and their evolution over time), and regional political dynamics are relatively rare, particularly in the post-peace agreement environment.³ However, we have studies on clan feud dynamics within Muslim Mindanao and research on the local political economy and the illicit sectors or "shadow economies", which have thrived due to a remarkable research initiative by International Alert (Lara and Schoofs 2013). Several case studies on municipalities, but only rarely comparatively, have been written (Quitoriano 2013; International Alert 2022) or the examination of specific empirical data presented (International Alert 2022). But generally, the conflict data has not been disaggregated at a subregional level for comparison or to enable discussion of possible subregional trends.

An essay by Adam (2017) focused on the duality of Muslim Mindanao as a "space of exception" in contrast with the rest of the country, which is presented as a "space of normality". But this dichotomy—whilst originating in a good analytical framework—also needs to account for the complexity of the highly heterogeneous situation in Muslim Mindanao and in various subunits of provinces, municipalities and *barangays*. An assessment of a real or perceived "state of exception" is perhaps less accurate than painting Muslim Mindanao and the Bangsamoro as a patchwork of different zones, reaching from zones of peace, through zones of contestation, to genuine zones or "spaces" of insecurity. Not only do we need to compare the Bangsamoro with other regions, but also to fragment it into different pieces in order to have a detailed look at myriad centres of violence and conflict.

Moreover, the ongoing irregular wars between the government and a number of insurgents (primarily the BIFF) could be categorized as civil wars, protracted low-level conflicts or even successful cases of counterinsurgency.⁴ But this conflict pattern is not the only phenomenon causing violence, especially in the Bangsamoro. Horizontal conflict is as prevalent as issues related to politics. Tools from the study of civil wars and political violence can help us to look at many incidents in the Bangsamoro. Still, the first step would be a rather fundamental question or puzzle: What types of violence persist in some of the Bangsamoro areas, especially those unrelated to criminality but rather the everyday political existence of individuals, citizens and rebels? For instance, violence alone by armed groups cannot guarantee control of the village—it has to be rather a tool among measures spanning (religious) authority, clan linkages and persuasion. The counterinsurgency literature speaks here about the so-called theory of competitive control (Kilcullen 2013); other studies emphasize factors of insurgent mobilization and survival (Bukit 2021; Engelbrecht 2021). A synthetic description and analysis can be developed by looking at violence—specifically armed violence—occurring in an area and relating it to the wider context of the existing civil wars.

METHODOLOGY

This chapter has its roots in the author's stay in Datu Piang for more than three years, working with Nonviolent Peaceforce, an international NGO. It is enhanced by additional perspectives gained whilst participating in the International Monitoring Team (IMT) from 2016 to 2019. The timeframe for the analysis is approximately five years. The rationale for that duration was to see the success or failure of a peace agreement unfold over a certain period, starting with the first significant breakthrough between the GPH and MILF: the FAB in 2012. The cut-off time for the study was the end of 2019, also to include empirical data from the Duterte presidency. The level of analysis focused on the municipal level, combining a micro-level look at the local dynamics within a conflict-affected province and a broader perspective on patterns and trends both within and outside the municipal level.[5] The qualitative data in this chapter is based on field research and historical information about conflict incidents in Maguindanao, media reports, participant observation and interviews with key actors. In addition, the author consulted internal working documents of the monitoring mission, such as case and verification reports. Most of the interviews remain anonymous and are not always noted in the text due to the sensitivity of the topic and the interviewees' ongoing involvement in the GPH-MILF peace process.

The main dataset for conflict incidents in both municipalities is drawn from three major sources: 1) the Bangsamoro Conflict Monitoring System (BCMS) of the World Bank/International Alert;[6] 2) incidents collected and recorded by the author during his active stay in Maguindanao; and 3) corrective data from newspaper archives and—in a few cases—oral testimony. After collecting the initial data, the set was standardized and criminal incidents were removed from the statistics (only a few criminal incidents were recorded from 2012 to 2017). Incidents of armed violence mainly were of three types: 1) horizontal (clan feuds, land conflicts, intra-MILF), 2) vertical (state vs. rebel), and 3) political violence (election-related or relative to political positions).[7] The non-exclusive reliance on the BCMS dataset was a deliberate decision in order to provide more specificity and texture to the discussion. Temporal disaggregation (the yearly progress) and agency (the actors launching violence) are duly considered.[8]

THE FRAGILITY OF "POST-CONFLICT" IN MINDANAO

While the GPH-MILF peace process contributed to a decrease in armed confrontation, everyday direct and structural violence in the southern Philippines continued in different manifestations (Lara and Schoofs 2013; ICG 2016). The current fragile condition is a situation of ongoing, relatively low-level violence marked by recurrent episodes of conflict. As an example, law enforcement operations against factions of the BIFF (one of the MILF splinter groups) had been occurring regularly in the last years; however, the frequency of these operations clearly increased in 2017 and led to a significant weakening of its factions. A focused military campaign also contributed to the gradual decline of the Abu Sayyaf Group in the Sulu Archipelago. Ceasefire violations between GPH and MILF from 2016–2019 were indirect results of such operations, which triggered misencounters. Thanks to the well-established ceasefire and peace structures, a repetition of the Mamasapano incident of 2015 did not occur.[9] Horizontal violence between different armed groups, including land conflicts, clan feuds and political violence, has also not disappeared. This conflict pattern, along with other cross-cutting issues, such as the proliferation of loose firearms, has been acknowledged by various studies (Torres 2007; Lara and Schoofs 2013; Lara 2014; International Alert 2022)[10] as fuelling insecurity in Mindanao. During Bangsamoro's political transition, clan conflict has further contributed to fissures in the region's development.

This current political transition into the new BARMM is one of the most interesting phenomena in the post-FAB and post-CAB environment. Violence is being kept as a legitimate option by "specialists in violence" (Bates 2008, p. 20) while its level is generally controlled. Conflicts often continue to be managed and not resolved. The fluctuating patterns of violence are noteworthy, with militant-related clashes and intracommunal conflicts sometimes occurring together but even more often in changing cycles. In any case, these local conflicts persist and are part of a daily routine for the Bangsamoro, as are their consequences. Since political violence, horizontal and vertical conflicts are local (and occasionally trans-local) in nature, it is thus important to examine the local environment and the fragility and fissures which give birth to such conflicts and violent incidents.

Until now, the provincial name Maguindanao alone has been sufficient to arouse feelings of unease and danger around the rest of the country. Populated by around 1.2 million residents and surrounded by paddy fields, rivers, marshes and mountains, Maguindanao is one of the oldest political entities in the Philippines, dating from pre-colonial state formation. Its development was primarily based on the cultivation of rice, exertion of royal authority—the *datuship*—and continuous expansion until the Spanish and American colonial powers subjugated indigenous leaders by confrontation, assimilation or co-optation. In recent times, apart from its general state of relative insecurity, Maguindanao experienced two major shocks of violence within a few years. First, the infamous Maguindanao massacre in 2009[11] and second, six years later, the bloody firefight in the rice fields of a town called Mamasapano. Whilst the former incident was an eye-opener for most about the dangerous nature of the feudal rule of the Ampatuan clan and political dynastic rule in the Philippines, the second incident dug the grave for the (then) Bangsamoro Basic Law (BBL) and a possible conclusion of the GPH-MILF peace process under (then) President Benigno Aquino III. Politicized and heavily debated, the incident was framed as a "massacre" by those sceptical of the peace process but a "defensive counter-attack" by the MILF, whose territory had been approached without prior agreed coordination (Vatikiotis 2017, p. 208).

Low-intensity conflicts in Maguindanao between the government and a variety of different armed groups followed as tedious, protracted campaigns developed suddenly into erupting bursts. Clashes between armed clans and other forms of communal violence have also continued, making Maguindanao the most unstable Bangsamoro province. Horizontal and vertical conflicts have often occurred in an "ebb and flow" fashion, with clan feuds gaining ground when militants have been on the verge of defeat and vice versa. Both patterns of violence have also intertwined, notably when it comes to the recruitment of militants (who joined an armed group for protection) and local elites as key actors in both conflict types.

A TALE OF TWO TOWNS

Although the two municipalities of Datu Piang and Shariff Saydona Mustapha are located in the same wider area of Maguindanao and have similar historical origins, they show nuanced differences in socio-economic development, governance and conflict dynamics.[12] As parts of Maguindanao, both towns are inside the heartland of the MILF, and each is an amalgam of different villages with unique histories of their own.[13] Both municipalities belong to the so-called Upper Valley of Maguindanao, dominated for decades by the Rajahs of the Buayan Sultanate. Both also constitute a periphery of Maguindanao in the sense that Datu Piang is relatively far from Cotabato City, the main economic hub of Central Mindanao/Cotabato region (about 1.5 hours by road), and parts of Shariff Saydona Mustapha are even farther away. Unsurprisingly, these peripheries have been carrying the burden of conflict and underdevelopment for a long time, and both have felt the impact of years of dynastic rule. Moreover, Datu Piang lies at a corner of the entity labelled the "SPMS-Box"—one of the most securitized areas in Maguindanao and the Bangsamoro—whilst Shariff Saydona Mustapha is at its core.[14]

Shariff Saydona Mustapha is a relatively new municipality in the second district of Maguindanao, consisting of sixteen *barangay*s with quite different backgrounds and characteristics. The town is a prime example of the electoral gerrymandering in the Ampatuan era.[15] Whilst some portions are easily reachable via vehicle and have road access, other locations are only reachable by boat or a walk through rice paddies along the marsh. Each of the sixteen *barangay*s was affected by violence in one way or another between 2012 and 2017. The majority of armed elements belong to the MILF, although a non-negligible part has been associated with BIFF. Thus, when on 4 June 2017, an effort was staged by Daesh-inspired elements to raise the black flag in a crucial position like a town hall or junction in Maguindanao, it was not a surprise that it occurred in Shariff Saydona Mustapha. This attempt was crushed by joint forces of GPH and MILF; however, no endgame followed. Before an intense battle between MILF and the Daesh followers occurred, several weeks of calm, unfruitful negotiations and manoeuvres had to pass. Yet, this was neither the end of IS-inspired elements of BIFF nor BIFF as a whole.

PROGRESSION OF ARMED VIOLENCE

The nature of violence has shifted in these *barangay*s over the years, albeit not in a more peaceful direction. The data collected for the period 2012–19 is broken down by type and location of the incident in Table 14.1.

TABLE 14.1

External Context	Year	Incidents in Datu Piang (-3 unidentified)			Incidents in Shariff Saydona Mustapha (-5 unidentified)			Internal Context
		State-Rebel	Rido (clan-based)	Political	State-Rebel	Rido	Political	
Framework Agreement on the Bangsamoro	2012	1	/	/	/	/	/	/
	2013	14	1	/	5	/	/	Consolidation of BIFF (January onwards)
Wealth Sharing Annex (July)								Operation Darkhorse I (July)
Power Sharing Annex (December)								
Normalization Annex (January)	2014	8	7	2	17	3	/	Operation Darkhorse II
Comprehensive Agreement on the Bangsamoro (March)								Emergence of ISIS/Daesh in discourse

TABLE 14.1 (continued)

Event	Year							Notes
BBL not passed after Mamasapano incident	2015	10	2	/	11	1	/	Mamasapano Incident (January)
								All-Out-Offensive (February onwards)
								First GPH-Daesh inspired group clash (November)
Duterte Presidency (June)	2016	7	4	/	8	/	2	July Ceasefire Incident
Drafting and Submission of new BBL (July)	2017	2	1	1	7	4	/	Marawi Siege (May)
Aftermath of Marawi	2018	/	/	/	3	/	/	Martial Law in Bangsamoro
Lead-up to BARMM	2019	2	/	/	5	2	/	ARMM to BARMM transition

Note: / indicates no recorded incidents.

The key findings flowing from the dataset underpinning the table include

- From October 2012 to December 2019, the municipalities experienced 64 (Datu Piang) and 73 (Shariff Saydona) incidents of armed violence. That makes it a rate of 0.65 incidents per month in Datu Piang and 0.74 incidents in Shariff Saydona Mustapha. This indicates the more constant and lethal progression of violence in the latter town.
- Vertical violence or state-rebel conflict has been both municipalities' most significant cause of violent incidents. The prevalence of government operations against the BIFF and BIFF's efforts to attack state security forces have been overall the most significant trademarks of the conflict dynamics in the two towns. This corresponds to the simple dictum that "rebellion matters".

- A significant part of both municipalities (> 60 per cent) was affected by armed conflict in the last five years. Several particular locations within the municipalities have been at the forefront of the hostilities due to 1) the presence of the military in the *barangay*, 2) the proximity of the non-state armed actors to the military presence, and 3) the contested yet overlapping character of the location. Vertical conflict was prevalent primarily in contested zones, as expressed by the factors above; horizontal conflict occurred almost always across the boundaries of the two conflicting parties (mostly intra-Moro violence), thus, contested areas as well.
- Rebel-initiated (insurgent) violence was more numerous but had less impact on displacement and injuries; state-led (incumbent) operations led to a less frequent but more lethal outcome.[16]
- Technically, the number—and to an extent, the impact—of incidents in both municipalities sank, especially in the year 2017. But the decrease was not significant, and the Marawi incident factor played a role as it bound some elements of BIFF's factions in support of the Abu Sayyaf Group (ASG)-Maute alliance (Placido 2017). Further, the bulk of the BIFF was engaging with local MILF and, later, the Armed Forces of the Philippines (AFP) in other parts of the second district.
- Both Shariff Saydona Mustapha and Datu Piang started as relative hotbeds of the BIFF insurgency: Datu Piang ceased to be such a base area through the years, whilst Shariff Saydona Mustapha witnessed the evolution of BIFF and remained both a centre of gravity and a centre of conflict.[17]
- Datu Piang had the bigger share of *rido* or clan-based feuding but managed them through a coalition of actors. The root causes were complicated and linked to immediate disputes and path-dependent continuations of old conflicts, potentially exacerbated by newer circumstances. Shariff Saydona Mustapha experienced relatively instantaneous horizontal conflict, mainly related to land or harvesting, and usually quickly pacified by the strongmen in the respective area.[18]
- In both municipalities, the degree of political violence as such was relatively low.[19] This can be explained by a relatively unchallenged formal power monopoly in Datu Piang exercised by the municipal

mayor (and his successor) and the absence of strong political institutions or powerful local officials in Shariff Saydona Mustapha (unlike other Maguindanao towns), which would make violence on a bigger scale unprofitable. In both cases, the non-state armed groups have not seen incentives to openly challenge local power on the municipal level, preferring a more symbiotic relationship.

Datu Piang used to be the seat of the Buayan Sultanate and has a rich and powerful history. In the 1950s, the municipality started to lose more and more territory to newly constituted towns and villages until, during the Ampatuan rule, it was left to stand on its own as a town connecting the adjacent province of Cotabato through the Rio Grande de Mindanao to the heartland of Maguindanao. Historically, parts of Datu Piang used to be rebel strongholds in the 1960s, and even today, a large portion of the municipality is in one way or another associated with the MILF.[20] Presently, the town consists of sixteen *barangay*s (fourteen along the river), most accessible via car. It takes at least forty-five minutes to travel from the main town centre to the farthest *barangay*.

Both municipalities have a formal governance structure, with municipal mayors, *barangay* captains and other line agencies. However, informal governance also matters, considering that more than 50–75 per cent of both municipalities' *barangay*s are also hosting members of armed groups and their relatives, some being even under relative control of these social groups, whilst maintaining overlaps with the formal governance structure (Adam and Verbrugge 2014; Espesor 2017). These movements usually gain traction and support by offering "concrete and practical solutions to the daily problems of substantial segments of the rural population" (Race 2010, p. 200). Once in place, these systems continue to prosper and even develop. The two armed groups deserving a closer look are the MILF and BIFF.

The MILF is significantly present in both municipalities through political structures/committees and military units such as the 105, 106, 118, 127 and the Field Guard base command (BC), belonging to the Bangsamoro Islamic Armed Forces (BIAF). No permanent camp structure is located in Datu Piang or Shariff Saydona Mustapha, but several communities, including hubs of MILF-BIAF, exist, often under different commanders and sub-commanders. Within the MILF organization, Datu Piang is nominally covered by 105 BC and Shariff Saydona Mustapha by 118 BC, notwithstanding residents of both towns who belong to different units.

In its original incarnation, the armed group that would come to be known as BIFF was a movement ("Bangsamoro Islamic Freedom Movement") that wanted the immediate liberation of the "Bangsamoro Homeland" without the seemingly exhausting avenue of peace talks which would lead to nothing. The original area of the BIFF coincided with the sphere of influence of the 105 BC of the MILF in municipalities along the Rio Grande River, separating Maguindanao province and North Cotabato (Franco 2013). One of these municipalities was indeed Datu Piang. In the course of the struggle against the government and after the death of its founder, the BIFF organization split into at least two existing factions, today respectively under Kagi Karialan and Esmail Abubakar (aka "Bungos"), and two more IS-inclined offshoots under Abu Toraife and followers of the late commander Salahuddin Hassan. Initial analysis of the BIFF's early stages focused on the "greed" aspect, attributing to the armed group a penchant for extortion and livestock raids. Whilst this may have been true in some cases, there were other elements with more significant weight, such as the setup of strategic/tactical base camps, the development of expeditionary attacks against other targets and the creation of subtle tactical alliances with other groups or individuals.[21] Throughout the years, BIFF has proved fairly resilient, even if its capacities have been significantly weakened.

MILF areas or territories/communities are diverse in the sense that unlike decades ago, there is no longer today a clear dichotomy between "the state" and "the rebels". State-rebel relationships have been steadily growing and have transformed everyday political and social interactions into a continuum on the ground, so we should talk more about an overlap of power and authority rather than outright contestation (Adam and Flaam 2016). This is also a consequence of the peace processes, which brought the armed structures of the MILF closer to the mainstream and gave political structures leeway to develop more legitimacy. Moreover, with the creation of the BARMM, the boundaries between state and rebels were further blurred. The real contestation seems to emerge from the fringes, i.e., other Moro actors exerting power in ungoverned zones and spaces.[22] The range of these actors could reach from political officials to mobile agents of violence, such as the BIFF, Maute and the ASG. In the core areas controlled by these actors, the state is considered a rival, and the contestation is often violent.

Whilst both municipalities have been affected by armed conflict from 2012 to 2019, both also enjoyed periods of relative peace. Three episodes are especially suitable to underline the dynamics of violence in Maguindanao and the possible continuation of those processes, provided that the supply of armed groups and means of violence remain constant. Whilst in *barangay*s of Shariff Saydona Mustapha, power remains contested between different actors and results in varying levels of conflict, the situation in Datu Piang is more balanced.

2013–14: The Battle for Ganta, Shariff Saydona Mustapha

The battle for control of Ganta in Shariff Saydona Mustapha is a remarkable case since it marked the end of the old or initial BIFF incarnation and arguably the beginning of a newly emerging BIFF. At the end of 2012, this *barangay* became the main area for the group to base after their first heavy battles with the government in mid-2012. BIFF used the time to build up military resilience and resources and train their forces in part of the *barangay*. Control was exerted mostly in this area only (Sitio Patawali), whilst there was, to some extent, a relationship with the rest of the *barangay*.[23] After the AFP took over Ganta during a military operation ("Darkhorse"), the dynamic shifted slightly. The armed group became more alienated from the community—also due to some political issues on the *barangay* level—as the BIFF wanted to grasp local political opportunities.[24] In addition, the presence of the AFP detachments always offered an opportunity for the rebels to harass and attack those locations. Most encounters happened wherever the military detachments were located—in contrast to previous clashes, which were a bit further extended, as the BIFF held significant geographical space. One of the defining qualities of the Ganta conflict was the leader of BIFF in the area, Ustadz Hassan Indal, who repeatedly urged his troops to hit military units as long as they were present in Ganta. After losing the stronghold, BIFF tried to retake the *barangay* but failed and dispersed into other areas of the SPMS-Box, setting new alliances and dynamics in motion.

The 28 July 2016 Incident

On 28 July 2016, clashes and firefights erupted between the AFP and the military forces of the MILF, the BIAF, in four different areas in the second district of Maguindanao. Three of the *barangays* were located in Shariff Saydona Mustapha, and the conflict started when elements of the military encountered the local MILF guerrillas—who were supposedly repositioned—and gunfire ensued. As with the 2015 Mamasapano incident, other armed groups joined the battle on the side of the MILF. The engagements lasted almost one day and only ceased in the evening through the interventions of the ceasefire committee and the International Monitoring Team. The affected towns and *barangay* were either MILF communities or close to those. The misencounter followed a period of proper coordination between government forces and the MILF in the context of prolonged operations against armed groups. But despite this coordination, human error triggered incursion and retaliation, which luckily were defused during the day so that a worse disaster was averted. The clash was also a reminder to both ceasefire structures that the absence of hostilities cannot be taken for granted and that the grassroots relationship between BIFF and MILF elements remains highly complex.[25]

2012–17: A History of Feuds in Datu Piang

Due to the presence of several commanders and elements of armed groups, particularly in the remote and riverside areas of Datu Piang, *rido* (clan-based feuds) tended to prosper, with some firefights lasting for several days. The logic of violence followed the logic of the eruption of *rido*, with incidents triggering clashes that, in turn, caused other disputes below the original conflict. Notwithstanding the gravity of this horizontal violence, Datu Piang maintained a cautiously calm profile in times of peace.[26] One *barangay* in Datu Piang, Ambadao, experienced a highly protracted feud primarily due to the power politics of influential leaders in a specific part of the municipality and their associations with external actors. In this case—in December 2014—an existing land conflict triggered the move of one party, which then set in motion a chain of events resulting in day-long firefights and the displacement of over 500 families. Some civilians were injured, livestock and material possessions were taken, and combatants were killed. Another clan feud involving an uncle and his nephew in Datu Piang and the opposite municipality of Midsayap reignited severely in early 2013 and reoccurred late in 2016/17. Although external factors such as political complexities and the anti-drug campaign under the Duterte administration played into the violence, the main conflict poles have rarely been fixed. Conflict resolution failed due to the absence of sustainable treatments for the root causes. These "sleeping *rido*" are one of the most imminent dangers for which the Bangsamoro must be ready.

The Garden of Forking Paths

Datu Piang's criminality rate was described as 75 per cent lower since the start of the anti-drug campaign and the ascendancy of Duterte to the presidency.[27] No ceasefire breach between GPH and MILF was noted in the municipality, and overall, things have moved from hidden tensions and conflicts towards a more understanding and coordinated relationship between the GPH forces, local government unit (LGU) and MILF so that communities do not have to choose exclusively anymore between the state and the rebels. The BIFF has stayed away from the town for a relatively long time, and the *rido* have been relatively under control in the sense that ceasefires between warring parties hold. In an interesting turn of events, during the Duterte era, army officials have also visited certain *barangay*s of Datu Piang to test their functionality and make assessments to monitor the proper governance by *barangay* officials. An expanding state reach thus supplements local governance's inherent weakness.[28]

Shariff Saydona Mustapha remained conflict-affected; by late 2018, a military operation was looming, targeting at least four *barangay*s of the municipality, and a similar pattern continued until 2019.[29] MILF members also regularly engaged the BIFF and the other, more IS-inclined groups.[30] Despite positive steps like creating a new municipal hall, the municipality still has difficulty performing properly and delivering services to all villages. The spaces of Shariff Saydona Mustapha are representations of protracted and tedious armed conflict at the periphery of the peaceful potential of the Bangsamoro. Moreover, although land conflicts and other forms of horizontal violence have not been massively reignited, vertical violence and clashes between militants and the government still occur.

CONCLUSION: QUO VADIS MAGUINDANAO?

Years into the Duterte presidency, the landscapes in Mindanao have been slowly changing. The state seems to be seizing the momentum in its assertion of sovereignty through the campaign against lawless elements, criminal syndicates and also a degree of cooperation with non-state groups, such as MILF or MNLF. Even the subsequent creation of the BARMM and the first years of the Bangsamoro transition is not only proof of Bangsamoro "self-determination", but also the willingness of Manila to devolve state functions to the region. Yet the frequency and duration of law enforcement operations, the proliferation of IS-inspired armed groups, political and armed conflict in pockets of insecurity, the war on drugs and lack of clarity about the political future of BARMM in the 2025 elections still sustain an overall volatile and fragile environment. Despite the CAB in 2014, "normalization", a term that encompasses a variety of measures to support the broader war-to-peace transition in the region, as part of the peace process is still in the starting blocks.[31] Small battles, sweeps and counter-sweeps marked by invisible tension and the absence of everyday normalcy permeate several areas, particularly in Maguindanao. Whilst some municipalities known as hotbeds of insurgency have shifted away from continuous strife and regular encounters between state and rebels and benefitted from some sort of governance, others remain in the insecurity trap.

The slow pace of bringing peace dividends to these contested zones, characterized by a certain absence of local government, contributes to armed conflict. Unsurprisingly, the most prominent and vocal local Daesh offshoot in Mindanao came precisely from spaces such as Shariff Saydona Mustapha: hard to access, difficult to govern, full of recruitment potential and still within the complicated clan and kinship line system of families. The question is whether the success rate for getting things done can be faster than the pressing tensions, fragilities and paradoxes on the ground. Or as one LGU official in Maguindanao said, "I am now 65 years old, and I don't think I will see proper peace prevail. The [former] President [Duterte] [has been] trying, but I am not sure it can be fixed as fast as he intends it."³²

Indeed, a good measure of the success of the new autonomous region will be how conflicts and political life are managed across the Bangsamoro. Two paths are likely: Municipalities will be contested, and violent (as seen with Shariff Saydona Mustapha) or somewhat pacified and less conflictual (as with Datu Piang). Whilst the peace process can undoubtedly diminish the risks of conflict eruption, structural constraints will always remain in a post-conflict society. Conflict is likely to stay when contestation is enmeshed with armed actors and less active local governments. Where contestation is managed, and by extension, this applies to a few towns and the whole region, the Bangsamoro will be a successful peace project.

Notes

1. There is not much disagreement that many peace agreements concluded between the Moro Fronts and the Philippine government in the decades after the mid-1970s remain actually contested in their implementation (Rood 2021).
2. This was just the culmination of a process which had been firstly nurtured in 2012 and then climaxed in 2015 with the first encounter between the Philippine government and a Daesh-inspired local armed group in the coastal municipality of Palimbang in Southern Mindanao. The first black flags on tricycles were spotted by several individuals as early as 2012.
3. This is also true for the main stakeholder of the peace process, the MILF. Moreover, issues inviting empirical study such as the different local manifestations of MILF or other groups such as the BIFF remain underexplored. The events in Marawi seem to have sparked a growth of material on the Abu Sayyaf and also the Maute Group or "IS-Lanao" (Rhoades and Helmus 2020; Arguillas 2021).
4. Despite the fact that MILF and the government signed a ceasefire agreement and two peace pacts, misencounters—isolated military engagements mostly due to a lack of movement coordination—could still occur.
5. With around 20,000 and 25,000 residents respectively for Shariff Saydona Mustapha and Datu Piang, the internal heterogeneity is limited and the municipal level is the most suitable lens for armed conflict.
6. http://conflictalert.info/.
7. A few incidents could not be identified as to the specific categorization under the three categories above.
8. See for instance the work of Kalyvas (2008).

9. In January 2015, a raid by the Philippine National Police to arrest a Malaysian terrorist was not coordinated with ceasefire mechanisms. In the resulting confusion, forty-four members of the PNP were killed as well as several members of the BIFF and MILF. See de Jesus and de Jesus (2016).
10. The year 2016 featured an increase in violent conflict incidents in all five provinces of Muslim Mindanao (International Alert 2017). The year 2017 followed largely a similar trend. In the following years, violence subsided once again, but it creeped back in 2022.
11. Also known as the Ampatuan massacre was the orchestrated killing of fifty-eight persons, including women and journalists, by armed men associated with the Ampatuan clan.
12. In late 2022, Maguindanao was divided into two parts: Maguindanao del Norte and Maguindanao del Sur.
13. For example, the Bakat village of Shariff Saydona was the seat of the Buayan Sultanate during the time of Datu Utto, a famous Maguindanaon ruler.
14. Its original meaning refers to the area boundaries of *Salbu-Pagatin-Mamasapano-Shariff Aguak*. Its first appearance was marked by the aftermath of the 2008/9 MOA-AD war when the MILF used areas inside the box to both withdraw to and from which to launch attacks.
15. Due to the different pieces of other areas which were carved out for the sake of giving an Ampatuan heir a municipality, conditions differ in each of the *barangays*. Saydona is carved out of parts of Datu Piang, Mamasapano, Datu Unsay, Shariff Aguak and Datu Saudi. Ever since it was created in 2009, it has been ruled by an Ampatuan descendant and did not technically fulfill the criteria for a municipality.
16. The impact aspect of this armed violence is a shortcoming of this chapter as reliable data on casualties was difficult to get by. Whilst displacement rates could be reasonably calculated, fatalities are more difficult to grasp and measure. The deduced trend was also confirmed by International Alert (2017, p. 52) in their report, "Guns, Drugs and Extremism: Bangsamoro's New Wars".
17. This outcome confirms some studies which stipulate that municipalities which have many neighbouring districts and towns are more likely to be affected by political and identity conflicts as opposed to illicit economies. See Capuno (2017), p. 17.
18. Both trends continued even during the BARMM transition period, when some *rido*-related clashes in Datu Piang reignited but feuding in Shariff Saydona Mustapha remained fairly instantaneous. Overall, Datu Piang still remained more at peace than Shariff Saydona Mustapha during 2020 onward.
19. Political violence mostly refers to election-related violence or violence pertaining to political motives.

20. As an example, one *barangay* is formally under the control of a *barangay* chairwoman, who is the wife of a senior MILF commander.
21. The origin of the BIFF lies indeed in the failed MOA-AD deal by the Arroyo government and the hostilities between the military and the MILF 105th Base Command led by Ameril Umbra Kato since 2008. After more than a year of firefights, Kato was demoted and replaced by his staff officer Zacaria Goma. Kato was not happy with the continuous peace talks and the compromises the MILF leadership entered and, in 2010, he broke off from the mainstream MILF. Whilst the central force seems to be initially gathered in Barangay Ganta of Shariff Saydona Mustapha, some BIFF cells have been also operating from semi-standing bases in North Cotabato and Maguindanao. The BIFF's modus operandi was directed towards military and police detachments primarily, but there have been cases where civilians were targeted as well.
22. *Barangays*, which have been dominated by MILF, have often morphed from "shadow governments" into more collaborative settings of local governance; ironically, the real parallel structures have indeed emerged from the fringes and were areas where the Maute Group thrived since 2014–15; the same would apply to certain BIFF areas.
23. In some cases, elements perceived as anti-BIFF inside Ganta were liquidated—a classic insurgent strategy.
24. Structures that could ease insurgents' attacks due to financial support or political cleavages.
25. The issue of coordination has remained at the forefront of other ceasefire violations in the years to come.
26. Moreover, since early 2016, the BIFF left Datu Piang mostly on its own, which constitutes another interesting puzzle.
27. This might be because a number of persons surrendered initially at the beginning of "Oplan *Tokhang*"—President Duterte's war on drugs—just like in other municipalities of Maguindanao.
28. A good indicator is, for instance, the surrender of firearms in various municipalities of Maguindanao, including Datu Piang.
29. Some *barangays* become conflict-affected as they are the entrance and exit areas of armed groups and the military to enter the main location of the opponent. In Shariff Saydona Mustapha's case, for instance, this is the *barangay* of Inaladan, which mostly experiences displacement but fewer encounters. However, as mentioned in the literature, the absence of direct violence from a specific area does not mean that a conflict's intensity is reduced (Kalyvas 2008).
30. Talking about a *barangay* in Shariff Saydona Mustapha and calling out Abu Toraife, one of the more radical militant leaders, a prominent MILF commander said in a video: "Look at Pusao. There are no other ruined areas here but Pusao. Not even animals are living there. It has turned into ruins, the houses

were destroyed, the mosques are destroyed, and the *madrasahs* are destroyed ... for you [Abu Toraife] have wreaked havoc on the face of the earth."
31. It includes, for example, the disarmament and demobilization of MILF fighters, the transformation of MILF camps into productive communities and amnesty for rebels.
32. Interview on 5 April 2017.

References

Adam, Jeroen. 2017. "Spaces of Exception and Spaces of Normality: Towards a Relational Understanding of Violence and Peace in Muslim Mindanao". *Asian Journal of Peacebuilding* 5, no. 1: 49–66.

Adam, Jeroen, and Helene Flaam. 2016. "'I Am Nobody': Grievances, Organic Members, and the MILF in Muslim Mindanao". Justice and Security Research Programme (JSRP) Paper 29. London: London School of Economics.

Adam, Jeroen, and Boris Verbrugge. 2014. "Informal Conflict Management in Exclusivist Political Orders: Some Observations on Central Mindanao". *Austrian Journal of South-East Asian Studies* 7, no. 1: 61–74.

Arguillas, Carolyn O. 2021. *The Challenges of Reporting Violent Extremism: Lessons from Mindanao*. Davao City: MindaNews Publications.

Bates, Robert H. 2008. "Probing the Sources of Political Order". In *Order, Conflict, and Violence*, edited by Stathis N. Kalyvas, Ian Shapiro, and Tarek Masoud, pp. 17–43. Cambridge: Cambridge University Press.

Bukit, Matthew L. 2021. "Bangsamoro Separatism and Classical Counterinsurgency: Reconsidering Revolutionary War in the Southern Philippines". *Studies in Conflict & Terrorism*.

Capuno, Joseph J. 2017. "Violent Conflicts in ARMM: Probing the Factors Related to Local Political, Identity, and Shadow-Economy Hostilities". University of the Philippines School of Economics Discussion Papers 2017-07, September 2017.

De Jesus, Edilberto C., and Melinda Quintos de Jesus. 2016. "The Mamasapano Detour". In *The Long Journey to Peace and Prosperity*, edited by Paul D. Hutchcroft, pp. 159–95. Mandaluyong: Anvil Publishing.

Engelbrecht, Georgi. 2021. "The Logics of Insurgency in the Bangsamoro". *Small Wars & Insurgencies* 32, no. 6: 887–912.

Espesor, Jovanie. 2017. "Waltzing with the Powerful: Understanding NGOs in a Game of Power in Conflict-ridden Mindanao". *Pacific Dynamics: Journal of Interdisciplinary Research* 1, no. 1: 66–83.

Franco, Joseph. 2013. "Attacks in Central Mindanao: Overestimating the Bangsamoro Splinter Group". *RSIS Commentaries*, 2013/149, 13 August

2013. https://www.rsis.edu.sg/wp-content/uploads/2014/07/CO13149.pdf (accessed 2 March 2023).
Hashim, Salamat. 2001. *The Bangsamoro People's Struggle against Oppression and Colonialism*. Mindanao: Agency for Youth Affairs – MILF.
ICG (International Crisis Group). 2016. "The Philippines: Renewing Prospects for Peace in Mindanao". *Asia Report N°281*, 6 July 2016. https://icg-prod.s3.amazonaws.com/281-the-philippines-renewing-prospects-for-peace-in-mindanao.pdf (accessed 4 March 2023).
International Alert. 2017. *Guns, Drugs and Extremism: Bangsamoro's New Wars*. Philippines: International Alert.
―――. 2022. *Conflict's Long Game: A Decade of Violence in the Bangsamoro*. Philippines: International Alert.
Kalyvas, Stathis N. 2008. "Promises and Pitfalls of an Emerging Research Program: The Microdynamics of Civil War". In *Order, Conflict, and Violence*, edited by Stathis N. Kalyvas, Ian Shapiro, and Tarek Masoud, pp. 397–422. Cambridge: Cambridge University Press.
Kilcullen, David. 2013. *Out of the Mountains: The Coming Age of the Urban Guerilla*. Oxford: Oxford University Press.
Lara, Francisco Jr. 2014. *Insurgents, Clans, and States: Political Legitimacy and Resurgent Conflict in Muslim Mindanao, Philippines*. Quezon City: Ateneo de Manila University Press.
Lara, Francisco Jr., and Steven Schoofs, eds. 2013. *Out of the Shadows: Violent Conflict and the Real Economy of Mindanao*. London: International Alert.
Majul, Cesar Adib. 1973. *Muslims in the Philippines*. Quezon City: University of the Philippines Press.
―――. 1985. *The Contemporary Muslim Movement in the Philippines*. Mizan Press.
Placido, Dharel. 2017. "BIFF Fighting alongside Maute, Abus in Marawi: Military". *ABS-CBN News*, 29 May 2017. https://news.abs-cbn.com/news/05/29/17/biff-fighting-alongside-maute-abus-in-marawi-military (accessed 4 March 2023).
Quitoriano, Eddie. 2013. "Shadow Economy or Shadow State? The Illicit Gun Trade in Conflict-Affected Mindanao". In *Out of the Shadows: Violent Conflict and the Real Economy of Mindanao*, edited by Francisco Lara and Steven Schoofs, pp. 49–85. London: International Alert.
Race, Jeffrey. 2010. *War Comes to Long An, Updated and Expanded: Revolutionary Conflict in a Vietnamese Province*. Berkeley: University of California Press.
Rhoades, Ashley L., and Todd C. Helmus. 2020. *Countering Violent Extremism in the Philippines: A Snapshot of Current Challenges and Responses*. Santa Monica, California: RAND Corporation.

Rood, Steven. 2021. "Mindanao Case Study". In *Handbook on the Prevention and Resolution of Self-Determination Conflicts*, by the Permanent Mission of the Principality of Liechtenstein to the United Nations, pp. 42–52. New Jersey: Liechtenstein Institute on Self-Determination, Princeton University.

Tan, Samuel K. 2010. *The Muslim South and Beyond*. Quezon City: University of the Philippines Press.

Torres, Wilfredo Magno III, ed. 2007. *Rido: Clan Feuding and Conflict Management in Mindanao*. Quezon City: The Asia Foundation and Ateneo de Manila University Press.

Vatikiotis, Michael. 2017. *Blood and Silk: Power and Conflict in Modern Southeast Asia*. London: Orion.

15

The ARMM Is Gone: Long Live the BARMM

Steven Rood, Veronica L. Taylor and Imelda Deinla

BACKGROUND

The Philippines is an overwhelmingly Catholic country. Its Muslim minority is a legacy of the ability of Muslims in the southern Philippines to resist political and geographic incorporation by the Spanish colonial authorities, the religious domination by the Catholic Church, and the indifference of the United States as a colonial power to petitions for Muslim self-determination. Consequently, the territory that Filipino Muslims occupied was included within the boundaries of the Philippine state during the period of direct rule by the United States (1898–1934) and again after the Philippines became fully independent in 1946. In the 1970s, cries for Muslim separatism grew in the face of increasing in-migration of Christian settlers from elsewhere in the country and increasing assertiveness and abuses by the government in Manila. Armed combat peaked in the early 1970s and continued off and on with periodic upsurges (2000, 2003, 2008) that displaced hundreds of thousands. For the more than forty years that the conflict continued, as successive peace agreements were reached between the government and the insurgents, the basic deal being struck was autonomy for Filipino Muslims to run their affairs within their own defined territory in return for dropping their demand for independence. A ceasefire was agreed upon between the Government of the Philippines and one of the major insurgent groups, the Moro Islamic Liberation Front (MILF), in 2001 (UN Peacemaker 2001). The ceasefire became increasingly effective until the 2012 signing of the Framework Agreement on the Bangsamoro.

SUCCESSIVE, SHAKY PEACE DEALS

Institutions to recognize the claims of Muslims in the southern Philippines were set up initially in 1976 as part of the so-called Tripoli Agreement, but this occurred during the authoritarian interlude led by former president Ferdinand Marcos Sr., and so this agreement yielded no genuine autonomy.

The Autonomous Region in Muslim Mindanao (ARMM) was authorized by the 1987 Constitution put into place after the ouster of Ferdinand Marcos in the 1986 "People Power Revolution". ARMM was established as a geographic and administrative entity and provided some autonomy to Muslims living within its boundaries. The Organic Law that established ARMM was revised after another agreement—the "Final Peace Agreement"—was reached with one of the major insurgent groups, the Moro National Liberation Front (MNLF), in 1996 (UN Peacemaker 1996). ARMM eventually had a geographic coverage of five provinces and two cities: Tawi-Tawi, Sulu, Basilan, Maguindanao, Lanao del Sur, Marawi City and Lamitan City.

ARMM had no fiscal autonomy at all. It was treated the same as a national government agency, going through the same budgetary process of approval by the national Department of Budget and Management and the Philippine Congress. The exception was revenue raised within the region, but since ARMM is the poorest region of the country, these funds were meagre. Not surprisingly, armed conflict in the southern Philippines continued through the period 1996–2018; some of it vertical insurgency against the state, but a great deal of it took the form of horizontal competitions for territory and influence and inter-clan feuding (*rido*) among local power elites (Lara 2019; Lara and Schoofs 2013; Torres 2014; Espesor 2017). Decades of conflict have taken their toll on the region's ability to function economically, much less be economically self-sufficient.

However, it was not the limited budgetary autonomy that most people referred to when they called ARMM a "failed experiment" (Legaspi 2011). Instead, those references are to decades of dysfunctional politics, electoral fraud, rampant corruption and continued violence in the region. For decades, the basic informal arrangement between the national government and regional elites in ARMM was impunity in return for vote fraud on behalf of national candidates. As long as local politicians could deliver votes for particular factions in the national capital, national authorities did not inquire too closely into the quality and processes of local government in ARMM. Internal revenue allocations by the national government to local governments became a new source of corruption and fierce, often violent, competition for elections among the local elites. Those allocations transferred funds from Manila intended for distribution at the city and *barangay* (community) level by elected office-holders. Competition to secure control of these funding pipelines was fierce, as was competition to secure control over the other scarce resource—land. The results of this resource competition in the shadow of continued armed conflict have been a set of dire social indicators (in education, health, nutrition, mortality and life expectancy and income) that are more reminiscent of low-income Africa than of dynamic Southeast Asia (Rood 2012).

After the last significant surge in violence in 2008, progress was made in negotiations with the MILF, the most significant remaining insurgent force in the southern Philippines. The Comprehensive Agreement on the Bangsamoro (CAB) was reached in March 2014, providing for enhanced autonomy for the region and greater resources for investment in return for the decommissioning of the MILF's armed forces. Unfortunately, progress on the necessary enabling legislation in the national Congress was halted in early 2015 as a national furore erupted after a botched police raid to capture a foreign terrorist within

ARMM, the so-called Mamasapano incident. The reckless pursuit of the bounty price for the terrorist led to the death of 44 police as well as those of Muslim fighters and civilians in the immediate vicinity, and it generated enormous negative publicity as it unleashed deep, latent anti-Muslim prejudices across the country (SWS 2015; de Jesus and de Jesus 2016).

REMOVING THE POLITICAL AND LEGISLATIVE ROADBLOCKS

Former president Benigno Aquino III had sought to make peace in the southern Philippines at the closing of his administration, but the Mamasapano incident ensured that his legislative time for doing this ran out. During the 2016 election campaign that followed, presidential candidate Rodrigo Roa Duterte, then mayor of Davao City—the largest city in Mindanao, the main island in southern Philippines—vowed to end decades of war and to address the legitimate demands of Filipino Muslims. As a long-time mayor of Davao, he had dealings with separatist insurgents over the years. Duterte won the presidency and, as a native of Mindanao, claimed personal and family connections to Muslims in the area.

By 2018, former president Duterte had made good on a significant part of that promise—he pushed through the passage of the Bangsamoro Organic Law (BOL), which represented a revised version of the Bangsamoro Basic Law (BBL) that had languished under the Aquino administration. His support for the BOL was personal and emphatic: the president argued that failure to implement a peace agreement negotiated with the MILF would embolden violent extremists. He cited the narrative of violent extremists who had taken over Marawi City in May 2017 for five months and their claims that negotiation is useless and only war is the answer to Muslim problems in the Philippines.

In January 2019, the BOL was approved by voters in ARMM through ratification in a plebiscite. Thus ARMM has been replaced with the Bangsamoro Autonomous Region in Muslim Mindanao (BARMM), which incorporates the regions in the southern Philippines that voted in favour of the BOL. The successful institution of the BARMM represents a signal achievement of the Duterte administration.

PROCESS

Shortly after taking office in 2016, the Duterte administration came up with a plan to restart the peace process that had stalled at the end of the Aquino administration. In the new plan, an expanded Bangsamoro Transition Commission (BTC) would submit a new draft law to Congress to implement the foundational CAB. By expanding the BTC, the new government could appoint members of the MNLF to the Commission to join other government nominees and the MILF (which had a majority membership). These new Commissioners were appointed in January 2017 and were able to submit a new draft law to the president in July 2017—whereupon it was transmitted to Congress for its consideration.

Nur Misuari, the founding Chair of the other major insurgent group, MNLF, refused to participate in this endeavour, claiming that the government should honour the 1996 Final Peace Agreement he had reached with them. However, he did not attempt to block this new legislative process; instead, he was persuaded to go along with another of President Duterte's initiatives, a proposed constitutional change to a federal system. If realized, the conversion of the Philippines from a unitary state to a federal system of government might include, for example, the designation of all of Mindanao as a state within this federal system. Ultimately, nothing came of efforts to federalize the Philippines. At the beginning of the next administration of Ferdinand Marcos Jr. in 2022, Misuari agreed to have his followers appointed to the new BARMM administration.

The very rapid passage of the BOL as a bill—something that had eluded the previous Aquino administration—can also be explained by the different political climate that resulted from the upsurge of violence in the clashes in Marawi City in 2017 (Arcala Hall, this volume). In January 2015, the Mamasapano incident had proven to be a roadblock in the passage of the earlier BBL, while in 2017, the clash in Marawi was seen as a reason to pass the new BOL. During the Marawi siege, the MILF cooperated with government forces to maintain a peace corridor to facilitate the evacuation of civilians from the war zone. There was also extensive media coverage of Muslim efforts to shield Christians from the violence inflicted by the supporters of Islamic State who had taken over the city centre (Lagsa 2017). On the whole, it was painfully evident that the city population suffering from the attacks was Muslim; this prevented the same sort of anti-Muslim backlash that had derailed the earlier effort to grant more autonomy to Muslims in the southern Philippines.

SCOPE AND CONTENT OF THE BANGSAMORO ORGANIC LAW

The new draft BOL in 2017 resembled the draft BBL that was being considered in 2015, with some changes. Like its predecessor, the BOL is a very comprehensive document. Functionally, it brings into being a state with a regional parliament, revenue-raising and taxation powers, and a full list of enumerated fiscal, economic, social, educational and environmental rights and responsibilities. The new Bangsamoro government is responsible for implementing everything from the provision of basic services in BARMM to delivering sustainable development (art. XIII, § 2), climate change policy (art. XIII, § 7), and gender equity (art. XIII, § 5) under the BOL.

The change between the draft BBL and the BOL with the most political impact was that the results for the ratification plebiscite would be considered for the established geographical coverage of ARMM as a whole rather than separately for its five constituent provinces (Tawi-Tawi, Sulu, Basilan, Lanao del Sur and Maguindanao) and two cities (Lamitan City on Basilan and the Islamic City of Marawi). In the January 2019 plebiscite, ARMM as a whole voted overwhelmingly to ratify the BOL, while the province of Sulu rejected it. Although Sulu provincial leaders filed a case in the Supreme Court challenging this provision of the BOL, absent a ruling in favour of the plaintiffs, Sulu is indeed included in the new BARMM.

The plebiscite was held in two additional cities that are geographically embedded in the area, Cotabato City in Maguindanao and Isabela City in Basilan. Voters in Cotabato City agreed to join BARMM, while those in Isabela City voted against it. Six municipalities in Lanao del Norte, adjoining Lanao del Sur, could possibly have joined BARMM. While the voters in those localities did indeed vote to join, the "mother" province of Lanao del Sur as a whole voted against the change to provincial boundaries, so the six municipalities remain outside

BARMM. A similar process for smaller units in Cotabato province led to 67 *barangay*s voting overwhelmingly to join BARMM, and 63 of the 67 were allowed to do so by their "mother" municipalities. These 63 are now referred to as a Special Geographic Area.

Congress made several changes in the 2017 draft before passing the BOL. Some of these made the law resemble previous organic laws passed under the autonomy provisions of the 1987 Constitution. For instance, in place of the listing of powers reserved to the national government, powers concurrent to the two levels and powers exclusive to the autonomous region, Congress simply listed the powers of the autonomous region and reserved all other powers to the national government. In a similar vein, as it had done in previous organic laws (not only for Muslim Mindanao but in the two previous attempts to create an autonomous region for the Cordillera that were defeated in plebiscites), Congress made the new BARMM subject to national laws.

The superior status of national law is particularly noticeable concerning the rights of indigenous peoples in the Bangsamoro. In the draft submitted by the BTC, this issue had been cast as an exclusive power of the autonomous region. In contrast, the BOL is made explicitly subject to the Indigenous Peoples Rights Act 1997 and requires the Bangsamoro Government to create a ministry to safeguard the well-being of indigenous peoples in BARMM—including their ancestral domain—and as part of education policy, a Tribal University System (art. IX, § 19) (Bangsamoro Organic Law, 2018). The BOL is also explicit that the UN Declaration on the Rights of Indigenous Peoples and the UN Declaration on Human Rights cannot be abrogated by BARMM laws.

The BARMM government will have considerably more resources than the outgoing ARMM. In particular, the fiscal transfers from the national government have been increased, and these will now be formula-driven (at 5 per cent of the collections from customs and internal revenue), giving the region fiscal autonomy for the first time. This fiscal autonomy is significant because the transfers from Manila had previously been subject to the discretion of the Budget Department and the Philippine Congress. The BOL also establishes a transitional ten-year Special Development Fund pegged at PHP 5 billion (about AUD 130 million) annually.

As part of its fiscal autonomy, it will also have the authority to raise revenue through issuing bonds and entering into loan agreements (art. XII, § 24), subject to national approval where these require sovereign guarantees.

Less welcome to the MILF is the explicit provision that operational control and supervision of the police regional office is lodged with the Philippine National Police (PNP) rather than the Chief Minister of the autonomous region, as the original draft had provided. The MILF had long said that a locally controlled police force, "responsible both to the Central Government and the Bangsamoro Government, and to the communities it serves", was a non-negotiable item, one that had been painstakingly arrived at in the peace negotiations leading up to the 2014 CAB. Former president Duterte, for his part, had long made it clear that he would not countenance a separate regional police force. His stance was unsurprising, given his reliance on the PNP for the prosecution of his signature "war on drugs". The MILF needed to compromise on this item to get the new law endorsed by the president, though this change has implications for peace in the region going forward. Many of the provisions of the "normalization process" (dealing with combatants and their arms) in the CAB are keyed to the establishment of a separate police force.

One of the important differences between the Final Peace Agreement reached with the MNLF in 1996 and the CAB reached with the MILF in 2014 is the disposition of insurgent forces. The 1996 Agreement called for the integration into the army and police of thousands of MNLF combatants (which often involved sons, nephews, or younger relatives as stand-ins) but was silent about the disposition of MNLF camps. Under the 2014 Agreement, there is no provision for MILF integrees' entry into the security forces (though under the BOL, requirements for entry into the PNP by MILF members are eased). Instead, MILF forces are to be decommissioned, and their camps converted into thriving civilian communities. Their arms are to be "put beyond use" under the supervision of an Independent Decommissioning Body made up of international and Philippine members rather than being surrendered to the government.

This decommissioning process had a symbolic start in June 2015 when 145 members of the MILF's Bangsamoro Islamic Armed Forces gave up their weapons and received resources and training for civilian livelihood opportunities. The next stage of decommissioning of 30 per cent of the MILF's forces was triggered by the ratification of the BOL—and the MILF estimates its force at 10,000 personnel and 2,000 arms (Arguillas 2019). While there are concerns about possible hitches in this process, the parties, particularly the Independent Decommissioning Body, continue to monitor progress, which is about two-thirds complete as of November 2022 (Sarmiento 2022; de la Cruz 2022).

TRANSITIONAL ARCHITECTURE

These stages in this process are called into question—in part since further decommissioning was tied in the so-called "Normalization Matrix" to the establishment of the Bangsamoro Police Force and to progress in curbing the private armies of local warlords in the region. Since an autonomous police force has been rejected in the process of crafting the new law, and there has been no progress on curbing private armies, this leaves the MILF forces with the prospect of being the only actors without guns in a volatile region that has been among the most heavily armed in the world (Engelbrecht, this volume). Further, the transformation of MILF camps into thriving communities and the socioeconomic support for decommissioned combatants have fallen behind schedule. Considerable work still needs to be done on this "normalization" aspect in the future.

As civilian governance is established in the new region and new authorities take office, there will surely be initial teething problems. The Bangsamoro Transition Authority (BTA), with a majority of members selected by the MILF, was appointed to exercise the new region's powers until the scheduled elections for the Bangsamoro Parliament in May 2022. Those elections were to fall simultaneous to the national elections in the Philippines, but the life of the appointive BTA was extended for three years until 2025. In the meantime, the BTA is mandated to avoid disruption of government functions while at the same time reorganizing the bureaucracy, which includes a phase-out of ARMM offices.

The BTA has legislative powers and is mandated to craft new codes governing administration, civil service, education, revenue, local governance and elections. As of late 2022, the first three Codes had been passed, while the latter three are being discussed in the region and parliament. Local elected leaders and other politicians, generally not aligned with the MILF, have interests that must be accommodated in crafting new rules for local government and elections (International Crisis Group 2023).

TRANSITIONAL JUSTICE AND RECONCILIATION MECHANISMS

A significant initiative under the BOL is the way in which transitional justice will be handled. A foundational element of the normalization plan in the CAB is the creation of the Bangsamoro Normalization Trust Fund (Bangsamoro Organic Law, Rep. Act No. 11054, art. XIV, § 2 (Phil.)). Still, uncertainty remains about both its scope and its funding sources (TPMT 2019). Decommissioning combatants requires adequate and legitimate socioeconomic programmes to replace membership in an insurgent group. An equally important element is the legal treatment of the MILF fighters—who will receive legal amnesty and how? Among the concerns raised is that some of the MILF nominees to the BTA need an amnesty in order to fulfil their duties in an open fashion (ibid., p. 21). President Duterte, at the end of his administration, issued amnesty proclamations, but the implementing Amnesty Commission had not been formed as of November 2022 (Arguillas 2022).

A more profound structural question is how BARMM will engage with justice and reconciliation processes. Forty years of armed struggle have produced deaths and atrocities perpetrated by actors on all sides. The CAB provided for the creation of a Transitional Justice and Reconciliation Commission (TJRC), which delivered a comprehensive report in 2016 recommending the establishment of a National Transition Justice and Reconciliation Commission for the Bangsamoro (NTJRCB). The BOL notes the TJRC report and tasks the Bangsamoro Parliament with

> enact[ing] a transitional justice mechanism to address the legitimate grievances of the Bangsamoro people and the indigenous peoples, such as historical injustices, human rights violations, and marginalization through unjust dispossession of territory and proprietary rights and customary land tenure (art. IX, § 1).

The TPMT notes that an Independent Working Group on Transitional Justice and Dealing with the Past exists, but the BOL casts this as a Bangsamoro, not a national, responsibility.

THE BARMM LEGAL SYSTEM

The calls for Muslim self-determination and, later, regional autonomy in the Philippines were concerned mainly with the recognition of territorial claims and distinct, local ethnic identities. In recent decades, however, the discourse of injustice has been linked to the right to a Filipino Islamic identity, particularly access to Islamic legal norms and institutions (*Shari'ah*). Many people in Mindanao understood the creation of the Bangsamoro to mean the creation of a region governed by fully Islamic law; elites in Manila were equally disturbed by this prospect (Deinla and Taylor 2015). The BOL delivers a fairly significant compromise that dilutes some of the promises of the CAB while making the justice institution designs more palatable to Manila and subject to national legal oversight.

Art. X of the BOL establishes a justice system "in consonance with the Constitution, *Shari'ah*, traditional or tribal laws, and other relevant laws" (art. X, § 1). The Bangsamoro Parliament is given the power to enact laws pertaining to *Shari'ah* on personal, family and property law (art. X, § 4) and on civil and commercial actions not covered by the national Code of Muslim Personal Law of the Philippines, as well as on criminal law covering minor offences.

While the classical sources of *Shari'ah* are listed in the BOL, it is silent as to the application of any particular school of Islamic jurisprudence, although Filipino Islamic jurists tend to favor Shafi'i jurisprudence as "more appropriate", given the beliefs of most Muslim Filipinos (Stephens 2011, p. 10). *Shari'ah* is limited to (and applies exclusively to) cases involving Muslims unless a non-Muslim voluntarily submits to it. Traditional or tribal laws apply to disputes of indigenous peoples, and the secular state law of the Philippines also continues to apply in BARMM (the regular state courts are retained). The legal pluralism of BARMM in practice gives rise to forum shopping and significant questions of conflicts of laws (Deinla 2018).

The *Shari'ah* courts within BARMM remain part of the Philippine judicial system under the supervision of the Supreme Court (as they were within ARMM). A significant change, however, is the creation of a *Shari'ah* High Court, a new appellate Court within BARMM (art. X, § 7). The formal status of judges within the *Shari'ah* courts is enhanced under the BOL, which requires judges at all levels of the *Shari'ah* courts (Circuit, District and High) to be regular members of the Philippine Bar with minimum periods of legal practice and at least two years' study of Islamic jurisprudence or *Shari'ah*. The time allowance by the Supreme Court to enable judges to qualify for the Philippine Bar (art. X, § 8) is a pragmatic recognition that not all serving or aspiring Islamic judges in the BARMM have passed the national bar exam, which is a notoriously difficult credentialing process. On the other hand, legal practitioners in the *Shari'ah* courts can continue to practise with their "special admission" qualification, to date earned on the basis of passing a much-abbreviated *Shari'ah* Bar exam.

FUTURE PROSPECTS

In preparation for electoral competition for seats in the Bangsamoro Parliament beginning in 2022, the MILF established the United Bangsamoro Justice Party (UBJP), secured its accreditation with the national Commission on Elections, and conducted training and activities for potential cadres. Political parties are notoriously weak in the Philippines (Hutchcroft 2019), so a programmatic party capable of winning elections and exercising power would be a unique contribution of the Bangsamoro to Philippine politics and governance.

In order to lessen the objections of established politicians and elected local officials, the UBJP initially said that it would only contest seats in the Bangsamoro Parliament, not positions in municipal or provincial offices. However, in 2022, when elections for the parliament were postponed until 2025, the UBJP ran candidates in several local races. A singular victory was over the incumbent mayor of Cotabato City, who opposed the city's inclusion in BARMM. Elsewhere the record was considerably more mixed, as the UBJP interacted with, and often lost to, traditional clan-based electoral campaigns (Englebrecht 2022a).

There are reasons for optimism when it comes to longer-run issues of violent extremism in the southern Philippines. The Philippine military and the MILF have emphasized that they believe a successful peace process is a vaccine against the Islamic State virus. The new governance architecture has the potential to decisively change the discourse about subnational violence, Islamic identity and resistance to the state in the Philippines. The narrative of the Bangsamoro struggle over the centuries has been a localized one that has consistently called for recognition of Muslim Filipinos' rights and justice claims. The veteran leaders of this struggle have decided that autonomy short of independence is the best way to pursue those rights—and the BOL places them in charge of that autonomy. If they make a success of this effort, the pool of indigenous recruits for violent extremism in the Philippines will grow smaller, both because the value of nonviolent means has been demonstrated and because it affirms a new narrative about that status and prospects for Muslims in the Philippines. This is very different from the narrative promoted by Islamic State—that the struggle is worldwide, that Islam is pitted against the rest, and a global caliphate is needed. There will be those who, for ideological or other reasons, are attracted to the Islamic State narrative. Having empowered Muslim leaders who are able to co-create a competing Bangsamoro narrative is likely to be of great effect since the fact that trusted locals deliver the message can be as important as the message.

Over time, the possibility of improved governance in BARMM would also help reduce radicalization indirectly. The great hope of regional autonomy, where political autonomy is supported by fiscal autonomy and secure transfers from the centre, is that it will create prosperity in a historically impoverished region. ARMM was synonymous with a stratified economy in which landed clans and titled lineages have done well economically and politically and a region marked by systemic corruption. BARMM will continue to be a region of great institutional diversity, where state (and now regional/State) institutions and non-state institutions jostle to provide public goods to citizens. The challenge of both the transition and sustained autonomy is whether local elites can co-create and formalize institutions that are more functional, inclusive and legitimate than the institutions that preceded them.

There are some other potential challenges to the BOL, but leadership and public support for the BOL and BARMM have been strong, particularly by the Muslims within the autonomous region. While some local politicians disapproved of the BOL in Sulu, Isabela City and expansion areas in Lanao del Norte, the local population has confidence in the MILF leadership to make BARMM work. There remains a challenge to the Supreme Court on the BOL by Sulu's leaders. Still, there is general optimism that this will be disregarded, considering a court that is seen as largely favouring state policy preferences. So far, the establishment of BARMM has not decisively affected local politics. However, the continuance of the political status quo is a big concern for the broader Muslim public, particularly the youth, who expects a "paradigm shift" with BARMM's establishment. Also, while vertical conflict between the state and MILF has largely ceased, conflict with other non-state actors remains a big problem. The task at hand for BARMM and MILF is enormous. But they need to make good on the promises, including the rehabilitation of Marawi City, and to make governance felt on the ground.

References

An Act Providing for the Organic Law for the Bangsamoro Autonomous Region in Muslim Mindanao, repealing for the purpose Republic Act No. 6734, entitled "An Act Providing for an Organic Act for the Autonomous Region in Muslim Mindanao", as amended by Republic Act No. 9054, entitled "An Act to Strengthen and Expand the Organic Act for the Autonomous Region in Muslim Mindanao", Rep. Act No. 11054 (27 July 2018) (Phil.), https://www.officialgazette.gov.ph/downloads/2018/07jul/20180727-RA-11054-RRD.pdf.

Arguillas, Carolyn O. 2019. "MILF to Initially Decommission 1,800 to 2,100 Weapons; 9K to 12K Forces". *MindaNews*, 25 January 2019. https://www.mindanews.com/peace-process/2019/01/milf-to-initially-decommission1800-to-2100-weapons-9k-to-12k-forces/ (accessed 11 December 2022).

──────. 2022. "100 Days of Marcos Jr.: Still No National Amnesty Commission". *MindaNews*, 10 October 2022. https://www.mindanews.com/top-stories/2022/10/100-days-of-marcos-jr-still-no-national-amnesty-commission/ (accessed 18 November 2022).

Deinla, Imelda. 2018. "(In)Security and Hybrid Justice Systems in Mindanao, Philippines". In *Hybridity on the Ground Peacebuilding and Development, Critical Conversations*, edited by Joanne Wallis, Lia Kent, Miranda Forsyth, Sinclair Dinnen, and Srinjoy Bose, pp. 217–34. Canberra: ANU Press.

Deinla, Imelda, and Veronica L. Taylor. 2015. "Towards Peace: Rethinking Justice and Legal Pluralism in the Bangsamoro". *RegNet Research Paper* No. 2015/63. https://dx.doi.org/10.2139/ssrn.2553541 (accessed 11 December 2022).

De Jesus, Edilberto C., and Melinda Quintos de Jesus. 2016. "The Mamasapano Detour". In *The Long Journey to Peace and Prosperity*, edited by Paul D. Hutchcroft, pp. 159–95. Mandaluyong: Anvil Publishing.

de la Cruz, Jovee Marie. 2022. "OPAPRU Slammed Over Missing List of Decommissioned MILF Combatants". *BusinessMirror*, 16 November 2022. https://businessmirror.com.ph/2022/11/16/opapru-slammed-over-missing-list-of-decommissioned-milf-combatants/ (accessed 18 November 2022).

Englebrecht, Georgi. 2022a. "Ballots and Bullets in the Bangsamoro". *International Crisis Group*, 20 June 2022. https://www.crisisgroup.org/asia/south-east-asia/philippines/ballots-and-bullets-bangsamoro (accessed 18 November 2022).

Espesor, Jovanie C. 2017. "Waltzing with the Powerful: Understanding NGOs in a Game of Power in Conflict-ridden Mindanao". *Pacific Dynamics: Journal of Interdisciplinary Research* 1, no. 1: 66–83. http://dx.doi.org/10.26021/874 (accessed 11 December 2022).

Hutchcroft, Paul D., ed. 2019. *Strong Patronage, Weak Parties: The Case for Electoral System Redesign in the Philippines*. Mandaluyong: Anvil Publishing.

International Crisis Group. 2023. "Southern Philippines: Making Peace Stick in the Bangsamoro". 1 May 2023. https://www.crisisgroup.org/asia/south-east-asia/philippines/331-southern-philippines-making-peace-stick-bangsamoro (accessed 5 May 2023).

Lagsa, Bobby. 2017. "Trapped in Marawi, Muslims Shield Christians from Terrorists". *Rappler*, 4 June 2017. https://www.rappler.com/nation/171901-civilians-rescued-marawi-muslims-protecting-christians (accessed 11 December 2022).

Lara, Francisco Jr. 2019. "Rust Never Sleeps: The Corrosive Power of Mindanao's Warlord Clans". *International Alert*, November 2019. https://www.international-alert.org/blogs/rust-never-sleeps-the-corrosive-power-of-mindanaos-warlord-clans/ (accessed 11 December 2022).

Lara, Francisco Jr., and Steven Schoofs, eds. 2013. *Out of the Shadows: Violent Conflict and the Real Economy of Mindanao*. Manila: International Alert.

Legaspi, Amita O. 2011. "Palace Calls ARMM a 'Failed Experiment'". *GMA News Online*, 15 February 2011. https://www.gmanetwork.com/news/news/nation/213067/palace-calls-armm-a-failed-experiment/story/ (accessed 11 December 2022).

Rood, Steven. 2012. "Interlocking Autonomy: Manila and Muslim Mindanao". In *Autonomy and Armed Separatism in South and Southeast Asia*, edited by Michelle Ann Miller, pp. 256–77. Singapore: Institute of Southeast Asian Studies.

———. 2019. "Finding Federalism in the Philippines: Federalism—'The Centerpiece of My Campaign'". In *From Aquino II to Duterte (2010-2018): Change, Continuity—and Rupture*, edited by Imelda Deinla and Björn Dressel, pp. 62–98. Singapore: ISEAS – Yusof Ishak Institute.

Sarmiento, Bong S. 2022. "TPMT, MILF: Bangsamoro Normalization Still Lagging behind Political Track". *MindaNews*, 23 October 2022. https://www.mindanews.com/top-stories/2022/10/tpmt-milf-bangsamoro-normalization-still-lagging-behind-political-track/ (accessed 18 November 2022).

Stephens, Matthew. 2011. "Islamic Law in the Philippines: Between Appeasement and Neglect". In *University of Melbourne Law School Centre for Islamic Law and Society: ARC Federation Fellowship Islam, Syari'ah and Governance Background Paper 9*.

SWS (Social Weather Stations). 2015. "Filipino Public Opinion on the Bangsamoro Basic Law and the Mamasapano Incident". https://www.sws.org.ph/downloads/publications/pr20150814b%20-%20Filipino%20Public%20Opinion%20on%20the%20BBL%20and%20the%20Mamasapano%20Incident_2015.pdf (accessed 1 December 2022).

Torres, Wilfredo M. III, ed. 2014. *Rido: Clan Feuding and Conflict Management in Mindanao* (expanded edition). Quezon City: Ateneo de Manila University Press.

TPMT (Third Party Monitoring Team). 2019. *Fifth Public Report, July 2017 – February 2019*. 11 March 2019. https://tpmt.ph/tpmt-fifth-public-report-july-2017-to-february-2019/ (accessed 3 January 2023).

UN (United Nations) Peacemaker. 1996. "Final Agreement on the Implementation of the 1976 Tripoli Agreement between the Government of the Republic of the Philippines (GRP) and the Moro National Liberation Front (MNLF)". https://peacemaker.un.org/sites/peacemaker.un.org/files/PH_960902_Final%20Agreement%20Implementing%20the%20Tripoli%20Agreement%20between%20GRP%20and%20MNLF.pdf (accessed 11 December 2022).

———. 2001. "Agreement on Peace between the Government of the Republic of the Philippines and the Moro Islamic Liberation Front". https://peacemaker.un.org/sites/peacemaker.un.org/files/PH_010622_Agreement%20on%20Peace%20between%20the%20GRP%20and%20MILF.pdf (accessed 11 December 2022).

Index

A
Abalos, Benjamin, 135
ABS-CBN, 176
Abu Sayyaf Group (ASG), 193, 201, 212, 258, 263, 266, 270
Adiong, Mamintal, 218–19
Advice to Debit Account (ADA) facility, 18
ageing population, 62
agribusiness, 67, 69, 119
Alvarez, Pantaleon, 163
Ambisyon 2040, 22
Amnesty Commission, 285
Amnesty International, 176
Ampatuan, 174, 259, 271n11
anti-narcotics campaign, 1, 172–73, 176, 182, 184. *See also* war on drugs
Aquino III, Benigno
  chief justice, selection of, 155
  corruption, and, 138
  economy during, 35, 51
  impeachment, and, 135, 153, 160–62
Aquino, Corazon, 135, 172
Armed Conflict Location & Event Data Project (ACLED), 176–77
Armed Forces of the Philippines (AFP), 209, 220–21, 263, 266–67
armed violence, 258, 261–69. *See also* political violence
Arroyo, Gloria Macapagal
  chief justice, selection of, 138
  impeachment, and, 133, 135, 157–58, 159–60, 161–62
  political machinations, and, 153
ASEAN, 14, 51
Asian Development Bank, 12, 24, 52
ATIKHA Overseas Workers and Communities Initiative Inc., 111, 117, 119–22
authoritarianism, 1, 6, 72, 143, 150–51
automobile industry, 69
Autonomous Region of Muslim Mindanao (ARMM)
  establishment of, 277, 278
  geographical coverage of, 281
  See also Bangsamoro Autonomous Region in Muslim Mindanao (BARMM)

B
Balikabayani, 119–20
Balikbayan box, 4, 109, 111, 112, 113–15
Bangko Sentral ng Pilipinas (BSP). *See* Central Bank of the Philippines

Index

Bangsamoro Autonomous Region in Muslim Mindanao (BARMM)
   creation of, 254, 265, 269, 279, 281–82
   legal system of, 286–87
   political transition in, 258, 285
   support for, 288–89
   See also Autonomous Region of Muslim Mindanao (ARMM)
Bangsamoro Basic Law (BBL), 259, 279–81
Bangsamoro Conflict Monitoring System (BCMS), 257–58
Bangsamoro Islamic Armed Forces (BIAF), 264, 267, 283
Bangsamoro Islamic Freedom Fighters (BIFF)
   origin of, 272
   territories of, 264–66
   trust towards, 213
   violent encounters with, 255–56, 258, 260–63
Bangsamoro Organic Law (BOL), 254, 279–82, 284–86, 288
Bangsamoro Parliament, 284, 286–87
Bangsamoro Transition Authority (BTA), 284–85
Bangsamoro Transition Commission (BTC), 280, 282
Barangay Police Auxiliary Teams (BPATs), 216
Bautista, Andres, 5, 130, 134–35, 162
bayanihan (community spirit), 198, 204
Bayanihan Constitution, 29–30
Bersamin, Lucas, 165
Bravo, Commander (Abdullah Makapaar), 212, 217
bribery, 161, 200. *See also* corruption
Buayan Sultanate, 255, 260, 264, 271

Budget and Treasury Management System (BTMS), 19–20
Budget Reform Bill (BRB), 12, 20–21
"Build, Build, Build" programme (B3P), 15, 48–51. *See also* infrastructure development
Bureau of Corrections (BuCor)
   modernization of, 201–4
   organizational practices in, 194, 196–200
Bureau of Fire Protection (BFP), 217, 219
Bureau of Jail Management and Penology (BJMP)
   budget of, 194–95
   modernization of, 201–4
   organizational practices in, 196–200
Bureau of the Treasury (BTr), 18–19
business process outsourcing (BPO), 28, 61, 63–64, 66

C

carbon energy, 80–82, 86–87, 96–97, 105. *See also* climate change; energy transition; Paris Agreement
Carpio, Antonio, 165
cash allocation, 17–18
Center of Psychological Extension and Research Services (COPERS), 238–39, 243, 248
Central Bank of the Philippines (BSP), 3, 25, 45, 47, 53, 64, 118
China, 2, 53
City Health Office (CHO), 239–40
civil-military operations (CMO), 211, 220, 226–27, 229
civil society organizations (CSO), 226, 244–46

clan feud, 213, 256, 258–59, 263, 267–68, 278. *See also* political violence
climate change, 78–79, 82–83, 90–91. *See also* carbon energy; energy transition; greenhouse gas (GHG), Paris Agreement
Climate Change Act (CCA), 4, 83, 90–91, 93, 101
Climate Change Commission (CCC), 89–93
CMO Coordinating Council (CMOCC), 220, 228
coal, 86–87, 96–97
Commission on Audit (COA), 19–20, 94, 137–38
Commission on Elections (COMELEC), 130, 134, 162
Comprehensive Agreement on the Bangsamoro (CAB), 254, 278, 285–86
Comprehensive Tax Reform Program (CTRP), 14, 51
Conditional Cash Transfer (CCT) Program, 17
Conference of the Parties (COP), 89
conflict
 horizontal, 8, 256, 259, 263, 278
 ISIS, and, 7, 192, 209, 216–17, 225, 261, 269, 280
 regarding land, 258, 267–68
 in Maguindanao, 257, 259, 266, 269
 vertical, 259, 262–63, 278, 289
Constitution, the
 creation of, 132–33, 150, 151
 impeachment under, 5, 130–36, 138, 156, 158, 160
 provisions of, 282
 review of, 29–31
Corona, Renato
 conviction of, 133, 139
 impeachment of, 135, 137–38, 153, 160–62
corporate income tax (CIT), 51
Corporate Recovery and Tax Incentives for Enterprise (CREATE) Act, 57
corporate social responsibility (CSR), 224
correctional system
 congestion, and, 192–95
 practices in, 196–202
corruption
 correctional system, and, 191–92, 194, 198, 202
 drug war, and, 174
 eradication of, 138
 impeachment, and, 132, 136, 152, 157–61
 See also bribery
Court of Appeals, 137
COVID-19 pandemic, 1, 57, 193
crisis management, 217–22, 228–29
cultural norms, 109–10

D

Daesh group. *See* ISIS
damayan, values of, 198, 204
Dangerous Drugs Board (DDB), 175
Datu Piang, municipality of, 260
 feuds in, 267–68
 violence in, 255, 261–64, 271
Davao Death Squad (DDS), 162, 172–74, 177
Davide, Hilario, 135, 137, 153, 157
De Castro, Teresita, 165
De Lima, Leila, 130, 155
democracy, 129–30, 150, 152–54
Department of Budget and Management (DBM), 17–20, 277

Index

Department of Education (DepEd), 19, 237
Department of Energy (DoE), 86–88, 91, 93–94, 100
Department of Health (DOH), 238–39, 241–42, 246
Department of Interior and Local Government, 202, 211, 230
Department of Public Works and Highways (DPWH), 19, 71, 219
Department of Science and Technology (DOST), 70–71
Department of Social Welfare and Development (DSWD), 219, 237, 243
Department of Trade and Industry (DTI), 64, 67, 69–71
Department of Transportation (DOTr), 15–16, 26
detention centres, 194. *See also* correctional system
digital revolution, 63, 70
Disaster Risk Reduction Management Councils, 211
Disbursement Acceleration Program (DAP), 139, 161
domestic workers, 63, 66, 73, 111–12, 115–16, 121
drug war. *See* war on drugs
Duterte, Rodrigo Roa
  Bangsamoro Organic Law (BOL), 254, 279–82, 284–86, 288
  "Build, Build, Build" programme (B3P), 15, 48–51
  drug war (*see* war on drugs)
  impeachment, and, 129–31, 133–34, 143, 153

E
Ease of Doing Business Act, 23, 28
economy, 35, 51, 62, 66, 71, 91

Electric Power Industry Reform Act (EPIRA), 83, 89–90, 93
  framework under, 97–98
  reforms under, 85–87
Energy Efficiency and Conservation Act (EECA), 83, 89–90, 93
energy transition, 78, 80–83. *See also* carbon energy; climate change; Paris Agreement
energy trilemma, 81–83, 93–94, 97, 99–100
Estrada, Joseph Ejercito, 133, 135, 137, 152, 157–58
European Union, 43, 53–54, 57
extra-judicial killings (EJKs), 54, 129, 134, 174, 177, 180. *See also* war on drugs

F
federalism, 29–31
Feed-in-Tariffs (FIT), 80, 87, 94–95
Filipino Muslims, 276, 277, 279, 286, 288
financial literacy, 110–11, 118–19
foreign direct investment (FDI), 26–27, 36
fossil fuel, 80–81, 86. *See also* carbon energy
Framework Agreement on the Bangsamoro (FAB), 253–55, 258, 277
Free Trade Agreements (FTAs), 53–54

G
General Appropriations Act (GAA) As-Allotment-Order (GAAAO), 17
GDP (Gross Domestic Product), 12–15, 17, 38, 40–42, 44, 50, 52, 60–62

global competitiveness ranking, 35–36
greenhouse gas (GHG), 79–81, 87, 89–93, 96. *See also* climate change
gross national income, 60
GSP+ (General System of Preferences), 54, 57
Gutierrez, Merceditas, 133, 135, 160

H
Hapilon, Isnilon, 209, 214
Health Quad Cluster, 237–46, 248–49
"Hello Garci" scandal, 159
House Committee on Justice, 132, 134–37, 139, 141, 158–60, 162–64
household consumption, 39, 47, 61–62
House of Representatives
  charter change, and, 31
  impeachment complaint, and, 132–34, 138–40, 157–59, 161–63
  "supermajority" in, 142, 156, 178
human capital, 16–17, 21, 54, 63
Humanitarian Emergency and Action Response Team (HEART), 218–20, 222, 224
human rights, 54, 174, 178–79, 184, 282

I
impeachment
  Constitution, under the, 5, 130–36, 138, 156, 158
  corruption, and, 132, 136, 152, 157–61
  Senate, and, 133–36, 138–39, 156–58, 161–63, 166. *See also* quo warranto

Implementing Rules and Regulations (IRR), 18–19, 237
income inequality, 3, 11, 21, 41, 90
Indigenous Peoples Rights Act, 282
"Industry 4.0", 54, 57
inflation, 25, 45–46, 47–48
infrastructure development, 14–16. *See also* "Build, Build, Build" programme (B3P)
INGOs (international non-government organizations), 237, 239–40, 245, 249, 257. *See also* NGOs (non-government organizations)
Intended Nationally Determined Contribution (INDC), 79, 92–93, 96, 100
interest rate, 43, 47, 50
Intergovernmental Panel on Climate Change (IPCC), 79, 91
internally displaced persons (IDPs)
  assistance for, 224, 229, 231, 238–40, 246
  evacuation centres, in, 219, 224
  home-based, 223, 237, 243, 249
  mental issues among, 247
Internal Revenue Allotment, 28
International Alert, 256–57
International Criminal Court, 2, 177
International Monetary Fund, 12, 52
International Monitoring Team (IMT), 257, 267
International Organization for Migration, 219
International Renewable Energy Agency (IRENA), 81
Investment Priorities Plan (IPP), 67
ISIS (Islamic State/Daesh)
  civilians killed by, 223, 229
  conflicts, and, 215–17, 225, 261, 269, 280

negotiations with, 221
See also Maute group

J
jail. *See* correctional system
Japan International Cooperation Agency, 48
Japan-Philippines Economic Partnership Agreement, 73
Joint Task Force Marawi (JTF Marawi), 215, 217, 220
Joint Task Group Ranao (JTG Ranao), 216, 220, 223, 225
judiciary, 137, 149–51, 158, 165, 193

K
Koop Balikabayani International, 120

L
labour migration, 63–65, 108–9
labour productivity, 43, 66, 71
Local Climate Change Action Plans (LCCAP), 92–93
Local Government Code, 28, 92
local government unit (LGU), 248, 250, 268

M
Maguindanao
  conflicts in, 257, 259, 266, 269
  province of, 255, 259–60, 264, 265, 271–72
Mamasapano incident, 258–59, 267, 279–80
Mandanas-Garcia ruling, 28
Manufacturing Resurgence Program (MRP)
  implementation of, 4, 41, 51–52, 68–70
  industry roadmaps under, 52, 57

manufacturing sector, 68
Maranao, 212–13, 226, 228, 247
Marawi
  attack on, 192, 204, 209–17, 230, 254, 280
  civil-military relations in, 210–11
  crisis management in, 217–21
  evacuation of, 221, 223, 236–37, 239, 248–49
  humanitarian response in, 223–25, 238–39, 241–46, 248–49
  zones, divided into, 214–15, 215–17, 221–22, 224–27, 229
Marcos Jr., Ferdinand, 3–4, 179
Marcos Sr., Ferdinand, 129, 143, 150–51, 179, 277
martial law, 179, 210, 226, 230
Maute group, 209, 212–13, 224, 226, 248, 266, 270. *See also* ISIS (Islamic State/Daesh)
mental health and psychosocial support services (MHPSS)
  clusters, 237–46, 248–49
  limitations of, 241–45
  providers of, 239–41
Metro Manila Subway Project (MMSP), 15–16, 26
migrants, 61, 109, 111. *See also* overseas Filipino workers (OFWs)
Mindanao, 254, 256, 258–60, 271, 282
Mindanao Railway Project, 15–16
Mindanao State University (MSU), 216
Misuari, Nur, 280
Morales, Conchita Carpio, 5, 134–36, 162
Moro Islamic Liberation Front (MILF)
  amnesty for, 285
  clashes, 217, 261, 263, 267, 271, 289

decommissioning of, 278
integration, and, 283–84, 287
peace process, and, 220–21, 254, 257–60, 268–70, 272–73, 277, 279–80
territories of, 212, 264–66
Moro National Liberation Front (MNLF), 213, 269, 277, 280, 283
Muslim separatism, 276

N

National Capital Region (NCR), 216, 223
National Climate Change Action Plan (NCCAP), 91–93
National Disaster Risk Reduction and Management Council (NDRRMC), 238
National Economic and Development Authority (NEDA), 26, 60
National Emergency Operations Command (NEOC), 214, 219, 228–29
National Energy Efficiency and Conservation Plan (NEECP), 89–90, 93
National Food Authority, 24
National Framework Strategy on Climate Change (NFSCC), 91–92, 101
Nationally Determined Contribution (NDC), 84–85, 92
National Power Corporation (NPC), 85–86
National Renewable Energy Program (NREP), 88–90, 93, 95, 100
natural calamities, 46–47, 237, 242, 244–45, 248
net-metering, 87–88, 94
New Bilibid Prison (NBP), 192–93, 197–98, 201

NGOs (non-government organizations)
development work, and, 219, 229, 243, 246
migrant savings, and, 110, 117–18, 120, 122–23
military units, engagement with, 212, 224–25, 228
relief assistance, and, 223, 231, 239, 249
workers' rights, and, 116, 119
See also INGOs (international non-government organizations)
non-tariff measures (NTMs), 53
normalization, 261, 269, 283–85
NPC-Small Power Utilities Group (NPC-SPUG), 86

O

Office of Civil Defense (OCD), 243–44
Office of the Chief Justice, 140, 153
Office of the Ombudsman, 132
Official Development Assistance (ODA), 16
"Oplan *Tokhang*", 173, 272. *See also* war on drugs
overseas Filipino workers (OFWs), 39
consumption habits of, 108, 109, 113–15, 117, 120, 122
domestic workers, 63, 66, 73, 111–12, 115–16, 121
organizations of, 111, 117, 119–22

P

Paris Agreement
commitments, 84–85, 96, 100
compliant towards, 79–83, 92, 99
See also carbon energy; climate change; energy transition

Peace and Order Councils (POCs), 211, 218
People Power EDSA Revolution, 151–53
Pernia, Ernesto, 22, 30, 43
peso, 3, 36, 43–45, 50
Philippine Daily Inquirer, 176
Philippine Disaster Risk Reduction and Management Act, 18, 23, 64, 85, 237, 246
Philippine Drug Enforcement Agency (PDEA), 177, 194
Philippine Economic Zone Authority (PEZA), 64
Philippine Electricity Market Corporation (PEMC), 87
Philippine Energy Plan (PEP), 86, 93
Philippine Government Electronic Procurement System (PhilGEPS), 19
Philippine Institute for Development Studies (PIDS), 31, 67
Philippine National Police (PNP), 172, 174, 194, 215, 222, 271, 283
Philippine Overseas Employment Agency, 63
Philippine Psychology Act, 246
Philippines Energy Efficiency and Conservation Roadmap, 89
PinoyWISE (Worldwide Initiative for Investment Savings and Entrepreneurship), 111, 119–21
police brutality, 2, 183
political violence, 8, 256, 258–59, 263, 271. *See also* armed violence; clan feud
poverty, 3, 11, 21, 41, 90
prison system. *See* correctional system
procurement, 18, 19

Psychological Association of the Philippines, 238–39
Public Financial Management (PFM) reforms, 17, 19–21
Public Telecom Policy Act, 64

Q

quo warranto, 136, 139, 140–43, 150, 153–54, 163–64

R

Rappler, 155, 175–76
recidivism, 192, 205
Red Cross, 215, 218, 223
remittances, 39, 44, 60, 63, 64, 110, 111, 117, 121
renewable energy, 80, 83, 86, 87–89, 93–95
rescue and retrieval operations, 221–23
reverse repurchase rate (RRP), 47
rido. *See* clan feud
Robredo, Maria Leonor, 5, 130, 134–35, 163
rules of origin (ROO), 57

S

Senate
  impeachment trial, and, 133–36, 138–39, 156–58, 161–63, 166
  shift in alliances in, 142
  trusted institution, as, 152
Sereno, Maria Lourdes, 5, 130, 138, 140, 153–56, 162–65
Shari'ah law, 286, 287
Shariff Saydona Mustapha, 255, 260, 261–64, 266, 269–70
social ostracism, 110, 115, 121, 123
social services sector, 16
South China Sea territorial claims, 2
Special Economic Zone Act, 64

Special Geographic Area, 282
spot market, 85
Supreme Court
  Chief Justice, removal of, 136–38, 149–50, 153, 163–65
  division within, 156
  fiscal transfers, decision on, 28
  impeachment complaint, and, 158–59
  satisfaction with, 152
  separation of powers, and, 139
  under supervision of the, 286–87
Sustainable Development Goal (SDG), 79

T
Task Force Bangon Marawi (TFBM), 230
Tax Reform for Acceleration and Inclusion (TRAIN) law
  effects of, 3–4, 14, 23, 46
  implementation, 24, 51, 80, 95, 97
Tax Reform for Attracting Better and High-Quality Opportunities (TRABAHO), 51, 57
tertiary education, 23
total factor productivity (TFP), 42–43, 56, 67
trade deficit, 3–4, 43–45, 53, 56, 72
Transitional Justice and Reconciliation Commission (TJRC), 285
Treasury Single Account (TSA), 19–20
Trillanes IV, Antonio, 130, 155
Tripoli Agreement, 277
turncoatism, 29, 141–42
typhoons, 237, 242, 244–45, 248
tyranny, 179

U
UN Declaration on Human Rights, 282
unemployment, 26–27, 35, 37–38, 63
UN Framework Convention on Climate Change (UNFCCC), 79, 84, 89–91
United Bangsamoro Justice Party (UBJP), 287
United Nations (UN), 79, 134, 237
United States, 2, 43, 53, 276

V
violence. *See* armed violence
violent extremist offenders (VEOs), 190–94, 197, 203–5
Volunteers Against Crime and Corruption (VACC), 134, 162

W
war on drugs
  brutality of, 2, 183, 184
  criticism on, 134, 156, 174, 177–80, 182
  death toll from, 171–72, 176–77
  extra-judicial killings (EJKs), 54, 129, 134, 174, 177, 180
  prison congestion, and, 193
  statistics on, 175–76, 180–81, 204
  See also anti-narcotics campaign
World Bank, 12, 42, 52, 56, 96, 257
World Economic Forum (WEF), 14, 48
World Energy Council (WEC), 81–82
World Health Organization (WHO), 239, 249

www.ingramcontent.com/pod-product-compliance
Lightning Source LLC
Chambersburg PA
CBHW040318300426
44111CB00022B/2943